ENTERPRISE IN AFRICA

Between poverty and growth

Edited by
KENNETH KING
and
SIMON McGRATH

INTERMEDIATE TECHNOLOGY PUBLICATIONS 1999

Intermediate Technology Publications Ltd
103–105 Southampton Row, London WC1B 4HH, UK

A CIP record for this publication is available from the British Library

ISBN 1 85339 478 5

Typeset by J&L Composition Ltd, Filey, North Yorkshire
Printed in the UK by Cromwell Press, Trowbridge

Contents

Foreword

It is particularly appropriate that the theme of this volume should be 'Enterprise in Africa'. It is a crucial issue in relation to the challenge for Africa because aid alone will not eliminate poverty in Africa. Aid will of course, continue to play an important role, but enterprise and partnership with business are absolutely essential and that is why this particular book is welcome to us, as I am sure it will be welcome in Africa.

Partnerships are a key theme for DFID and for development, as is coherence between different departments and of policies; partnerships with non government organizations, with international agencies such as the UN, but above all with developing countries. There will no longer be the notion of donors and recipients but a partnership between two countries; doing things we agree together; working on a common agenda.

Let us think about the size of the task that we face: 23 per cent of the world's population living in abject poverty – 1.3 billion people. Our White Paper's title is *Eliminating World Poverty*. This requires setting ourselves targets to eliminate poverty with other countries and institutions with which we work.

At the heart of these is halving the number of people in poverty by 2015. Of course, there are sceptical voices who say that it is not our concern or that the goal of really eliminating poverty is fantasy. That is nonsense. If you were to come down as a visitor from Mars and look at the wealth in the world, the wealth under the ground in terms of natural resources, in the seas, the food that we can produce, and look how unequally distributed it is, you would see that if it was more equally distributed then poverty could be eliminated. It is also in our interests to do so. It is not just a moral imperative; it is important from our point of view in the rich North. If you look at the high correlation between poverty and conflict, you will see that poverty is the main cause of people fighting over limited resources – just to survive, just to exist. Poverty is the principal cause of poverty around the world; conflict which, if it is allowed to continue, will in the long term cost us far more.

In Africa the challenge is the greatest: 40 per cent of the continent's population is below the absolute poverty line. Child mortality under the age of five is the worst of any region. The number of children in primary education is actually reducing in some countries. One of our targets in the White Paper is to get every child into primary education. It is believed that life expectancy could worsen in the next 5 to 10 years as a result of AIDS unless we take the kind of action we as a government are proposing in our White paper.

But at the heart of our strategy is the need to build stronger partnerships, above all between the governments of developed and developing countries, as well as the voluntary sector and business. What does that mean in practice?

First, it means working effectively with governments to provide a much more favourable, enabling environment for businesses to flourish in a way that provides faster growth and opportunities for the poor. Unless we have faster growth, these countries will not be able to be pulled out of poverty and that is why, although the

Multilateral Agreement on Investment (MAI) was started and continues in the OECD, our recent report shows that it has great potential for investment in developing countries, particularly in Africa. Governments need to involve business in an open and transparent manner in policy dialogue. One important example of this is the issue of corruption. Private industry needs to work together with civil society and government to create a culture and framework of governance that does not tolerate corrupt behaviour in or out of the state. That is a big challenge but a challenge that we must face. Also the formal business sector can become pro-active champions of the poor and disadvantaged – and that is what we are urging as well.

Second, it means thinking creatively about approaches and initiatives that are pro-poor, as far as business is concerned, as well as pro-profit. They must think of what can be done to help poor people as well as to make profits. We are ready to back with financial support, and other support, any new ideas. In Kenya we are working with the banks, for example, to help them develop financial products which are accessible to small-scale entrepreneurs who have traditionally lacked access to services from the formal banks. It is in this area of small and medium entreprises, which this book discusses, that we see a great potential.

Third, it means adopting socially responsible business behaviour. There is a recognition by business that by investing in the communities in which they work, they are investing in their own future as well. This is an issue of competitiveness as well as philanthropy. But to increase economic growth in Africa we need to attract higher levels of foreign investment than at present. That is why the MAI is so important. The issue for Africa is not exploitation by foreign investors but the need to attract more foreign investment. We need to overcome in Africa the perception that has been held by investors, created over 25 years. There are signs that this is taking place. A recent Harvard report showed very rapid improvement in the leading reforming countries and high levels of optimism within those countries that things will continue to improve. That is already being reflected in higher investment in Uganda, in Ghana, and in Tanzania. Those three countries received US$580 million foreign direct investment between them in 1996.

This book examines in more detail how small and medium-size enterprise can help; in Kenya, South Africa, Ghana and elsewhere where British finance and expertise are being linked to African enterprise and initiative to restore the growth of the informal scetor which provides jobs and contributes to the reduction of poverty. We also need to find a way to promote greater stability and to encourage enterprise and development. We can help by improving taxation systems and financial markets. We also can help with perceptions of and criteria for investment. We will continue to work to create a more secure and stable political environment. It is important that we should be investing in human development through basic education, health and clean water.

In many parts of Africa the pattern of decline has been halted. Our Department for International Development wants to build on those successes with governments that like us are committed to tackling and eliminating world poverty. We shall go through country-to-country partnerships with them and build up a country programme in which we share their ideals and commitments to eradicate poverty.

George Foulkes
Under Secretary of State
Department for International Development, London

Preface

This book links small enterprise research and policies with broader development debates on the elimination of poverty and the promotion of growth. it cuts across the interests of academics, practitioners and policymakers in many disciplinary areas. This transdisciplinary concern with policy, practice and theory is characteristic of much work in the Centre of African Studies at the University of Edinburgh, and in particular its more than thirty years of annual African Studies conferences, all of which have drawn experts from many different aspects of area and development studies.

The conference of mid-1998, which was the starting point for this volume, was supported by the Binks Trust, the Foreign and Commonwealth Office and the Department for International Development. Together, they brought to Edinburgh most of the authors represented in this book.

The significance of the debates in this volume to the British development efforts is illustrated by the foreword provided by George Foulkes, the Parliamentary Under-Secretary for International Development. He makes clear that it is appropriate to revisit out thinking about enterprise in Africa at the very time that his and other development agencies are refocusing their understandings of both poverty and growth in development co-operation. But for development to be genuinely participatory then it is clear that a vision that goes beyond aid will be essential. As George Foulkes argues, enterprise development is an important element of such a shared vision. As part of a coherent, locally owned industrial strategy, it also has the capacity to contribute significantly to both the poverty reduction and growth strands of development. At what we all hope is a turning point in Africa's economic development, this volume brings together authors from Africa, Europe and North America, with rich experience of researching enterprise, in order to broaden and deepen our understandings of the challenges and opportunities facing the millions of African small and micro enterprise.

Kenneth King
Director
Centre of African Studies
University of Edinburgh

Authors' Biographies

Susanna Adam holds a doctorate from the University of Bremen for her study of the indigenous training system as found in Ibaden, Nigeria. She has subsequently worked as a consultant assisting in the development of curriculum and delivery mechanisms for improved training for the African informal sector.

Abigail Barr is a researcher at the Centre for the Study of African Economies, University of Oxford. Her work focuses on the role of social capital in determining economic outcomes in Africa. Current research interests include ethnic networks in the Ghanaian and Ethiopian manufacturing sectors and the effects of resettlement on social capital in rural Zimbabwe.

Jacques Charmes is an economist and statistician. Director of Research at the French Scientific Research Institute for Development and Co-operation (IRD, formerly ORSTOM) and Professor of Economics at the University of Versailles – St Quentin en Yvelines, he has been involved in the design and analysis of many labour-force, living standards and informal sector surveys in Africa, north and south of the Sahara.

Hans Haan is a development economist who has carried out work related to the micro- and small enterprise sector since the early 1980s. He worked in various countries in Africa, most notably as an ILO expert (1980–82) involved in research on the 'informal sector' in Southern Africa, and again for the ILO in Ghana and Kenya (1993–1996) as the project manager of the FIT programme. Haan is currently living in Amsterdam and working as an independent MSE-consultant.

Lawrence Honny obtained his PhD from the University of Bradford. He was formerly a research fellow and lecturer at the Centre for Development Studies and School of Agriculture at the University of Cape Coast, Ghana. He is now a consultant engaged in project panning, performance and impact evaluation.

Andy Jeans, Programme Manager with APT Enterprise Development, has worked in small enterprise development in Africa and South Asia for 15 years. Particular interests include innovation and cost-effectiveness in approaches to the provision of services to small enterprises.

Susan Joekes has been for many years a Fellow of the Institute of Development Studies, University of Sussex. She has also been on the staff of the International Center for Research on Women in Washington DC. Her work is mostly on gender analysis in relation to international trade and labour markets; and natural resource management and environmental change.

Wanjala Kerre is Associate Professor of Technological Education at Moi University, Eldoret, Kenya. He is a regular contributor to national and international work on the links between education and technology, particularly focused on the informal sector.

Tony Killick is Senior Research Associate of the Overseas Development Institute, London; and Visiting Professor of the University of Surrey. His principal interests are in the areas of economic policies in developing countries, and in the ways in which the policies of international agencies impinge upon developing countries.

Kenneth King is Director of the Centre of African Studies and Professor of International and Comparative Education at the University of Edinburgh. He has worked for many years on international education and training, the African small enterprise sector and aid policy.

Dorothy McCormick is Senior Research Fellow at the Institute for Development Studies, University of Nairobi, where she has been involved in teaching and research since 1988. Her main research interests are in enterprise development and industrialization in Africa.

Simon McGrath is Research Fellow at the Centre of African Studies, University of Edinburgh. His research interests are in the links between overall economic development in Africa and the roles of education and training, small and micro-enterprise development, and international co-operation.

George Manu, based at the ILO International Training Centre in Turin at the time of writing this chapter, has now returned to Ghana, where he is Chief Executive Officer of Empretec, a leading MSE support organization.

Fra von Massow is a Social Development Consultant specializing in gender, social policy and planning for rural development, including micro-enterprise development in Africa. She is currently Team Leader of the Micro Research: Health and Education project, Ethiopia (Oxfam Policy Department), where participatory research methodology has been applied. Fra is an Associate of the Development Planning Unit, University College London, and a member of the Gender Programme at the DPU.

Donald Mead has spent nearly half of his forty-year career as a development economist in the Third World, mostly in Eastern and Southern Africa. For the last half of this period, he was a Professor of Agricultural Economics at Michigan State University, where he has been engaged in extensive research on the characteristics of small enterprises and their policy and project needs.

Thandika Mkandawire is the Director of the United Nations Research Institute for Social Development. He is an economist with a long experience in the promotion of comparative research on development issues. From 1986 through 1996, he was Executive Secretary of the Council for the Development of Social Science Research in Africa (CODESRIA), in Dakar.

Poul Ove Pedersen, Centre for Development Research, Copenhagen, has carried out research on regional and industrial development in both Africa and Europe. Presently he is engaged in a project on the impact of globalization on Africa, where especially he studies transport and related services.

Christian Rogerson is Professor of Human Geography, Department of Geography and Environmental Studies, University of the Witwatersrand, Johannesburg, South Africa. He has major research interests in small enterprise development, local economic development and urban and regional studies.

Introduction

Enterprise in Africa: new contexts; renewed challenges

SIMON MCGRATH and KENNETH KING

New contexts

Thinking about small and micro-enterprises in Africa has a long history but debates about their nature and prospects, and whether and how to support them, have continued without resolution in academic, practitioner and policy circles. This book is an attempt to examine the current nature of some of these debates. In so doing, it asks where the evidence is that justifies key theoretical, policy and practical beliefs in the field. However, it is equally mindful of the importance of broader intellectual trends in shaping our understanding of the possibilities for policy and practice. Therefore, it attempts to bring together the consideration of new contexts with that of the evidence regarding central challenges that have been and remain important for work in the field of enterprise development.

Pro-poor policy

At the macro-level of development policy, a new orthodoxy appears to be emerging at the end of the 1990s which is shifting the primary focus of development back on to the eradication of poverty (Riddell 1997; King and Buchert 1999). This has led to a greater sense of economic growth being a means to this ultimate end, rather than the central goal of development and aid. Such an overall shift in the language of development spoken by donors will necessarily be put into practice in a number of ways. This book considers some of these and the implications that a pro-poor policy has for enterprises and small enterprise development policy. Moreover, the subtitle of this book: 'between poverty and growth', points to the continuing challenge in this sector of getting an appropriate balance between a focus on poverty and one on growth.

Renewed confidence about African economic growth

The shift towards a pro-poor policy is, at least implicitly, a critique of the weakness of structural adjustment strategies over a decade and a half. Critics have long argued that the focus on macroeconomic 'fundamentals' under this approach increased poverty levels for large numbers of Africans and undermined, rather than supported, African development (e.g. Chossudovsky 1997; Fine 1998; Marais 1998). However, it is important to note that ideological shift towards pro-poor growth has been taking place at the same time as economists have become more optimistic about Africa's economic growth (Holman 1997; Killick this volume) and African politicians such as Thabo Mbeki have begun to talk of an 'African Renaissance'. Moreover, it appears that structural adjustment remains on the policy agenda as a policy tool even when its broader ideological support seems to have been undermined. As this book will show, structural adjustment has had major impacts, both positive and negative, upon the health of small and micro-enterprises (SME) individually and collectively. Several chapters highlight the complex relationship between the macroeconomic situation and the situation of those in the SME sector. It is equally clear that any new balance of the relative emphasis on poverty and growth will have major implications for SMEs, altering the emphasis of support programmes or the policy and economic environment they face.

New thinking about development

The recent rethinking of the importance of poverty and growth needs to be viewed in the context of longer term socio-economic trends. Looking backwards, it is now apparent that the time that the informal sector was 'discovered' in the early 1970s was one in which the world economy was undergoing fundamental changes. The 'golden age' of Keynesianism in the OECD countries was collapsing and the international system of fixed exchange rates had just been abandoned. A sharp economic downturn forced large companies, and the capitalist system in general, to seek new ways of maintaining or deepening capital accumulation. This led to the increasing internationalization of production, trade and investment: resulting in the current phenomenon of globalization (McGrath 1999).

Alongside this came a widespread shift in the way in which work was organized. Mass production increasingly became challenged by flexible production as the leading way of organizing manufacturing activity. Through an emphasis on smaller economic units and informalization as a means of flexibilization, the new approach increased the emphasis on small and micro-enterprises as key economic agents in the North. This inevitably influenced the way that such enterprises came to be viewed when Northerners took on the role of donors and advisers in the South. Moreover, in combination with the trend of globalization, flexible production seemed to be something that Southern economies could not ignore.

When the ILO employment mission visited Kenya in 1972 it was self-evident that the state was at the centre of development strategies. The intervening quarter of a century has seen intellectual fashion seriously undermine this 'given' of previous thinking. The subsequent emergence of a neo-classical orthodoxy in development economics saw the state more as a problem for development than as the principal agent in its achievement.

In the light of the apparent failure of African states to act in such a manner, the notion of an African developmental state became discredited, as

Mkandawire's chapter explores. Instead of the African development state, the imagery was of the African 'vampire state' (Frimpong-Ansah 1992). Notions of the weak state also developed and contributed in turn to an interest in political research with the role of non-state actors in development. This, of course, mirrored trends in development practice as support to African development increasingly bypassed, though never totally abandoned, the state-to-state route. Privatization of aid in the North led to increasing prominence of NGOs. In Africa, local perceptions of the limited and problematic nature of state intervention became coupled with North-South NGO partnerships which sought to circumvent the role of the state both at the recipient and donor levels.

Intellectual fashions of the 1990s, centred around globalization and post-modernism, have also served to downplay the nation state as an analytical tool, thus helping to reinforce perceptions of the state as but one, highly problematic, actor on the developmental stage (McGinn 1996).

Changing trends in small enterprise development

Many of the above trends have also been linked to the emergence of new thinking in small enterprise development (SED). SED was clearly the logical focus as part of a neo-liberal view of development, and many NGOs have emerged in this area. As the field developed rapidly so an orthodoxy began to emerge that micro-credit was the most effective and efficient tool available. By the time that the Consultative Group to Assist the Poorest (CGAP) was established in 1995 it appeared that micro-credit was the single tool that could transform the lives of the very poorest (CGAP 1995). However, soon after, the Donor Committee for Small Enterprise Development began to emphasize the importance of placing credit alongside what it termed as 'Business Development Services' (the full range of advisory, training, etc. supports) as part of a package for SED (Gibson 1997).

Thinking about small and micro-enterprises has also evolved at the theoretical level. The importance of thinking about flexible production systems for small and micro-enterprise theory has already been alluded to. This trend has seen a growing concern with the enterprise as part of a nexus of relationship and structures. Linkages between SMEs and with larger firms, and the geographical and sectoral clusters of enterprises and organizations that are formed as a result, have become important areas of research as several of the subsequent chapters indicate. The rules that enterprises operate with, and the structures that help or hinder their performance, have also been given a heightened profile. Institutions (in North's [1990] sense of rules of the game), trust and enabling environments have also become important landmarks in the conceptual landscape of SME studies. Here it is important to note that recent interviews with entrepreneurs in Kenya[1] strongly emphasized the

[1] Fieldwork by Kenneth King (February/March 1999) to be written up subsequently.

importance they placed on issues of state transparency, reduced corruption and a 'level playing field'. Thus, this debate about the rules of the game is a popular one as well as an interest of theorists and donors.

Rethinking education for development and for self-employment

By the start of the 1990s the notion that the school should be a key provider of vocational skills and knowledge had been seen as inappropriate by the World Bank and some other donors, e.g. ODA. This view was rejected, however, by African governments, as Kerre's chapter illustrates. Nonetheless, as African education became even more aid-dependent and donor-driven in the 1990s, and basic education moved to the centre of donor, and increasingly recipient thinking, so vocational schooling seemed to lose ground, as countries such as Ghana and, currently, Kenya began to stress the merits of narrowing their school curricula, with vocational subjects being one of the prime victims (McGrath 1997 and 1998b).

Until quite recently such vocational preparation, and its parallel in training institutions, was designed for the formal sector alone. However, the growing policy interest in the informal sector gradually brought in its wake a two-pronged concern with orientation and preparation for work in SMEs that has increasingly influenced training policy in the 1990s.

First, there has been a parallel realization of the existence of a skills development tradition within the SME production sector. Most systematized in West Africa, under the 'traditional apprenticeship' system, but present elsewhere, such training has been an important source of skills and socialization to SME working practices (King 1977 and 1996; Fluitman 1994). As the literature on this phenomenon has developed, there have been tendencies both to celebrate this modality of skills development as indigenous, self-reliant and vibrant, and to argue for the need to intervene in order to address perceived deficits in skills and, typically, the theoretical knowledge underpinning them.

The second approach has been to seek to reorient formal education and training towards socialization and preparation for SME (self-) employment. At school level this included very major curricular reforms, particularly in the 1980s, such as under the Kenyan '8–4–4 system'. The technical skills development side of school-based interventions has lost ground during the 1990s in the light of the basic education drive. However, the notion of enterprise education seems to have remained immune from the Fosterite critique and is a major aspect of the current South African Curriculum 2005 reform (King 1997), and is a central theme of the background paper for the International Congress on Technical and Vocational Education (UNESCO 1999).

The emergence of transdisciplinarity

One of the characteristics of academic research on small and micro-enterprises in recent years has been its crossing of disciplinary boundaries.

This book gives some sense of this through chapters which come from individuals with disciplinary homes in education, geography, politics, economics, statistics, business studies and development studies. Research on SMEs is in some ways an early exemplar of the growing trend towards transdisciplinarity, where it is the problem rather than the traditions of the discipline which are at the heart of research (Gibbons et al. 1994). However, too often over the quarter of a century lifespan of 'SME studies' the reality has not lived up to the potential. Instead, SME research has been compartmentalized into a 'development studies approach to SMEs', a 'business studies approach to SMEs', and so on, with findings and insights struggling to cross semi-permeable boundaries. The opportunity provided by the thinking about the new ways in which knowledge is produced and disseminated (Gibbons et al. 1994) is to break down such boundaries and create SME studies that are reflective of learning across multiple disciplines.

Issues

The changes outlined above form a backdrop for debates about the future of African small and micro-enterprises at the dawn of the new millennium. In the second section of this chapter our attention will shift towards an exploration of a series of important issues for understanding and intervening in the SME sector in Africa. These issues will be discussed in greater detail in the chapters that follow, but their rehearsal at this point serves to foreground the relationships between them and provides a framework through which to read the debates of the book as a whole.

What are the implications of pro-poor policies for African SMEs and for organisations engaged in supporting them?

It is important to acknowledge the complexity of the relationship between the poverty eradication and growth objectives of development policy. It is also vital that research gets behind the rhetoric of the apparent shift to see what exactly it entails in terms of policies and practices. Much of this volume explores these issues in greater detail and asks how consistent the new discourse is with the needs and aspirations of SME actors. In particular, it asks whether growth and poverty eradication are in fact served best by a targeting of the poorest, or whether the role of successful enterprises and employment generators is worthy of more attention.

What is the relationship between the dynamics of the SME sector and broader economic trends?

Several of the subsequent chapters highlight the ways in which broader macroeconomic fortunes create both push and pull pressures on the SME sector. As the sophistication of such analysis develops, it becomes important to ask what overall macroeconomic policies would best support the SME sector. An understanding of SME–macroeconomy relations also permit new insights into policies such as structural adjustment and liberalization. Moreover, a deeper awareness of the dynamics involved should also lead on to a consideration of how best SME interests can be fed into national policy processes. Several chapters point to obstacles in this regard. These include the weakness of informal sector associations (Haan), the continued urban bias in policy making and thinking about SMEs (Rogerson) and the androcentric nature of macroeconomic policy and its impact on female-owned SMEs (von Massow).

Is the SME sector a continuum or a series of segments; and what are the implications of its structure?

Much of the debate in this book is concerned with examining the internal characteristics of the SME sector. This leads to an equally crucial focus on the degree of fit between the reality here and the models of the SME sector used by policy makers; and the implications their differences have for interventions in the sector. A series of oppositional categories fill the book's pages: urban–rural; male–female; white–black; emergent–survivalist; traditional–modern; developers–survivors, alongside pictures painted of the diversity of multiple segments or types of enterprise.

Another tension is also evident: that of universalistic versus targeted policy. There is a tendency to talk of a national small enterprise policy without sufficiently highlighting the crucial issue of whether such a policy is built upon an assumption of a generic SME or has a view about a range of SME realities.

By exploring the issue of classification, several chapters are able to ask important questions about policy. Rogerson shows how the South African SME policy notionally uses three types of SME, but in practice privileges emergent black enterprises: a reflection that links back to the poverty-growth policy debate. By providing a gendered SME typology, von Massow links the discussion of small enterprise development to the wider debates on gender and development. These and other chapters encourage the reader to ask who are the intended beneficiaries of specific policy interventions and what the relationship is between SED and development policy more generally.

A questioning of whether the sector is best classified as a continuum or as a series of segments (with permeability as a subordinate issue) is also useful as a way into understanding SED and development policy. The notion of segmentation highlights the barriers to progress that individual enterprises face, and forces the reader to ask what these barriers are and how, if at all, they can be broken down. It also raises the important issue of whether a policy that acknowledges such segmentation and attempts to reflect it in a notion of target groups, runs the risk of reproducing segmentation. Past interventions in the lives of the poor, such as rural education and income-generation projects, have been strongly criticized for keeping the poor in ghettos of 'relevant' provision. It remains a challenge to conceive of programmes that reflect individuals' and communities' present realities without foreclosing opportunities for transformed livelihoods.

Again, this can lead us back into the debate about the overall goal of development. So far, this introductory note has talked about pro-poor policy but it is worth for a moment highlighting the potentially crucial distinction between poverty eradication and poverty alleviation. Ameliorating the conditions of target groups may well be a central aspect of poverty alleviation. Poverty eradication, the stated goal of the British development White Paper, however, would surely require the withering away of target groups through radical transformation of their livelihoods and lives.

An emphasis on a continuum highlights the possibility of such a transformation, but also reminds the observer that enterprises can also decline as well as grow. To understand the dynamics at play in movement along a continuum, we are encouraged by several chapters to look at the effects of the macroeconomic position on the relative balance between involution and evolution in the SME sector. In addition, it is important to ask, as von Massow does, what is the motivation of the entrepreneur in engaging in business activities. In spite of the assumptions of neo-classical economics, entrepreneurs are individuals with complex sets of needs, aspirations and opportunities, who cannot simply be reduced to 'rational' economic agents engaged in profit maximization.

How straightforward is intervention in the SME sector?

Much of the success and vitality of the SME sector, where it exists, is a function of its ability to stay outside the ambit of the state. Moreover, it must be remembered when considering the issue of intervention in the sector that the reach of both state and donors is limited. Nonetheless, interventions are occurring and new ones continue to be planned and debated. A focus on the linkages between macroeconomic and SME realities and a concern with the internal structure of the SME sector provide valuable route markers along the path to understanding the nature of and prospects for such interventions in the sector. Mkandawire highlights the political choices that are involved in promoting small rather than large enterprises. Choices are evident too in Rogerson and von Massow's accounts of policy biases.

The book highlights other reasons to be cautious about interventions. In our later chapter we note the dangers inherent in trying to extend the reach of the state and formal systems to areas that have remained largely beyond their ambit. It is clear that the authors in this volume eschew the two extremes: on the one hand of pushing a strong formalization agenda (as can be seen in our account of the South African learnership proposals – see McGrath and King this volume and McGrath 1998a); or, on the other, following de Soto (1989) down the path of radical deregulation. Rather, the emphasis here is twofold. First, the authors acknowledge that policies are not neutral and that interventions need to be considered for their differential impact on different groups. Second, they note that there are weaknesses in the way that the SMEs do things, for instance in the area of skills development. However, they are also aware of the weaknesses of state attempts to intervene in the sector to make things better. When state systems are struggling to deliver on their traditional goals, there is reason to doubt their ability to serve new goals and new clienteles.

What is the role of the state in supporting small and micro-enterprises?

The *1997 World Development Report* (World Bank 1997) has been taken as reflecting a shift in the World Bank's long-held hostility to the state. In a number of African countries new governments have emerged which seem more competent and confident. Equally, there are a number of better established political systems, in Botswana, Ghana and Uganda, for instance, which seem to be success stories on some level. However, there are also reasons for caution in stressing the role of the state. The notion of the developmental state in the context of globalized financial markets seems to be brought into question by the recent experiences of the Asian 'tigers'. The proposed Multilateral Agreement on Investment seems to enshrine the power of the market over the state.

SME studies of course are about enterprises and enterprise. As such, the field has tended to be more naturally inclined towards celebrating the market than the state. Mkandawire's contribution, however, posits the argument that African development requires coherent industrial policy. Moreover, one distinguishing feature of that coherence is the balancing of SME needs with those of larger firms.

Important insights into the possibility of industrial policy both for the SME sector and for wider economic development are likely to emerge from the experiences of South Africa. An aspect of the policy tensions that Rogerson talks about there is between the Department of Finance/World Bank sponsored Growth Employment and Redistribution (GEAR) strategy with its neo-classical orthodoxy about fiscal discipline and liberalization, and the Department of Labour/Department of Trade and Industry continuation of an industrial policy tradition, with SMEs seen as a key element alongside larger business and the state (McGrath 1998a). The Job Summit of October 1998 illustrated the on-going nature of this internal South African debate.

What are the appropriate roles of institutions and infrastructure in small enterprise development?

A discussion of the role of the state is closely linked to a consideration of issues of institutions and infrastructure. Several chapters highlight the failure of formal infrastructure, organizations and regulatory systems to support small and micro-enterprises. Barr shows how much of the networking activity of the SMEs that she has studied in Ghana is conditioned by their vulnerability and are risk minimizing rather than productivity enhancing. Pedersen highlights the crucial role of reliable intermediaries in a climate where trust is difficult to give except on the basis of a long relationship or familial ties. Moreover, echoing Barr, he identifies lack of trust as a key obstacle to technological development. In these chapters, and that of McCormick, it appears that African SME clustering and networking cannot capture the benefits suggested by the international literature because they are concerned with establishing and maintaining trust rather than with innovation. It is the lack of such institutional frameworks as the effective access to enforceable contract under the formal legal system that is at the heart of this dilemma.

These insights are important. As we noted above, there has been a tradition in SME literature to emphasize the pernicious impact of regulation on SMEs. Work such as that of Barr, McCormick and Pedersen encourages a far more sophisticated reading of the relationship between regulation and SMEs. It requires policy makers and analysts to consider exactly how a particular piece of regulation, or its absence, affects small and micro-enterprises and whether any action can be taken that would improve the situation. Moreover, remembering Mkandawire's caution that a policy preference for the SME sector is for one group of capitalists over another, it is incumbent on the policy community to examine who are the winners and losers from any proposed or enacted policy. As the discussion about segments versus continuum has already shown, the assumption of homogeneity of experience and interests is false.

How can education and training best support the development of SMEs?

Several chapters show a belief in the importance of technology and skills as tools for the upgrading or transformation of the SME sector. There are a number of discrete elements to such an emphasis. As Jeans shows, there is still much mileage in the intermediate technology route to small and micro-enterprise uplift. We have already noted how the environment in which SMEs operate often causes them to be risk minimizers rather than active technological upgraders. This is something that the technology NGOs are concerned to change. One approach that has been tried in recent years has been that of an alliance with informal sector associations (ISAs). Haan's chapter reviews some of the evidence for this and points to the great difficulties that have been experienced. However, both he and Jeans point to examples of more successful interventions.

The need for intervention in the SME sector in search of technological improvement has been made in a number of major projects in recent years. The Nigerian Open Apprenticeship Scheme was one of the largest of these. However, Adam's chapter paints a picture of an artisanal sector in Ibadan that appears not to have made the technological breakthrough the intervention expected. Instead, she highlights declining skill levels and technological competence, a picture mirrored by work from other places, most notably Kumasi, Ghana (Powell 1995).

It is evident that there are still questions about how skills and technologies can be successfully transferred into and within the sector and how they can be upgraded. Honny, Kerre and our own later chapter consider some of the evidence that exists for formal education and training interventions designed to promote SME development. We are concerned in part with the very fundamental questions that remain unanswered about the ability of formal education and training institutions to support informal sector activities. Nonetheless, we wish to emphasize the importance of skills development for both formal and informal economic activities and to encourage the exploration of appropriate mechanisms to deliver on this. Our concern with the evidence for success of current programmes should not be taken to imply that we find the current policy emphasis on a lean school curriculum[2] and basic education unproblematic. Rather, we are conscious of the failings of the Education for All discourse (WCEFA 1990) to pay adequate attention to the question of what future it is preparing children for.

Where is the evidence for current policies?

As we argue at greater length in our later chapter, the link between education and enterprise is very poorly understood. Adam's contribution is one of the very few existing that seeks to ask where SME skills come from and to make explicit the role of the school in preparation for SME production. Instead, it is far more common to argue, on the shallowest of evidence, that more schooling is good for the SME sector. Not only is this questioned by the evidence proffered by Mead; it ignores crucial issues of causality (Charmes) and fails to open the 'black box' of the school (McGrath and King). As we note, the methodological challenges of opening the black box and of accounting for non-school factors are such as to make it extremely difficult to talk authoritatively about education and training's contribution to SME performance.

Problems of evidence exist more widely in the field of SED. Manu's chapter is an attempt to question the alleged effects of enterprise development programmes. He powerfully uncovers a series of assumptions that inform policy and practice and shows that their grounding in evidence is poor. Charmes also points to the limitations in data that continue to undermine the basis for interventions.

Much of the discussion of this book reinforces the view that policies are frequently built on the sandiest of evidential ground. However, to go thus far

---

[2] In its most extreme form reduced to local language, colonial language, mathematics and science.

would be simply to repeat much of the literature critical of African development of the past two decades. Rather, it is important to note that policies reflect negotiations and compromises, whether explicit or implicit, between societal groupings, with claims about evidence used in complex ways as weapons of diplomatic warfare. Examinations of evidence cannot exist apart from the identification of vested interests in the arena of small enterprise development.

What would a methodology for SME studies look like?

Earlier in this chapter we touched upon the growing importance in the academic discourse of the concept of transdisciplinarity. At that point, and subsequently, we used the term 'SME studies' as a shorthand for research that is done on the SME sector. For a moment we propose to take this term further and ask whether there are important methodological insights that emerge from the following chapters that could form key elements of a unified curriculum of SME studies. The intention is not to propose that such a quasi-discipline is needed. Rather, its 'virtual reality' allows us to foreground some key issues for those concerned with understanding SMEs.

Most of the points here are reiterations of earlier comments. We have already highlighted the lack of data that lies behind much of the policy and practice of intervention. We have noted that there are serious methodological challenges inherent in opening the black box of education and in establishing causalities. Studying the SME sector is often a matter of researching the hidden, because those being researched are often reluctant to be opened up to the gaze of the state. Charmes's methodological discussion is a particularly pertinent and provocative one in this regard. Another facet of the hidden face of the SME sector is too often the gender perspective. Several chapters (e.g. Joekes and von Massow) underscore the importance of such a perspective when researching or intervening in the SME sector or the wider economy.

It is a strength of SME research that it draws on so many disciplinary backgrounds. However, as we have already noted, too often the sector is viewed within the narrow confines of disciplines. As educationalists, we are conscious of when work on technology fails to take account of the latest thinking in our own field, when it turns to the role of education in technological development, or when economists use measurements such as 'years of schooling' that seem to have no analytical value within our own discipline. Often the converse is equally true. At the heart of the rationale for this book has been the need to develop conversations across those backgrounds. The intention was to make a contribution to reducing such instances of misunderstanding. More importantly, however, it was also to seek to harness the power of having outsiders asking the questions that insiders have learnt to take for granted, and for sharing the great wealth of insights that exist when knowledge and skills are pooled across disciplines.

Although we have pointed to the popularity of transdisciplinarity as a concept, we are aware that it has to be developed in practice. In a situation in Britain where academics are still primarily valued for their contributions to disciplines and for their conversations with their disciplinary peers, it is important to have books like this which recognize neither the division between disciplines nor that between academics, policy makers and practitioners.

A note about the structure

The pursuit of such a synoptic vision better allows this book to address certain key issues, such as the influence of external discourses and forces on the SME sector. This introduction is followed by Part 1, which seeks to locate the subsequent debates about the SME sector in broader contexts of macroeconomic prospects, trade patterns and political disputes. Part 2 looks at the overall structure and internal dynamics of the SME sector. Part 3 looks at issues of linkages, clusters and associations. The fourth and final Part considers the role that education, training and technology can play in small and micro-enterprise development.

Part 1
Micro-Enterprises, Macro-Contexts

1 Have Africa's economies turned the corner?

TONY KILLICK[1]

Introduction

It needs no elaboration here that the economic performance of most of Africa's[2] economies over the last three decades has been generally abysmal, both absolutely and by comparison with other developing regions, and that this has created a highly adverse economic climate for the development of African private enterprise, including the small and medium-sized enterprises which are the special concern of this book. Africa has experienced slow growth of GDP, particularly when compared with other developing regions; and a wide range of other economic indicators also reveal Africa's performance to have lagged far behind (although some comparisons on the educational and health fronts are less adverse).

However, although estimates vary substantially, there appears to have been a notable revival in recent years, beginning in 1994 or 1995. Optimistic statements have been coming from the World Bank and other donor agencies, as well as from African sources, suggesting that Africa's economies have at last turned the corner and that, with continuing policy efforts, the recovery will be sustained. But will it, or will the later-1990s prove to be a false dawn? It is proper to be wary. After all, it is easy to see reasons why donors and others might have an interest in putting the best possible gloss on what is currently happening. They badly need an African success story, given the volume of aid that has been devoted to the continent, and there is always the possibility that talking up the present situation, by encouraging investors, will itself help sustain the recovery. We all want to believe in a long-term recovery and that may influence professional judgements. But maybe the up-turn is temporary? The world economy, after all, has been booming, creating an encouraging

[1] I should like to acknowledge valuable research assistance by Shondeep Banerji, the encouragement of Kenneth King and a small grant from the Foreign and Commonwealth Office. Without any of these ingredients this chapter would not have been possible. It will also become clear that I owe a considerable intellectual debt to the paper by Paul Collier and Jan Gunning referred to in the text.

[2] This chapter is about Sub-Saharan Africa (SSA) and references in it to 'Africa' should be read as referring to SSA.

environment but one which, as the East Asian problems remind us, should not be taken for granted for the longer term. Maybe the African 'boomlet' is due to good luck, to favourable shifts in the terms of trade, or in world interest rates? Maybe, at least until *el niño*, favourable weather has been responsible? Africa's economies are, after all, still predominantly agricultural. Maybe the regional averages recorded for SSA are biased upwards by the outstanding records of just a few countries, with most others still mired in stagnation? Relatedly, we should remember that 1994 was the year of the devaluation, after 46 years and after serious recessions in many Franc Zone countries, of the CFA franc: maybe the overall regional figures are unduly influenced by an essentially once-for-all response by the CFA countries, catching up on the income losses of earlier years?[3]

The purpose of this chapter is to provide a preliminary view on this matter: preliminary because it is still too early to do more than arrive at a highly provisional judgement, to say nothing of the generally appalling shortage of reliable data on recent trends in Africa. The first section sets out growth and other economy-wide performance indicators and also looks at the country spread and persistence of the growth. The approach of the remainder of the chapter is to examine the extent to which the growth recovery has been underpinned by improvements in Africa's economic 'fundamentals', on the grounds that the growth is unlikely to be sustained unless some important fundamentals have also been strengthened. The second section very briefly surveys the existing growth accounting literature on Africa in order to identify a list of candidate 'fundamentals', and the third part then examines trends in some of these, before a conclusion.

Recent trends and some disaggregations

Tables 1.1 and 1.2 set out fuller information on the continent's recent economic growth, together with some other performance indicators.[4] There are significant differences in the numbers presented in these tables. These are due both to differences in data sources and in the type of average presented. Table 1.1 is based on IMF data and reports weighted means, including preliminary estimates for 1997. Table 1.2 is derived from the World Bank's *Development Indicators* series and the data presented are median values. Unfortunately, available data for this table go only to 1995. Being medians, these averages give far less weight to extreme values in the series and treat all country data

[3] This line of explanation is given plausibility by data in Dhonte (1995), showing the extent to which the overall stagnation of SSA in 1985–94 was statistically due to economic deterioration among CFA countries.

[4] The figures in the table do not fully agree with the data in the published version of the *World Development Indicators*. Reasons include incomplete information, particularly about PPP valuations and weighting systems. Also, the data in Table 1 are *median* values, not means, in order to overcome problems created by extreme values and to avoid the need to address the weighting issue.

Table 1.1: Key macroeconomic indicators for Sub-Saharan Africa[a]

	1992	*1993*	*1994*	*1995*	*1996*	*1997[b]*
1. Change in real per capita GDP (%)	−3.9	−2.4	−0.6	1.7	1.6	0.8
2. Gross investment as a % of GDP						
(a) Whole region	16.3	15.8	17.0	17.3	17.0	16.4
(b) Franc Zone	12.5	13.9	16.3	16.1	17.6	17.0
(c) Non-Franc Zone	17.2	16.2	17.1	17.5	16.9	16.3
3. Overall fiscal balance (% GDP)[c]	−9.1	−8.6	−7.8	−6.1	−5.8	−4.6
4. Broad money growth (%)	32.6	27.3	44.1	28.2	30.3	17.8
5. Consumer price inflation (%)	37.7	39.1	44.4	40.5	32.8	13.2

Source: Fischer et al. 1998 (from IMF databases).
Notes: (a) Weighted means
(b) Preliminary
(c) Excludes grant receipts.

Table 1.2: Growth and other performance indicators for Sub-Saharan Africa to 1995 (per cent p.a. except as indicated)

	1980–90	*1990–95*	*1994*	*1995*
1. Growth of total GDP				
(a) whole region	2.8	2.4	3.7	4.2
(b) SSA except Nigeria, RSA & Franc Zone	2.9	2.9	3.7	4.2
(c) Franc Zone only	2.9	1.1	2.1	4.5
2. Sectoral growth rates (whole region)				
(a) agriculture	2.8	1.3	2.6	3.0
(b) manufacturing	4.5	2.4	1.8	2.9
(c) services	3.6	1.9	3.0	4.1
3. Export value growth				
(a) whole region	5.1	2.7	3.7	13.7
(b) SSA except Nigeria, RSA & Franc Zone	4.3	3.4	10.5	8.7
(c) Franc Zone only	6.2	1.8	−0.8	25.8
4. Inflation				
(a) whole region	9.8	10.9	23.2	11.0
(b) SSA except Nigeria, RSA & Franc Zone	14.4	22.5	15.7	18.6
(c) Franc Zone only	4.3	8.8	33.2	8.0
5. Gross investment (% GDP) (whole region)	18.7	17.7	17.3	16.4
6. International reserves (months of imports) (whole region)	1.61	2.22	2.48	2.67

Source: World Bank World Development Indicators, 1997a and b, 1998 & CD-ROM.
Note: Median values.

as having equal weight. There are obvious advantages and disadvantages to both types of calculation. What is clear from both tables, however, is that, while Africa's recovery is noteworthy by comparison with what went before, its speed is less than giddying. At least the decline in per capita incomes has been reversed (Table 1.1) but the positive growth of the most recent years is still fairly slow, with average incomes in 1997 still below the 1991 level.

We should not exaggerate the extent of the recovery. When we turn to look at price stability, the differences between the two tables are great, largely because of Table 1.2's low weight given to extreme values. However, it is difficult to discern any strong trend in inflation from either table; up to 1996 the recent record seems about in line with that for the 1990s as a whole. The most intriguing figure is the IMF's estimate of sharply lower inflation in 1997 (Table 1.1, line 5). Table 1.2 provides some indication of an improving balance of payments, with reserves (relative to imports) apparently on a rising trend, even though imports have also been growing, and we shall later note an improving export record.

From whence is the growth coming? Before looking at country disaggregations, see Section 2 of Table 1.2, providing sectoral growth rates. From these it seems that the services sector (although this is actually a conglomerate of a wide range of public and private activities) is the fastest growing: a fact of some importance for the growth of small-scale enterprises, for economies of scale are less marked in many service activities than they are, say, in manufacturing. Agriculture has also been performing above its longer-term trend rate. There is little sign of any reversal of de-industrialization, with manufacturing the slowest-growing sector in 1994 and 1995. Exports have been doing quite well, however, particularly in 1995 (Table 1.2, item 3(a)) but unfortunately these figures are based on export values (volumes not available) and thus include price changes (although the UN (1998: 20) provides export volume data suggesting growth in the 6–8 per cent range for 1995–97.

What about the geographical breakdown? The data on which Table 1.1 is based were prepared for the SSA region as a whole, for SSA excluding Nigeria and South Africa, for SSA excluding also the Franc Zone countries, and for the Franc Zone alone. Weighted means were also calculated for all series and these would give more prominence to the contributions of Nigeria and South Africa. In fact, however, exclusion of these two countries alone (as 'special cases') made little overall difference to the results obtained. More interest attached to the results that also excluded the Franc Zone countries because of the stagnation of most of these economies prior to the January 1994 devaluation and their revival since. Table 1.2 brings out two other features which are particularly noteworthy for the CFA countries: (a) the extraordinary turnaround that occurred in their export performance between 1994 and 1995: an outcome which must surely be related to the devaluation; and (b) the jump in their inflation rates in 1994 (also presumably an effect of devaluation) and its subsequent decline in 1995.

Table 1.3 takes the task of country disaggregation a little further by asking how widespread the recent growth has been. For this purpose, we have included some highly provisional estimates for 1996 (see the note to Table 1.3). First, we looked for countries that had consistently achieved GDP growth of 5.0 per cent or more (not a particularly high hurdle) during each of the years 1994–96: see section (A) of the table. Only three countries passed this test: Angola, Togo and Uganda (Togo's substantial growth in 1994, when most other CFA countries remained quite depressed, is best understood as a rebound from the political uncertainty and economic recession of 1991–93). As at 1996, these three made up only 6 per cent of Africa's total population. An additional three countries – Guinea, Mauritania and Mozambique – passed the lower hurdle of at least 4 per cent growth in each of the years, and these account for a further 4.5 per cent of the region's population: see section (B) of the table. Note that two of these countries are recovering from devastating civil wars. For them we may merely be observing a temporary catching-up process rather than a movement on to a steeper long-term trend line.

A different approach is taken in section C, which records the proportions of countries with specified growth levels in each of the years recorded. This provides a more encouraging picture. We see there a rather steep increase in the proportions of countries with reasonably strong growth records, together with a halving between 1994 and 1995 of the proportion of countries whose GDPs were shrinking or growing at under 1 per cent (remember that most

Table 1.3: Consistency in GDP growth, 1994–96

	1994	*1995*	*1996*[a]
A – Countries with GDP growth of at least 5% in each year			
Angola	7.7	6.3	(16)
Togo	13.0	8.2	(13)
Uganda	6.1	11.2	(10)
B – Additional countries with growth of at least 4% in each year			
Guinea	4.0	4.6	(5)
Mauritania	4.4	4.6	(4)
Mozambique	5.4	4.3	(7)
C – Proportions of countries with strong and weak growth records			
4% p. a. or more	42	59	63
5% p. a. or more	23	36	40
1% p. a. or less	30	15	17
Number of observations	43	39	35

Source: World Bank World Development Indicators, 1997a and b 1998 & CD-ROM.
Note: 1996 figures are more than usually approximate, being derived as the growth rates implicit from comparison of 1990–95 and 1990–96 growth averages.

countries have population growth rates of 2–3 per cent p.a.); there were only six such countries in both 1995 and (provisionally) 1996.

In other words, the numbers of countries participating in the growth is quite substantial and apparently rising, although consistency is a problem. Note also that the two giants of the region, Nigeria and South Africa, have not led the growth recovery, and IMF data indicate that they have continued to lag through to 1997 (Fischer et al. 1998: Table 2).

Identifying the fundamentals: the African growth literature

To go beyond the growth rates we need to enquire into the sources of growth in African economies, to examine to what extent these too have improved and are likely to continue to do so. There has in recent years been an appreciable amount of research into the sources of growth in Africa and from these it is possible to extract a substantial number of candidate fundamentals, or explanatory variables. Unfortunately, there is not yet consensus about the causes: each author has his own model, resulting in a rather rich mix of significant variables.

At the same time, there is a fair degree of agreement about at least some of the more obvious variables. No attempt is made in this chapter to develop and test any particular model. The approach is eclectic. Table 1.4 lists all the candidate fundamentals that receive some serious degree of support in the existing empirical literature. As the table note states, some of these can be expected to be closely related to each other but until more definitive results are available it is not possible to narrow the list further with confidence. Fortunately, it is not necessary for the limited purposes of this chapter to postulate some definitive model: the variables listed in Table 1.4 can be defended as plausible potential influences. They are placed into four groups, roughly according to the speed with which they can change and their responsiveness to policy, from the 'Givens' of Part A of the table to the policy variables in Part C. It is impossible to discuss each of these within the confines of this chapter, although the table provides a very brief commentary on each, together with source citations where appropriate.

One point that should be noted, however, is that, other things being equal, Africa's initial low levels of income and development predict that the continent should have experienced average long-term growth, rather than the contrary (see item A6 of Table 1.4): the 'catch-up' hypothesis which underlies most modern growth theory, on the grounds that the highest returns to capital should be obtained in the economies with the greatest capital scarcities. Perhaps, then, the tendency towards catch-up is at last asserting itself? If so, that bodes well for the sustainability of the recovery.

This consideration helps explain the apparently limited attention paid in Table 1.4 to the influence of investment. There is little dispute that low past levels of capital formation have made a major contribution to SSA's economic

Table 1.4: Influences on economic growth in Africa

Variable	*Expected Sign*	*Comment*
(A) 'GIVENS' (change slowly or not at all; exogenous or insensitive to policies)		
1. Nearness to equator	-	Ram (1997) finds this a highly significant, robust and quantitatively substantial variable. Explanation: adverse impact on soils, agricultural productivity and human health. Also Sachs and Warner (1997).
2. Weather/climate	+/-	Weather (especially rainfall) has obvious short-term impact on agricultural yields. A long-term declining rainfall trend in low rain-change areas has exerted negative effects (Collier and Gunning 1997: 13).
3. Natural resource	+/-	Despite contributing to GDP and exports, the balance of opinion now predicts a net negative outcome, via Dutch Endowment Disease, etc. (Sachs and Warner 1997: 348).
4. Landlockedness	-	Raises transport costs and risks, reduces gains from trade (Sachs and Warner 1997). There is a high incidence of this in SSA.
5. Population growth and economic dependence	+/-	Despite potential benefits from technical progress and scale economies, net effect often found to be negative (Sachs &Warner 1997; Hadjimichael et al. 1995; Ghura 1995; etc), via reduced K: L and productivity growth.
6. Low initial income	+	Note this is a positive factor. Occurs via 'catch-up' – higher returns to capital. A basic feature of modern growth theory. But contingent on other country characteristics.
7. Contagion effects	-	Slow-growing neighbours have negative effect (Easterly and Levine 1998). Average African country's neighbours grew at only 0.5% p.a. in 1960–90. East Asia equivalent: 4.2%.
8. Smallness of domestic market	-	Limits industrialization possibilities. Aggravates effects of closed-economy biases (Killick 1994).
9. Terms of trade	+/- (-)	Exert strong short-term influence. Also, a long-term tendency to deteriorate (Hadjimichael et al. 1995) (see also B8).
10. World real interest rates	+/-	Found by Ghura (1995) to have been significant and substantial negative influence on SSA growth in 1970–90.

Table 1.4: *Contd.*

(B) – INTERMEDIATE VARIABLES (less slow-changing; somewhat responsive to policy)		
1. Low domestic saving and investment (S&I)	-	SSA severely hampered by low past S & I. Capital stock per worker and as per cent GDP falling or static (Collier and Gunning 1997). Both public and private investment are important (Khan and Kumar 1997; Oshikoya 1994).
2. Foreign aid	+/-	Should have positive effect by augmenting domestic saving but could induce lower saving, Dutch Disease, reduced policy credibility, etc.
3. Heavy external indebtedness	-	'Debt overhang' effect. Discourages investment. Elbadawi et al. (1997a) find this to be significant drag on private investment.
4. Slow technological progress	-	Difficult to capture satisfactorily in growth regressions. SSA believed to lag behind other regions, leading to slower productivity growth. Collier and Gunning (1997, Table 1) show growth in 1971–91 to have contributed only 0.2% p.a. to output growth, against 1,3 per cent for all developing countries.
5. Poor human capital	-	Knowledge, skills, vigour, education and health. SSA disadvantaged by very low initial levels and continuing lags in quantity and quality (Killick 1994, etc).
6. Financial shallowness	-	Poor level of development of financial services; poorly functioning financial markets. Expected to be significant brake on growth but shows up only weakly in growth regressions.
7. Poor infrastructure	-	Depresses productivity, raises risks. SSA particularly disadvantaged (Hayami and Platteau 1997: Table 3). Elbadawi et al. (1997b) find this to be a significant negative influence. Also Easterly and Levine (1998).
8. Primary product dependence	-	SSA export structure has diversified less out of PPs than other regions. Fosu (1996) finds PP exports to have weaker growth-inducing effects.

(C) - POLICY VARIABLES		
1. Exchange rate competitiveness	+/	Together with C2, various studies emphasize importance of quality of macro-policies (Hadjimichael et al. 1995; Burnside and Dollar 1997; Ghura 1995; etc). Importance of Franc Zone response to CFA devaluation.
2. Fiscal and monetary	+/-	As for C1.
3. Public services	+/-	Adequacy of these as affecting human capital, returns to private investment, improvement of productivity, 'social capital'. Negative effects of poor past quality stressed by Collier and Gunning (1997).
4. Policies affecting openness	+/-	Most growth equations find openness a strongly positive influence (Sachs and Warner 1997; Collier and Gunning 1997; Hadjimichael et al 1995). Past policies have been particularly protective (e.g. Ng and Yeats 1997) but have become less so in recent years. Growth particularly influenced by export performance (Ghura 1995).
5. 'Market friendliness'	+/-	Past policies regarded as antithetical to market mechanisms with strongly negative results (World Bank 1981, etc). But very difficult to catch in growth regressions.
(D) – POLITICS, INSTITUTIONS, 'SOCIAL CAPITAL' (influencing choice of policies and most of 'intermediate' variables).		
1. Weak institutions / 'social capital'	-	Includes weak rule of law, enforceability of property rights, ethnic fractionalism, 'patrimonialism', corruption, political instability. Importance stressed by Hadjimichael et al. (1995); Collier and Gunning (1997); Killick (1994); etc. Easterly and Levine (1997) find ethnic divisions to have a powerfully negative growth effect. See also World Bank (1997a) for evidence of negative effects of various aspects of weak 'social capital'

Note: Several of the variables are quite closely related to each other. Thus, only some of them could appropriately be included in any one regression equation.

stagnation, with most, although not all, investigators finding investment to be a significant explanatory variable. However, this begs the question of why investment has been so low. The indications are that returns on investment are particularly low in Africa (Collier and Gunning 1997: 16; Elbadawi et al. 1997b), quite the contrary of what the catch-up hypothesis predicts (although we should remember it is a 'contingent' hypothesis, depending on other country characteristics), so we need to ask why this should be, to probe below the investment figures, which is what some of the other variables listed in Table 1.4 seek to do.

We should also observe that there remains uncertainty about how much stress should be placed on the relative influence of policy and non-policy variables. The overwhelming stress from donor agencies, as well as academic researchers, has been on the quality of policies, especially macroeconomic management (see sources cited in Table 1.4; also Fischer et al. 1998) but it is worth remembering that some of the studies cited there also find exogenous shocks to exert a potent influence. We should also record Easterly et al.'s (1993) examination of the sources of differences in country growth rates, finding that shocks exerted as much influence on outcomes as policies, cautioning against over-emphasis on what can be achieved through policy improvements alone.

Have the fundamentals improved?

We turn now to investigate the extent to which the fundamentals identified in Table 1.4 exhibit signs of improvement, in ways that throw light on whether the recent growth recovery is likely to continue over the longer term. We shall have to do so selectively, of course, because some of the variables in Part A of the table are invariant 'givens' (landlockedness, nearness to equator, etc.) and also because of restrictions imposed by data availabilities. First, has Africa's recovery been a matter of good luck, the by-product of favourable world economic conditions, or of good weather?

Good luck? Examining a 'given' such as weather, it is not possible to reduce this to a single statistical indicator. However, it does appear that weather conditions were reasonably favourable in much of the region during 1994–96, contributing to the above-trend agricultural growth in 1994–95 recorded in Table 1.2 (item 2(a)), a result which appears to have continued in 1996, with a provisional growth rate for agriculture of 4–5 per cent in that year. It appears that conditions were a good deal less favourable in 1997, and what is being attributed to the effect in 1998, but for the years for which we have growth data, it appears that favourable weather helped to some modest extent.

What about the commodity terms of trade, fluctuations in which can exert a strong short-term influence on economic growth among African countries? There is need for some caution here because different estimates of SSA's terms of trade provide substantially varying results. What is evident is that it would be impossible to explain the growth recovery as a consequence of terms of trade movements. The long-term downward trend has continued in the 1990s. This was broken only by a very slight improvement in 1996 (largely the result of temporary rises in petroleum prices), which particularly helped a few oil-exporting countries, but which has been followed by substantial commodity price falls since mid-1997, accelerated by the spill-over effects of the East Asian crisis. Overall, SSA's post-1993 growth recovery has been achieved in the face of adverse terms of trade movements.

What of world interest rates, rather surprisingly found by Ghura (1995) to exert a significant and substantial influence on growth on the continent? Here too the evidence is unambiguous: world real interest rates in the relevant period have tended to rise, with inflation declining faster than nominal interest rates. Here again, it seems that Africa's recovery cannot be explained as simply a contagion effect from a worldwide economic boom. Overall, it seems that a 'good luck' line of explanation of Africa's growth recovery can be firmly ruled out. The weather helped a little until 1996, but a booming world economy did not translate into terms of trade and interest rate shifts that added to Africa's recovery.

One other of the given, or only slow-changing, variables is worth mentioning: population growth. While SSA, with North Africa and the Middle East, remains the region with by far the fastest-growing population, it seems that the rate of increase is gradually declining in SSA (% p. a.):

1980–90: 3.0 1990–95: 2.6

This is also reflected in declining fertility, with the crude death rate still falling gradually despite the ravages of AIDS and other diseases (total fertility rate, number of children):

1980: 6.7 1990: 5.7 1996: 5.6

Bearing in mind the negative sign of population growth in most growth regression results, this trend, while far too gradual to explain the post-1993 growth recovery, can be expected to make it a little easier to sustain the improvement into the future. Indeed, given the strong connection that also flows from economic growth to declining fertility, there may be a virtuous circle at work here, albeit of modest strength.

Intermediate variables: investment, human capital and others

We turn now to variables listed in Table 1.4 as intermediate in nature: less slow-changing; more amenable to manipulation through policy changes. Does the recent behaviour of these help explain Africa's growth recovery and can we infer from them anything about the likely sustainability of the process?

The recent behaviour of domestic saving and investment is particularly important in this connection, not only for their direct growth-inducing effects but also because of what they might tell us about sustainability and the extent to which underlying determinants may also be changing. Unfortunately, the news here is not encouraging. Recent saving investment levels relative to GDP remain as low, relative to other regions, as they have throughout the 1990s, a statement which is true of both private and public investment (see Table 1.1, item 2). Domestic saving has also remained stuck at similar levels. Some qualifications are necessary, in that there has been some revival of investment among some of the faster-growing African countries, particularly within the Franc Zone, where private investors appear to have been initially encouraged by the incentives created by the 1994 devaluation. Even in these countries, however, the ratio appears to have levelled off at the overall regional average of around 17 per cent of GDP.

Overall, however, it does not appear that the African growth recovery has been primarily investment driven, i.e. has been based on the more productive use of existing resources. No doubt there remains much scope for more of that, but it is equally clear that growth could not be sustained indefinitely through such means. Gross investment rates of well under a fifth of GDP are simply inconsistent with adequate long-term growth, and the continued depression of private investment levels suggest that there has not, as yet, been any decisive improvement in expected returns and risks. This conclusion is reinforced by the continuing extremely low levels of foreign direct investment coming into Africa, a point that will be taken up later.

One related point to note, however, is that post-1993 growth has been achieved despite falling aid levels, a feature which might be read as rather reinforcing those who see aid-dependence as ineffective if not actually harmful, but which could equally well be seen as reinforcing the earlier point that the growth recovery has been achieved despite adverse external factors:

	1991	*1994*	*1996*
Aid as % GDI	35.3	34.1	27.8
Aid as % imports	18.0	18.4	12.7

One of the factors identified in Table 1.4 as probably having exerted a drag on investment in the past is the external debt overhang, by reducing the expected returns on investment, raising perceived risks and competing away public revenues which could otherwise be devoted to capital formation. There have, of course, been successive initiatives to provide debt relief to low-income SSA debtor countries, of which the most recent is the 1996 'Heavily Indebted Poor Country' (HIPC) initiative. Although many would argue that they still do not go far enough, the concessions now on offer have begun to make a real difference and the overhang (conventionally represented by total debt relative to GNP) has fallen appreciably since its peak in 1994. Debt service payments have been slower to come down, because of the growing share of multinational creditors in the total debt stock, but these too are estimated to have fallen in 1996.

These improvements might have played some role in the recent growth recovery, although it would be much easier to be confident about this had we not already observed the absence of any appreciable recovery in investment. Assuming that debt ratios continue to decline, as they should under the terms of HIPC, this should exert a positive influence on future investment, although the position is likely to vary greatly from debtor country to debtor country.

Proceeding through the 'intermediate' factors listed in Table 1.4, what now of trends in technological progress? Here we can offer only the most fragmentary evidence, in statistics on the utilization of commercial energy and of fertilizers in agriculture:

Commercial energy use per capita (kg)	1980: 249 1992: 258 1995: 237
Fertilizer consumption (kg/ha.)	1979–81: 16.0 1994–96: 13.2

It would be absurd to try to draw any strong conclusions from such straws in the wind and it may be that, for agriculture at least, the impression of inertia which they convey is false. Progress is being made with the spread of hybrid varieties and improved techniques in the agricultural sectors of a number of African countries, even if elsewhere there is little progress.

What is clear, however, is that the above numbers offer no clue as to the sources of the recent economic growth, nor any encouragement for the sustainability of this. The suspicion remains that the pace of technological progress remains slow in Africa and that the gap with the rest of the world is widening rather than narrowing.

What of the human capital situation? This too is notoriously difficult to capture with any simple statistical series. We offer three indicators: adult literacy as a broad measure of the stock of people with at least a minimum level of education; the ratio of pupils to teachers in primary schools, as providing some (highly imperfect) idea of the quality of education on offer; and the infant mortality rate, as an indicator of trends in health standards:

Adult literacy (per cent)	1980: ? 1990: 44 1995: 56
Primary pupil:teacher ratio	1980: 39 1993: 36 1995: 41

Infant mortality (deaths per 1000 births)	1980: 115 1992: 97 1996: 91

Again, the evidence is painfully inadequate. The improvement during the 1990s in adult literacy is a positive sign (although the rate of improvement in a previously stationary and normally only slow-changing statistic is suspiciously rapid, raising questions about the reliability of the statistics), but the pupil:primary school teacher ratio shows no improvement. Indeed, it seems quite possible that the quality of education provided has deteriorated, as governments have sought to reconcile protecting the employment of teachers with overall budgetary stringency by cutting back on maintenance, school books and other inputs. The infant mortality trend is also an encouraging one. If it is representative of the general trend in health (notwithstanding AIDS, etc), it could help sustain growth in the future, although the gradual, long-term nature of the trend rules it out as an explanation for the upsurge in economic growth of the most recent years.

Unfortunately, we have been unable to find meaningful up-to-date statistics on trends in financial deepening, which is the next of our 'intermediate' variables and we are in a not much better condition regarding infrastructure. The only straw in the wind there is that data on telephone availability per 1000 of the population, although varying widely according to the measure chosen, all indicate an increasing trend. There are no continent-wide time-series data on trends in transport and other forms of infrastructure, although it is most unlikely that improvements (if any) in such capital-intensive items could have been rapid enough in recent years to stimulate much of the increased growth, especially given the continued depressed levels of public investment.

Are policy improvements driving the recovery?

We turn now to some of the policy variables set out in Table 1.4. Here too we have only highly incomplete data. By common consent, the exchange rate (particularly the real exchange rate) is a policy instrument of the first importance in the trade-dependent economies of Africa, influencing the production of tradeable goods; the prospective returns on private investment; the inflation rate; and government tax revenues. It is evident that the last decade or more has seen the adoption of far more flexible exchange rate policies in Africa than held through the 1960s, 1970s and through into the 1980s. We have already signalled the 1994 CFA devaluation as an important event for the performance of the Franc Zone countries.

What of recent movements in this variable? The World Bank publishes index series for trends in real effective exchange rates (REERs) among its *World Development Indicators*, but there is only a limited number of observations for African countries, and only for 1990 (the base year), 1995 and 1996. A mixed story emerges from these:

- All except three (Burundi, Nigeria, Sierra Leone) of the 15 countries for which there are estimates had REER levels in 1996 which were below the 1990 level, indicating a tendency towards depreciating rates. Among non-CFA countries there were seven depreciating countries, against three appreciators.
- Between 1995 and 1996 the number of countries whose REERs appreciated (i.e. became less competitive) exceeded those who depreciated in the ratio 3:2. This is probably the result of the Franc Zone arrangements, where the nominal rate has been fixed since January 1994, resulting in a gradual tendency towards appreciation, with the CFA franc tied to a French franc which in turn, is part of the EU Exchange Rate Mechanism, i.e. is effectively tied to the Deutschmark. However, most of the appreciations were minor.
- Averages for these 15 countries give mixed results. The (unweighted) means (1990 = 100) for 1995 and 1996 were 86.9 and 88.7 respectively. Equivalent median values were 91.7 and 87.7. Either way, no strong trend is revealed. It is the depreciation below the 1990 level which is the more significant.

What of the quality of other aspects of macroeconomic management?

The general perception is that macro-policies have improved and, particularly, that governments are being more careful to avoid large budget deficits that can be financed only through monetary expansion. A degree of support for this proposition is provided by data in Table 1.1, with fiscal deficits apparently on a declining trend (although for all items it would be wise not to place much weight on the 1997 provisionals). We sought confirmation of these budgetary trends from the World Bank's *World Development Indicators* database (but with observations available only for 1994 and 1995) by examining statistics on the extent of budget financing by domestic borrowing, which is probably the best single indicator of the macroeconomic quality of fiscal policy. Unfortunately, however, there are complete observations for a mere eight SSA countries, and this small sample is clearly biased in favour of governments with relatively high standards of management (and hence fiscal reporting). For what they are worth, the data for these countries indicate that the scale of domestic deficit financing diminished in four cases and worsened in the other four: no clear trend.

There is rather more information on monetary developments. The indicator we use here is of the growth of broad money supply (M2). Table 1.1 (line 4) provides weighted means which, if we leave the 1997 estimate to one side, reveal no clear trend. There are *Development Indicator* data for 1992–95 (with the number of observations varying between 37 and 42).

Mean values were seriously distorted by extreme values (e.g. Zaire's M2 grew by nearly 7000 per cent in 1994) but by using medians we obtained the following rates of (current price) monetary growth (per cent), which are markedly different from those in Table 1.1:

1993: 12.8 1994: 31.4 1995: 15.0

Comparing the above, as well as the Table 1.1 statistics, with the real growth of the economies in question indicates that money supply was still growing well ahead of demand, and this can be related to the data on inflation trends in Tables 1.1 and 1.2. Of course, inflation is not purely a product of fiscal and monetary policies. Exchange rate movements also exert a strong influence, as may price trends in the rest of the world and the influence of weather on food supplies (although we have seen that the latter was moderately benign during the years we are studying). Nevertheless, the absence of any clear deceleration of inflation (with the unreliable exception of the provisional 1997 estimate) does raise questions about the extent of improvement in macro-management.

This, in fact, must be the overall judgement on the quality of macroeconomic management. To the extent that we can draw any conclusions from the poor evidence available, it is that no strong improving (or deteriorating) trend emerges. Once again, we are unable to utilize this set of variables to provide any strong explanation of the growth recovery. We can also relate this conclusion to the weak demonstrated ability of the 'structural adjustment' programmes of the IMF and World Bank to exert a decisive impact on the quality of macroeconomic policies (Killick forthcoming: 2) and the limited number of African governments regarded by those agencies as pursuing satisfactory macro-policies, although it is true that most of the evidence pre-dates 1994.

Openness

The background here is the strong connection found in a number of studies between increasing openness and economic growth (Table 1.4, item C(4)). If only by virtue of their smallness, Africa's economies are, of course, highly trade-dependent. However, this does not necessarily mean that they are open, in the sense of having policies and practices in place which maximize the gains from trade and encourage inflows of capital from the rest of the world. We earlier noted evidence that Africa as a region has particularly high protective barriers (Ng and Yeats 1997). Once again, we are not in a position to offer direct evidence on recent continent-wide changes in policies towards trade and capital flows, and are restricted to examining changes in the economic variables most likely to be influenced by such changes in policy.

First, there are the following data on the value of international trade (exports plus imports) relative to GDP in recent years (per cent):

1992: 63.0 1993: 56.0 1994: 71.3 1995: 68.6

If we take the first two years as representative of the pre-recovery situation and the latter two as belonging to the recovery period, then there does appear to be a noteworthy overall increase in this indicator of openness and we can also recall the earlier discussion of the positive role of export expansion in recent economic growth. However, the statistical basis for this generalization is fragile.

The other indicator we can use is inflows of foreign direct investment. It is well known that little such investment has occurred in the past, despite increasing attempts by African governments to convince investors that they should bring in their money. The following figures are median values for inflows, expressed as percentages of GDP:

1992: 0.41 1993: 0.97 1994: 0.62 1995: 0.88

It is difficult to derive much encouragement from these figures and the indications are that the 1996 data do not display any overall improvement. In all years the figure is below 1 per cent of GDP. We might also recall the data given earlier showing foreign aid to have declined sharply in 1996, although this is not a good indicator of openness.

To sum up, instead of lamenting the absence of direct evidence on various other relevant aspects of policy – not least measures policies affecting 'market friendliness' – it is best to conclude this section by admitting that we have been unable to find strong policy reasons for the growth recovery. There is no firmly-established improving trend in any of the macroeconomic indicators we have been able to deploy, with the partial exception of budgetary trends, although the longer-term movement towards greater exchange rate flexibility has been important, contributing to the export expansion of the most recent years.

The role of politics and institutions

Beneath (often irrational-seeming) economic policy choices there lie political institutions and interest systems which yield their own logic. As summarised in Table 1.4 (D), various authors have sought to establish a link between political systems in African countries, their policies and their economic performance. Economists increasingly recognize the importance of bringing such political and institutional factors into their analyses, which it has become fashionable to bundle under the heading of 'social capital': a vague concept which refers, *inter alia*, to such factors as the rule of law and enforceability of property rights, the extent and predictability of corruption, ethnic fractionalism and other sources of political instability.

There is presumably little dispute about the economic importance of such factors (to say nothing of their importance for human rights), nor about the fact that quite a substantial amount of potentially important political change has occurred in SSA in recent years. Alienation from the state and discontent with governments has often reached an intensity which enforced changes. Governments find it increasingly difficult to keep control of press and electronic media. Old-style *de facto* one-party states with apparently irreplaceable leaders, like Moi's Kenya or Mugabe's Zimbabwe, look increasingly like endangered species. There have been more multi-party elections; a few leaders have been voted out of office (although more have had themselves re-elected). In principle, these developments should be good for public accountability (and hence probity), for transparency (and hence market friendliness), for the rule of law and for political stability (both reducing the perceived riskiness of investment).

This is over-simplistic, however. For one thing, researchers looking for associations between types of political system and economic performance world-wide have found little correlation. Here is an area where the 'East Asian miracle' (now looking a little jaded) has unwelcome implications for Africa. Strong governments with 'autonomous' policy makers seem there to have produced the best results but that is not necessarily the direction in which Africa has been travelling.

There are other reasons for not drawing a simple connection between political liberalization and improved economic policies. Democracy brings its own distortions to economic policy-making, among them the electoral cycle. To give but one example, but from a country which has been widely extolled as illustrating the benefits of Washington-style economic policy reforms, a persuasive argument could be made out for the proposition that Ghana's public finances and monetary stability have yet to recover from the loss of fiscal discipline which resulted from the first multi-party elections in 1992.

Multipartyism may also be a vehicle for heightened, rather than reduced, ethnicity, with all that may entail for clientelism and the misdirection of public resources. Moreover, political liberalization will not necessarily do much to restore the often seriously eroded capabilities of state institutions to design and implement improved policies. For these and other reasons, the formalities of Western-style parliamentary democracy cannot be assumed to translate into the economic policy advantages which are often assumed, even where they result in improved human rights observation.

In short, it is not obvious that the processes of political change (while desirable for other reasons) that are under way will necessarily bring a net improvement in economic policy choices. Even liberalized governments still struggle to achieve credibility; there remains much public uncertainty about the outcomes and a perceived danger that reforms may be reversed. Although the situation varies greatly across countries and the overall trend is a slowly improving one, the perceived riskiness of investing in Africa remains generally high, with credit rating agencies still giving SSA by far the worst risk rating of all regions. The absence of any revival of investment in Africa's growth recovery could be seen as a predictable outcome of these continuing uncertainties and of the unsatisfactory institutions which underlie them.

Conclusion

Most short-term forecasts for GDP growth in SSA are moderately optimistic, expecting growth of 4–5 per cent in 1998. May we then conclude that Africa's economies have indeed turned the corner? Certainly there are some reasons for optimism. We have shown that the accelerated growth of the last few years is not confined to some small group of countries, with well over half growing at 4 per cent or more. This is important, not only because it stands to benefit large numbers of people, but also because its multiplier effects help lagging neighbouring countries step up their growth too (Easterly and Levine's (1998) positive contagion effects). Moreover, we have shown that the growth recovery cannot be put down just to good luck. While the weather has indeed been kind until recently, the improved economic results have been achieved in the face of generally unhelpful trends in the terms of trade and in world interest rates. International efforts to reduce external debt burdens may help encourage investment and limit the diversion of government revenues away from economically productive uses. Even some of the more deep-seated constraints show signs of improvement, of which slowing population growth and improving health and education indicators are noteworthy. Moreover, there have been some important policy changes, most notably towards more flexible and competitive exchange rates, plus a tentative trend towards improved fiscal balance, and there has been a welcome and long overdue improvement in Africa's export performance; and we should always remember that there are potentially huge gains if the continent can begin to take advantage of its catch-up potential by improving the returns to be had from new investments.

Against these encouragements we must set some more negative considerations, however. First, while the growth recovery has been reasonably widespread, we saw that few countries have managed to sustain consistent above-average growth year by year, and two of the few that have done so are in war recovery situations. We noticed too that the region's economic giants, Nigeria and South Africa, have not been in the vanguard of the recovery; both of them face formidable (but different) political-economy difficulties. Our analysis has also thrown some doubt on the extent and spread of economic policy reforms in the directions of improved macro-stability, market friendliness and openness, although the availability of evidence here is particularly inadequate. A most serious factor for the sustainability of accelerated growth is the continued depressed levels of public and private investment, which remain at levels incompatible with sustained rapid growth. The continuing low levels of private investment (including foreign direct investment, which, on a net basis, remains almost negligible) suggest that there has as yet been little fundamental improvement in investors' perceptions of the balance between risk and reward. They, it seems, are betting against the persistence of the growth recovery. Rebuilding reputations and confidence can be a slow process.

No doubt perceptions are influenced by the intractable or slow-changing nature of some of the more fundamental constraints summarized in Parts A and B of Table 1.4, of which the poor stock of human capital, the associated weak ability to make productive use of modern technology, the parlous condition of the physical infrastructure, and the weakness of the institutions of the state suggest themselves as of particular importance. The severity and intractability of these constraints help to explain why Africa's economies have responded only rather weakly to the improved price incentives associated with structural adjustment programmes, which, in turn, raises questions about the sustainability of the policy changes. Lastly, there are questions about the extent to which recent political changes are likely to strengthen the conditions for growth and provide reassurance against policy and institutional reversals in the future.

On balance, these considerations warn against any facile assumption that Africa can at last look forward to a prolonged period of catching up: not merely with other regions but even with the modest living standards it used to have. There are at least more grounds for optimism today than there have been for a long time. But the obstacles remain extremely large and the danger of regression is ever present. The one safe conclusion is that outcomes are likely to differ greatly across the countries of Africa, just as they do at present. The African entrepreneur must pray that he or she has been born in the right country.

Finally, we should bear in mind the appallingly poor state in which African most socio-economic data remain. The evidence presented above is highly incomplete, often out of date, no less often unreliable. Country data change bewilderingly from one year to the next; some look implausible. Anyone who has worked with the detail of Africa statistics knows how easy it is to slip into a morass. Any conclusions about Africa's prospects may hence be unsafe – except that improving on this situation ought surely to be a top priority, promising large returns.

2 Developmental states and small enterprises

THANDIKA MKANDAWIRE

For a volume on small enterprises, it may seem odd that one draws attention to the role of the state, especially in its full-blooded 'developmental form'. The widespread view of the relationship between the state and the small enterprise sector is that the less the state interferes the better, and this for both doctrinal and practical reasons. Against this view, I argue that even in a strategy that is 'friendly' to small enterprises, the state needs to play a developmental role way beyond that of the Smithian 'state as watchman' or the 'minimalist' state sanctioned by the 'Washington consensus'. The development of SMEs presupposes a proactive and interventionist policy and state capacity to pursue such policies. I shall argue that one of the effects of SAP in Africa has been precisely to erode the capacity of the state to carry out these measures. Consequently, any strategy designed to stimulate SMEs and articulate them dynamically and synergistically with other sectors will need a more active and revamped state.

Although much of the writing on small enterprises tends to succumb to a Manichaean discourse in which 'small is beautiful' and big is ugly, realistic strategies have generally involved 'walking on two legs' within a fairly coherent industrial policy. If industrialization based on highly protected large-scale industrialization has not been a resounding success in Africa, the case for a small enterprises-based development strategy is not closed. Allowing for learning effect, scale economies, external effects and less than perfectly competitive markets, a case can still be made, even on the basis of neo-classical theory, for a policy that encourages large-scale industry or consolidation of small enterprises into larger ones, and pushes for an economy that is 'bimodal' or that encourages the dominance of large-scale enterprises. That, after all, was the approach that characterized the South Korean strategy of industrialization in which large-scale conglomerates (*chaebols*) have played a leading role in the economy (Amsden 1995; Chang 1996). The role that the SMEs ultimately play will depend on the relationship they have with the large-scale enterprises.

I define a developmental state as one whose ideological underpinnings are developmental and which seriously *attempts* to deploy its administrative and political resources to the task of economic development. Proxies such as 'tax efforts' and expenditure patterns can be used to measures such 'seriousness'. The main force behind such an ideology has usually been nationalism, inducing nations to seek to catch up with countries considered as more developed or to firm the resource base for national defence and security, etc. Can the state in Africa play a developmental role with respect to both large and small enterprises? Although it is now widely admitted that the Asian states played a central role, it is still suggested that the African state cannot.

I have elsewhere argued that neither Africa's own history nor the practices of the most successful developmental states suggest that the edification of developmental states in Africa is impossible (Mkandawire 1998). Many of the things that are said to hamper African states from playing the role of a developmental state were quite prevalent in the Asian developmental states, and were often used in a deliberate manner to spur accumulation. It is true that some of those features are now blamed as the underlying as 'crony capitalism' that caused the Asian crisis, although only yesterday they were hailed as aspects of the 'embeddedness' of state policies in society and as evidence of close and synergetic collaboration of the state and the private sector (Evans 1997b).

Although I talk about small enterprises (SMEs) I shall specifically be referring to capitalist small enterprises, partly because when one talks of small enterprises in Africa one is usually not talking about small decentralized state enterprises or even co-operatives but of small, individually owned firms, and particularly those that rely on wage labour and are considered as the 'missing middle' in African economies. This is not simply a reflection of an ideological bias but because it immediately places the small enterprises in a context in which other classes may support or contest their emergence. In addition, these wage-labour-using SMEs are the most dynamic and offer the most promising opportunities for getting out of the subsistence or coping syndrome of many of informal sector activities in Africa today. And finally, the discussion of small enterprises within the capital-labour nexus problematizes the SMEs' relationship to the state not only as recipients of state favours but also in terms of their capacity to influence state polices in light of other claims on the state by other social classes, such as labour. The recognition that we are dealing with wage labour rather merely self-employment means that a whole range of labour issues arise. These labour aspects extend beyond the much vaunted job creation and touch upon such questions as earnings, labour market segmentation, lack of legal protection and the irregular nature of work, which are fraught with ideological and political conflicts. States play a central role in mediating the relationship between employers and employees and in many ways shape the relative balance of forces between them.

What do developmental states do with respect to small industry?

States can promote or support SMEs on both the supply and demand sides. Different authors writing on Africa have stressed a different side of the problem and have then argued that either supply or demand was a major constraint on the expansion of SMEs. This is, in a sense, a fruitless discussion since the relationship between supply and demand has the characteristic of a cobweb. Rapid growth in demand can reveal supply factors as the constraints.

However, after a while, supply may overtake demand giving the impression that it is demand that is a constraint. This yields a 'cobweb' movement of the supply and demand relationship. Consequently, depending on conjuncture and the types of questions asked, either supply or demand will be a constraint. State policy must therefore constantly consider both blades of the scissors.

On the demand side, policies aimed at supporting small enterprises have included demand simulation: one major determinant of the well-being of SMEs is overall economic growth. Consequently, state policies that stimulate aggregate demand and growth are of major interest to SMEs. The type of adjustment that African countries have pursued during the last 15 years has centred around economic stabilization and demand restraint and has thus been essentially deflationary, resulting in miserly rates of growth and hardly any increase in investment. Poorly devised trade liberalization has flooded domestic markets with imported goods because no policies to enhance domestic industries to produce some of these goods competitively were introduced simultaneously. Besides macroeconomic policies, the state can pursue sectoral or industrial-level policies that can support the growth of SMEs. The state can reserve selected items for exclusive production on the small scale, and can subcontract certain activities to SMEs.

On the supply side, the state can improve the functioning of markets by providing infrastructure (including industrial estates) and through pushing for certain organizational forms that exploit synergy and resolve co-ordination failure and reduce risk. It can facilitate acquisition of technological capability through its training programmes and extension services and through articulating small enterprises with large enterprises. The state can provide financial support through provision of subsidized credit or through the creation of 'rent-making' opportunities. Writers on Asia point to 'contingent rents' which have been used to encourage contests among private firms for government incentive and co-ordination schemes (Yanagihara 1997). Such rents are paid to reward growth enhancing activities by private firms. The presence of 'rents' might serve as an encouragement to more investment. Much of the writing on Asia, at least up until the current financial crisis, took it for granted that the creation and allocation of rents by the state had played a central role in both creating a nationalist capitalist class and in promoting accumulation (Jomo 1994).

In countries such as South Korea we find that financial assistance is the most critical form of support for SMEs. The Korean government has made extensive use of parastatal finance institutions, targeted credit, and credit guarantee schemes. Government intervention in finance was so pervasive that the line between private and collective support was blurred. Most SMEs sampled in a World Bank study used at least one collective institution of financial support, and rated them very positively (Kim and Nugent 1994). The point of the Asian experience is that the use of 'rent-seeking' as an argument against a more active developmental state is simply not credible. Rent seeking usually involves redistribution of income from one-group to another. The effect of such redistribution on growth depends on its impact on incentives and the use to which the 'winners' use the surplus in their hands. The relevant issues are: 'rents' for whom and with what reciprocal obligations for receivers of such rents?

The obvious message here is that there is a need for various form of 'rent-creating' policies and for the revival of 'development banking' in Africa, and not the *ad hoc* arrangements for funds for the promotion of small enterprises that we see today in Africa. There is also a need for industrial policies within which SMEs' policies are imbricated. Such roles require a much more active role for the state than that implied in the regulatory state that current programmes of 'good governance' are pushing. They presuppose a state committed to, and with the capacity for, social transformation.

The African case: reducing the capacity of the state

In sharp contrast to the situation outlined above, is the African case in which the trend has been towards the weakening of the state's capacity to perform these roles. In the more doctrinaire literature, small enterprises are the essence of competitive capitalism, unfettered by state intervention or state-supported monopolistic practices of large-scale industries. This view stems partly from the fact that in Africa the state has been associated with development strategies which have favoured large-scale parastatal enterprises or private firms dominated by trans-national corporations (TNCs). Such strategies have provided protection of markets; subsidized infrastructure; produced human resources appropriate to the requirements of large enterprises; practised credit rationing that provided cheap credit to large firms. These measures constitute, in the eyes of the critics, the 'distortions' that have hampered the growth of small enterprises in Africa through their discriminatory effects. The financial repression they have engendered has crowded out small enterprises from financial markets; zoning laws have discriminated against the private sector; the skills produced in the polytechnic schools have been the wrong ones for small enterprise. The litany of discriminating practices could go on. In light of such discriminatory practices, it is argued that the current wave of reining in the state is the best that could happen to small enterprises. In liberalized markets, small enterprises are expected to out-compete the hitherto heavily protected dinosaurs in both domestic and export markets. The removal of such policies would presumably favour small enterprises by creating a 'level playing field'. It will also induce potential entrepreneurs to move away from rent-seeking activities to directly productive activities. It will expand the domestic market for small enterprises by shifting demand away from import-intensive consumption patterns to ones favouring domestic goods. It will encourage competition in which small enterprises have (inherent?) advantage. It will open financial markets to enterprises hitherto kept out by financial repression. The growth of small enterprises will increase employment and, therefore, improve income distribution. All this follows not from any proven case that this is indeed what happens under structural adjustment but from a set of axioms that lead ineluctably to these conclusions, given the underlying assumptions.

One logical consequence has been that adjustment policies were aimed at 'rolling back the state'. While it is true that any kind of response to the fiscal crisis of the state may have justified drastic reductions in state expenditure, both the cognitive prism through which the problem was seen and the actual solutions proposed led to a drastic erosion of the capacity as a state by squeezing the state through fiscal constraints and by splitting it through increased fragmentation of control over public money between state institutions and a multitude of donor initiatives. One could add here the pillage of the state through asset-stripping and 'fire sales' through privatization. The effect of all this is captured by Janice Aron (1996) thus:

> The state in Africa has come full circle to the small government of precolonial days; but with the additional hystereris effect from past shocks of a seriously depleted current institutional capability, deterioration in the current quality and scope of social services and infrastructure provision, coupled with a fiscal position highly vulnerable to changes in foreign aid. (117)

Such a state cannot be expected to be of much use to the private sector, even of the small-scale type. No wonder 'capacity building' is now a major buzzword in the donor community.

Contradictory rationales and ideologies for small enterprises

With the demise of the state's position in the policy-making arena, policymaking in Africa has become nearly a free-for-all affair with the result that a whole range of rationales are advanced for policies pursued by the main actors, each of which has carved a niche for himself. The values and ideologies underpinning the support for small enterprises vary from the laissezfaireist neo-liberalism of de Soto (1989), through the 'employment creation' view of the ILO, to the humanitarian quest to reinforce 'survival' strategies for the poor. Although the principal actors behind these strategies often act as if their views converged, the objectives behind the promotion of small enterprises vary and are not always compatible. There is therefore a need to address the mutual compatibility of these views and their implications for the trajectory of growth of the small enterprise. Among the most frequently asserted objectives are:

- efficient utilization of resources

- employment generation
- innovative entrepreneurial development ('seedbed' role)
- stimulation and democratization of capital accumulation by redressing regional or ethnic imbalances
- regional development
- national control of the economy
- poverty alleviation
- increasing flexibility of the economy
- ensuring sustainable development through the use of environment-friendly small-scale technologies.

Even if all these objectives were pursued by one agent, they would need some prioritization and deliberate measures to reconcile them. Over the years, the dominant justification for small-scale enterprise has shifted. In the 1970s, the ILO approach related small-scale enterprise to strategies of 'growth with equity'. In more recent years, small enterprises have been defended on the basis of either static allocative efficiency (Steel 1993) which rarely spells out exactly how this relates to growth objectives, and often derives equity implications from neo-classical first principles (i.e. factors of production receive their correct returns), or on grounds of 'livelihood' or 'sustainable development' strategies which tend to relegate growth and efficiency considerations to a secondary position. Such a view is in sharp contrast to one that sees SMEs as the bastion against transnational capitalism and predatory states. For some, the emergence of such SMEs, especially in their informal form, signals the resurgence of civil society in Africa (Chazan 1987). This view, often held by NGOs, is concerned mostly with the 'social side' of enterprises and with associative types of enterprise, even though the bulk of micro-enterprises are individual or family. In the more openly pro-capitalist defence of SMEs the arguments takes a more Schumpetarian twist and stress the fundamental role of entrepreneurship in capitalist development. It should be noted here that the Schumpetarian vision is based on capitalism's capacity for 'creative destruction'. Those emphasizing the creative role often ignore the other half which may contradict the objectives of other supporters of SMEs. A dynamic SME sector may lead to the 'destruction' of some 'livelihood' activities and will lead to greater social differentiation as the rate of graduation is accelerated and many of the small enterprises go under, forcing the owners to engage in distress sales of their labour to the more entrepreneurial survivors of the competition.

Obviously, the various rationales underlying support for SMEs need to be reconciled, assuming they can be reconciled at all. Policy makers need to be cognisant of the inherently contradictory thrust of the various rationales. Such reconciliation or cognisance does not seem to be taking place in the African situations in which disparate sets of actors are engaged in promoting small enterprises. In Kenya, for instance, Aleke Dondo reports that there were 100 SME promotion programmes implemented by a variety of organizations, including the national government, bilateral and multilateral donors, private capital and NGOs (Dondo 1998). This leads not only to a fragmentation of assistance to the small enterprises, but also makes the reconciliation of the above objectives virtually impossible. Thus, programmes by some agents to promote SMEs through finance offered on commercial terms can be undermined by competition from heavily subsidized producers of the same commodities. It is this multiplicity and conflicts of objectives that obfuscates the success criteria that are used to judge a particular strategy for the promotion of small enterprises in Africa.

Absence of industrial policy

'Industrial Policy' has been one of the pillars of development policy among virtually all the high-performing Asian countries. It has also been one feature of their policy that the World Bank has been least comfortable with and that it has systematically downplayed. The *East Asian Miracle* (World Bank 1993) finally acknowledged the significant role of the state, although in a back-handed manner especially in respect to industrial policy and its reduction of a complex set of proactive state policies into a vacuous 'market friendliness'. The *1997 World Development Report* (World Bank 1997) seemed to have endorsed a more positive role for the state. Closer reading suggests that what is being proposed is not a developmental state but a regulatory one. For Africa, the World Bank has continued to insist on a 'minimalist state' position. This clearly emerges in the 1994 *Adjusting Africa* and the 1995 *Bureaucrats in Business,* where the World Bank retreated to its more familiar ideological terrain in which a 'developmental state' borders on an oxymoron.

However, even when it has admitted industrial policy for Asian development, the World Bank has counselled African countries against it, usually on the grounds that it requires skills and discipline that African states do not have. Even if industrial policy had worked in the successful economies, African states were too weak and too prone to 'capture' by vested interests such that the pursuit of such policies would produce perverse outcomes. Consequently the most important case against 'developmental states' in Africa is no longer faith in flawless markets, but rather the view that whatever the degree and extent of market failure, African states cannot correct them in ways that do not make things worse. What emerges in the literature on Africa is that what has obviously worked in other 'late industrializers' is simply a non-starter in Africa. Interestingly, World Bank micro-level specialists still see possibilities and the need for micro-level intervention by the state. Thus a recent World Bank study on industry in Africa argues that:

> there is no a priori reason why Africa should not benefit from some form of infant industry protection to promote learning in domestic firms, as

has been evident in the cases of most successful developers in this century. However, given previous experience with such policies, critical issues related to appropriate administration, monitoring, enforcement and, most importantly, time-bound elimination of these trade policies need to be carefully addressed. (Biggs and Srivastava 1997)

The demise of development finance

Virtually all studies on constraints on the growth of small enterprises point to problems of finance. In the neo-liberal interpretation this has been blamed on credit rationing induced or practised by states. The neo-liberal literature not only criticized 'financial repression' for distorting markets and retarding the development of the financial sector, but made several claims regarding the efficacy of financial liberalization as an instrument of development of small enterprises. More specifically, interest-rate ceilings, coupled with credit rationing, led to inefficient allocation of resources. This manifested itself in the use of capital-intensive techniques even in situations of mass unemployment and cheap labour. Such policies also discouraged risk-taking and rationed out risky but potentially high-yielding economic activities. The positive and high interest rates enhance efficiency of investment by discouraging projects with low returns and by encouraging the choice of more labour-intensive policies.

It is argued that 'financial repression' in the form of interest rate ceilings, preferential treatment of large-scale enterprises have starved small enterprises of the necessary finance. Financial liberalization would create a 'level playing field' which would favour small enterprises. In the simplistic 'financial repression' literature, financial liberalization would not only increase loanable funds (by stimulating savings) but would end credit rationing by the state and thus open doors to investors hitherto excluded from borrowing from the formal financial institutions. In the event, this has not happened in Africa. While reforms have failed to stimulate total savings, they have led to savings being increasingly channelled through the formal financial sector that is not accessible to SMEs.

Imperfections and credit rationing in the credit markets are not merely caused by 'financial repression' but are inherent to any realistically defined financial markets. And much of what is happening in the post-adjustment phase confirms the message of these theories. Liberalization has done little to end the credit rationing that has hitherto been blamed on state interventionism. Steel and associates attribute this slow growth of credit to the private sector (especially to the small enterprises) to a number of factors: the inertia of past practice whereby 'the historical orientation of banking systems toward serving the import-export trade and the public sector limited their interest and experience in serving small indigenous clients' (Steel et al. 1997). Second, the post-reform emphasis on profitability and portfolio soundness has reinforced the bias towards large enterprises. One result was that while small enterprises suffered from a severe shortage of working capital, the banks were awash with excess liquidity. The argument then is whether credit rationing by the private sector is inherently superior to that imposed by the state. The answer will depend partly on how competitive the banking sector really is. One outstanding feature of financial markets in African as well as other developing countries is their fragmented oligopolistic nature. Even in the age of financial liberalization the large number of new banks does not significantly erode the position of the few oligopolies owing to the skewed distribution of assets, deposits and capital among existing firms. The banking sector in African countries is highly concentrated, not only because of the financial repression by the state but also because of the inherent nature of the banking system in these countries: the smallness of the financial markets, the strategies of the Metropolitan banks to which they are attached, the economies of scale in banking, etc. Consequently, there has been little improvement in the access of SMEs of finance from the formal financial institutions.

Small enterprise as a 'seed bed' of a national capitalist class?

The role of small-scale industry in development can be seen from two perspectives. From one perspective, a development process based on small-scale enterprise is envisaged as not only possible but as good in itself because it presumably ensures more employment, greater equity and a more autonomous development process. For others, small enterprise is a logical point of departure towards more complex forms of organization at later stages of development. It is, for better or worse, the breeding ground for future veritable 'captains of industry'. The 'petty bourgeoisie' spawned by the SMEs are to grow into a veritable national bourgeoisie. This point has been the subject of running debates in Africa, especially among the Left. Some have doubted the possibility of the transformation or the graduation of the petty bourgeoisie into a national bourgeoisie. Indeed, the once-dominant dependency school ruled out such a possibility on the grounds that either the 'dependent state' was congenitally incapable of supporting anything more than 'comprador activities', or that the transnationalization (and now globalization) processes have obviated the need for such a national bourgeoisie and have foreclosed the option; or that the asymmetric nature of centre-periphery relations tended to produce class structures that were not conducive to SMEs, especially in situations where they were in competition with transnational capital. The various epithets suggested that, at best, Africa could produce only 'lumpen bourgeoisie', 'drone capitalists', 'comprador elements', 'dependent capitalists', etc. not up to the 'historical mission' of development in Africa.

Over the years, developments elsewhere, and in Africa itself, have undermined the empirical foundations of such a view. However, the problems they raised with respect to the capacity of the African capitalist class, their relationship with the state and foreign capital are still highly pertinent. The current adjustment programmes have simply side-stepped these issues by insisting on the rather vacuous 'enabling environment' for all capital, irrespective of nationality. Indeed, in their insistence on instituting a level playing field they effectively exclude policies that would favour local capital against transnational forms. It is interesting to note that the African leaders that have embraced structural adjustment most ardently still entertain a jaundiced view towards national capitalists and incessantly hurl vilification and insults at them. They do not seem particularly persuaded that such SMEs deserve special measures from the state. Even among those governments that are not particularly hostile to small enterprises, it is simply taken for granted that SMEs will somehow muddle through on their own, partly in response to the growth of large-scale industries. No particular policies are required.

This brings us to the nature and capacity of African capitalist classes to respond to state initiative – a poorly studied area. The first set of capabilities includes 'industrial capabilities', which include entrepreneurial, managerial and organizational and technological capabilities. The lack of such capabilities is a recurring theme in the literature on SMEs in Africa, so that creative and ingenious though they obviously are, they are rarely able to 'manufacture up' by moving up the technological ladder to technologically sophisticated processes. One can, of course, continue to grow even in the absence of such moving up the technological ladder as is suggested by the case of Hong Kong; however, such a strategy, dependent on an infinitely elastic supply of labour, cannot be the basis for long-run growth.

The second set of capabilities are of a political nature

The literature on social capital and the importance of synergy between the public and private sectors suggests that development is facilitated if a well organised private sector engages a strong state. As defined by Evans (1997a: 3), the idea of synergy 'implies that civic engagement strengthens state institutions, and effective state institutions create an environment in which civic engagement is more likely to thrive'. The absence of such synergy is a recurring observation in the relationship between states and small enterprises.

What factors influence the outcome of the bargaining relationship between government and business? Stephen Haggard (1998) identifies the following:

- the nature of political institutions and the extent to which they provide opportunities for business access to, and control over, the policy agenda
- the preferences and political capacity of the private sector: organizational preferences of the private sector, ability to mobilize broader support from other segments of the population, and the ability to withdraw political and economic support.

Neo-liberal political economy, while favouring markets, has had difficulties in dealing with 'really existing capitalism' in which capitalists are organized and collectively can exert pressures on the government. It has simply assumed that such activities by capitalists constitute rent-seeking and have, therefore, negative effects on growth. Consequently where growth has taken place, neo-classical economists have either downplayed the role of the state or assumed that the private sector has had no access to policy-making bodies, which are presumably insulated from any rent-seeking activities of enterprises. Both Marxist and Weberian literature take the intimate relationship between the state and the capitalist class for granted. In the Marxist literature, the very nature of the capitalist state was that it would have complementary relations with the capitalist class. In the extreme the state simply acts on behalf or at the behest of the capitalist class. In other versions the structural positions of the capitalist in the economy imposed limits as to what the state could do against the capitalist class. For one, its fiscal needs and its needs for legitimacy (through employment and economic well-being) required capitalist co-operation. A capitalist 'strike' through the withdrawal of investment would lead to fiscal and political crisis. Neo-Weberian analysis of the state–business relationship in the high-growth Asian economies also emphasize the existence of effective frameworks for the exchange of information between the state and business through the institutionalization of deliberative or consultative bodies and policy dialogues between the state and business (Haggard 1998; Hsaio 1995; Koo and Kim 1992; Root 1998). The basis of such a consultative process is the possibility of mutually beneficial outcomes. The internalization of the 'national projects' by business requires high degrees of trust and motivation, resulting in what Evans (1992) has referred to as 'embeddedness' partly intended to overcome problems of information asymmetry, co-ordination failures and moral hazard.

If capitalism is to be politically viable in Africa, it will have to have some national anchoring based partly on the capacity of the indigenous capitalist classes to direct state policy toward their gaining access to factors of production, towards strengthening their position *vis-à-vis* foreign capital, and toward providing an 'enabling environment' for indigenous capitalist investment by facilitating institutions of stabilizing capital–labour relations and supplying technical services and physical infrastructure. For political legitimacy the capitalist class will have to convince critical sections of the nation that its 'project' of capital accumulation is in the national interest. Can SMEs constitute an important political force in this context? The question arises from the evidence which suggests that such capacity in Africa is extremely low. There are both historical and political reasons for such weakness of the SMEs *vis-à-vis* the state. At independence the SME sector was small, largely because colonialism had suppressed the emergence of such a class so that, unlike say India, the business class played a marginal role in the struggle for independence and could easily be dislodged from whatever key positions it may have occupied in the liberation movements (Boahen 1985). The absence of an indigenous capitalist class, with sizeable capital and organizational resources and entrepreneurial skill, obviated the need for the new states to form alliances with such classes for its development 'project'. It also limited the capacity of the capitalist class to 'capture' state policies.

In addition, only in rare cases, if ever, has the indigenous class constituted an important base of state revenue. In the mineral-rich economies the state had access to revenue either through direct ownership of the mines or through royalties and other rents obtained from foreign-owned mines. In other economies, the state had direct access to peasant surpluses through the marketing boards bequeathed by the erstwhile colonial masters without any mediation by an indigenous capitalist class, not even a merchant class. This irrelevance to the state's fiscal well-being has in a sense compromised the class's economic leverage over the state.

Furthermore, both the invidious comparisons of African capitalists with idealized capitalists elsewhere and the fear of capture by rent-seekers or patron–client networks have led to a negative and naïve view of the interrelation between public power and private interests, a view which pre-empts or precludes the possibility of building positive coalitions between the state and the business community. The presumption is simply that a state–capitalist relationship in Africa can be only collusive, and not synergistic and mutually reinforcing or benignly co-operative and collaborative (see for instance Lewis 1994: 441). As a consequence, in the African case, the call for state autonomy has been tantamount to call for 'isolation' by delinking of the state from its social roots while subjecting it to external 'agents of restraints' through a battery of conditionalities and technical assistance. The Bretton Woods Institutions (BWIs) have sought to free the state from the 'capture' by distancing the state from local vested interests. This alienation of the state is supposed to provide the necessary autonomy to ensure decisions that enhance national interests. Paradoxically, the BWIs have doubled their efforts to encourage 'government-business cooperation' (Moore and Hamatal 1993) although it is not always clear over what the co-operation would be and what each of the partners would be bringing to the table. The general view seems to be that such co-operation will enable reforming states to garner political support from the business class, which may not always appreciate that the current reforms are in their long-term interests. Forgotten in all this are constraints imposed on national governments with respect to what they can do for domestic capital. Here, one is not referring to the demands for a level playing field and the exigencies of some of the international conventions to which African states are partisan, but also to the political atmosphere that the new ideological dispensation imposes. African policy-makers are torn between the laissez-faireist pressures of the 'Washington Consensus' and the rhetoric that African governments create 'enabling environments' for the private sector by more proactive government–business relationships.

Compounding matters has been the hijacking of key state functions by international financial institutions, further distancing the state from local capitalists. Indeed, contrary to their self-perception as the guarantors of private capital, the BWIs are a source of extreme insecurity among local capitalists. Wanton liberalization of markets without careful consultation with business classes; privatization that provides no special privilege to local capitalists; cessation of directed credit or 'development finance'; high interest rates: all these underscore the distancing of the state from local capitalist interests and the pre-eminent position of international financial institutions' interests and perceptions in policy-making. They definitely do not produce the much vaunted enabling environment for small businesses. The comings and goings of BWIs' missions are as much a source of uncertainty in the SME community as the movements of commodity prices. Will they devalue the currency? Will the Minister of Finance be changed? Will privatization be accelerated and thus force the government to engage in 'fire sales'? Should one wait for the Paris Club meeting before investing? Will the government comply with the conditionalities?

Although much of the focus in the literature is on how states in Africa destroy the developmental capacity of small enterprises, it is important to recall that an active role assumed by states was not always the result of hostility to private investment caused by a putatively visceral anti-capitalist reaction induced by the colonial experience. The fact of the matter is that in the immediate post-independence period most African governments pursued what were known as 'industrialization by invitation' strategies in which the attraction of foreign capital played a central role. Bereft of powerful business interests, African states were less receptive to local business interests and more attentive to those of foreign capital. Many of the policy measures that eventually worked against small-scale industries were designed to attract foreign investment. Protective measures for industry were often part of the package of incentives demanded by, or intended to attract, foreign capitalists. So was access to cheap credit. It was the reticence of foreign investment that pushed African governments towards increased reliance on parastatals and joint ventures and escalation of the battle to attract foreign capital using a battery of incentives. The reticence of foreign investment was accompanied by a suspicion and even hostility towards indigenous capital by African states even in those countries that were avowedly capitalist in their ideologies. The 'mistake' of African governments was that having failed to attract foreign capital, they never really seriously considered the option of domestic capital partly because of the political unease African leaders felt about the emergence of a national capitalist class and partly because of genuine doubts that such a class could assume the leading role in industrialization. In some cases it was felt that the emergence of such capitalists would complicate future transitions to socialism; the assumption being that nationalization of industries in which the state already played a major role, and which were owned by foreigners, would provide fewer political barriers. Another political argument came from the authoritarian thrust of African politics, which sought to block the emergence of alternative sources of political power.

In addition to all this have been problems of self-organization internal to the SMEs themselves. In many cases they have failed to shield themselves from divisive forces stemming from society at large, political divisions, ethnic solidarities, religious loyalties, sexism, etc. We should here add the 'collective action' problems likely to be encountered by a sector consisting of many and disparate actors. Attempts by outsiders to jump start the process by organization of SMEs in Africa have apparently yielded little. Most of the associations formed with the assistance of external funds have survived only as long as foreign funds were forthcoming (cf. Haan this volume). With the end of foreign funding, 'free rider' problems have undermined the financial basis of associations though lack of compliance to membership requirements.

Conclusion

Although neo-liberal policies have contributed to the ideological respectability of small enterprises in African policy discourses, they have also tended to undermine the state's capacity to be of much use to SMEs. One thing stands out clearly: the emergence of a dynamic and modern SME sector dominated by a national capitalist class is not facilitated by laissez-faire regimes that international financial institutions have sought to impose everywhere in Africa. Evidence from a wide range of experiences with capitalist accumulation suggests that the emergence of a national bourgeoisie is fostered or even planned by the state, or nurtured in a 'hothouse' fashion by the state (Marx 1962). The creation of a national bourgeoisie will pose innumerable political, ideological and even ethical questions. The measures required may include privatization, but it seems to me that privatization is probably much less important than stimulation of capitalists to invest in new and competing activities. More pertinent to our discussion is that privatization in Africa should be as a strategy for the transfer of state assets to a strategically placed domestic private capital or as an instrument of creating a national bourgeoisie. However, as I have argued elsewhere, privatization in Africa has not been premissed on that objective (Mkandawire 1994: 161). It has been largely driven by fiscal concerns of the state; faith in the inherent superiority of private enterprises; ideological aversion to state ownership; and the unfounded belief that public investments always crowd out private investment. For all the talk about globalization, the edification of capitalist accumulation in a specific country depends ultimately on national characteristics (class formation, resource base, etc.) and policies towards both foreign and domestic capital. Historically, the domestic class assuming this role has been referred to as a 'national bourgeoisie'. If capitalist accumulation is to take place, such a class will have to serve as a catalyst if for no other reason than that Africa is unlikely to constitute an attractive place for foreign capital for some time to come, partly because of the continent's 'image problem' and partly because of the way financial markets are constituted and the marginal position of Africa in these markets. The crisis in Asia will simply reinforce this segmentation and Africa's exclusion from financial markets. Both the global flows of foreign investment and the exigencies of development of national economies place the largest burden of private investment on domestic capital.

The point here is that it will be prudent for African policy makers to work on the assumption that capitalist accumulation will be largely national for much of Africa. Indeed, given Africa's very tarnished image, confidence by Africans in the continent's future will be of prime value in resuscitating investment. The small enterprises can serve both as a seed bed of such a capitalist class and can provide some of the political support to capitalist accumulation in Africa. This will require that the efforts of individual enterprises are embedded in a broad developmental effort with fairly coherent objectives and strategies for the SMEs. More specifically, the state will have to play more than a merely regulatory or custodial role by assuming clearly developmental tasks. There is nothing either in African economic and political history or the experiences of other developmental states that makes it inherently impossible for African states to play such a role. Strategies that disable the state in the hope of strengthening SMEs are self-defeating.

3 Gender, property rights and trade: constraints to African growth

SUSAN JOEKES

Introduction

This chapter argues that gender-based constraints have contributed to the weak supply response of African agriculture to export opportunities. The distribution of gains from trade is also highly inequitable in gender terms.

The organization of the chapter is as follows: the first section is a summary exposition of a new variant of international trade theory which suggests that the potential for African exports prospects rests, at this stage, on developing export capacity in high-value primary products. The second section sets out a gender analysis of the African smallholder farming system. It identifies the household-level institutional constraints facing African women that prevent them, whether as farmers or as providers of family farm labour, from allocating resources to production in such a way as to enhance productivity and maximize revenues, and from enjoying an equitable share of farm cash income. The third section draws attention to a new, high-value primary product category that seems to offer good prospects for trade, and which may also have the developmental merit of bypassing the gender constraints in smallholder farming.

Africa's trade potential

The example of many fast-growing developing countries suggests that Africa should look to international markets as a possible source of growth. But while participation in trade could contribute to accumulation and growth, African countries should not follow the Asian example in respect of the commodity composition of trade. Instead, they need, at this stage, to forge a new path focusing on high-value exports of primary commodities.

The key phrase in the above statement is 'at this stage' because the argument refers not to any absolute 'African' condition but to the present state of the economic resource endowment of the region. The crux of the argument is the classical proposition that the optimal pattern of trade depends on a country's resource endowment, because this determines its comparative advantage relative to that of other countries. Comparative advantage is realized through prices. The market price of an abundant resource tends to be low, and that of a scarce resource to be high. This prompts the increased production of goods and services whose factor input requirements match resource price relativities. In the context of trade, variation in countries' resource endowments, none being inherently 'worse' or 'better' than others, translates merely into specific indications for the trade pattern each should adopt.

The most influential neo-classical formulation of the theory of comparative advantage, the Heckscher-Ohlin theorem, takes capital and labour as the basic resources. Wood has put forward a different specification which fits the facts of the pattern of North-South trade flows much better (Wood 1994; Wood and Berge 1994; Berge et al. 1994).[1]

First, Wood proposes that capital should not be included, taken as a basic, site-specific resource. The evolution of global financial systems has made capital fully and highly internationally mobile. Instead, he proposes that the two locally fixed building blocks of an economy are labour and natural resources. But labour has to be differentiated into three categories because (Wood argues) its value as an economic resource differs according to skill or education level: uneducated labour is not a resource from the perspective of modern industrial production, because some basic level of education in the workforce is an absolute requirement in that sector. More technologically advanced processes require even higher levels of skill. The production of primary commodities does not require a low level of formal skills in the workforce but it does require a large input of natural resources (in terms of mineral ores or cultivable land for agriculture). This points to a fundamental dichotomy in types of production in relation to trade. Whereas primary production requires a high ratio of natural resource inputs to labour (especially skilled labour), secondary or industrial sector production requires the reverse on the factor input side, i.e. a high ratio of labour – especially skilled labour – to natural resources.[2]

For empirical application of the model, simple, readily available indicators can be used for both types of economic resource. Labour skills are measured by the average years of education per worker, more precisely by average years of schooling in the population of working age. This conforms to the observation throughout the developing world that the average number of years of schooling in industrial workforces is higher than in agriculture and basic services such as commerce and personal services. Natural resources are measured by land area in relation to adult population, which serves as a rough but surprisingly good proxy for natural resource availabilities of different types. Land area indicates both the potential for agriculture, forestry and/or livestock rearing, and the probability that mineral reserves of some kind exist within the territory.

The resource endowments of different countries and regions are found to

[1] What follows is a very simple presentation of the elements of Wood's analysis relevant to the subject of this chapter, drawn from these sources.

[2] Within manufacturing industry, variations in the technological level of production map on to variations in requirements for labour of different skills levels, but this aspect of the theory is not taken any further in this chapter.

differ dramatically. Aggregating to regional level, the patterns of resource endowment and composition of exports are as follows.

Figure 3.1 plots resource endowment ratios for six different regions. The angle of the slope from the origin indicates the resource ratio. East Asia has the highest ratio of skills to land, followed by South Asia and Latin America (which have similar ratios, although Latin America is the more richly endowed both in skills and natural resources). Africa has the lowest endowment of skills, the largest endowment of natural resources and, by a long way, the lowest ratio of skills to land.

There are also strong variations in export composition by region and country, as Figure 3.2 shows. The composition of exports conforms well with the pattern of endowments.[3] Africa, as the region with the highest endowment of land relative to skilled labour, has by far the highest proportion of any region of unprocessed primary products in its exports. Among developing countries, East and South Asia have the highest share of manufactures in their exports. Latin America falls neatly in between Asia and Africa in terms of the ratio of manufactures to unprocessed primary products in exports, as predicted.

The lesson to be drawn from the model in this context is that countries (and regions) should, in seeking gains from trade, be guided by their resource endowments. Although concentration on labour-intensive manufactured exports was appropriate to the East Asian countries at the beginning of their export-led growth path, it is not an appropriate path for African countries to follow now. It is not adequate or correct to base trade policy merely on the fact that African countries are 'low wage' economies.

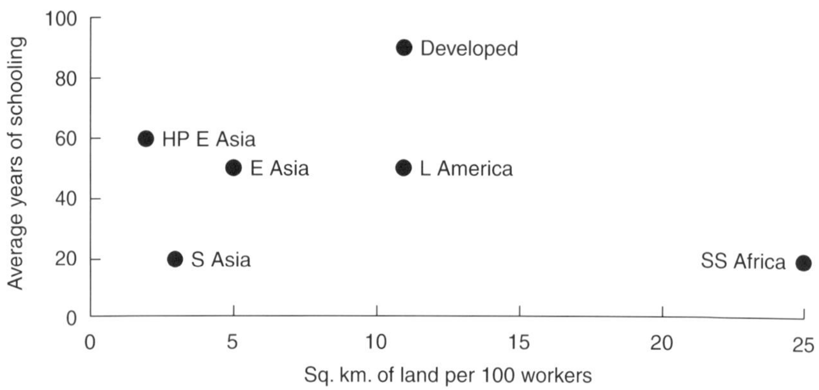

Figure 3.1: *Regional factor endowments*

[3] Regressing endowments on the commodity composition of exports reveals a highly significant relationship at country level, but this is not the place to present these results.

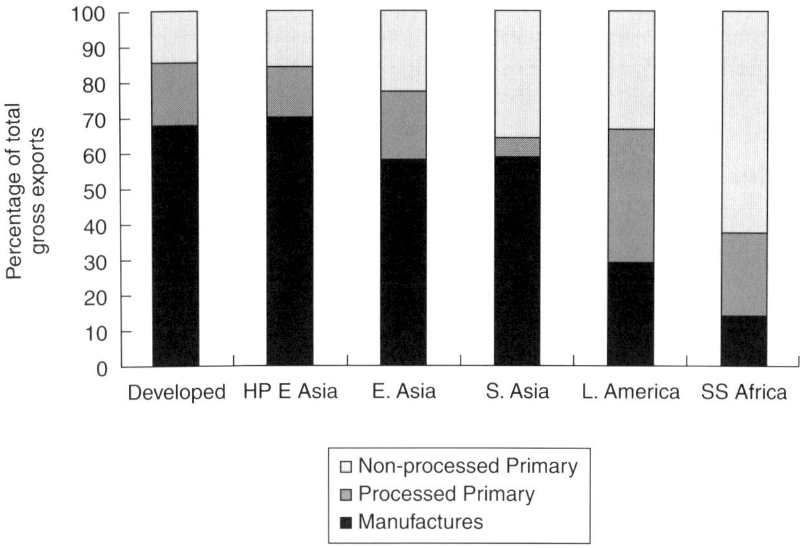

Figure 3.2: *Regional export composition*

Trade in primary production can contribute to aggregate economic growth just as manufactures can. By raising investable surplus, it will facilitate improvements in education and skill levels and facilitate productivity growth in the indigenous manufacturing sector, sufficient to enable it to become internationally competitive in other sectors in due course (UNCTAD 1998). The problem for African producers is to identify and realize profit from high value-added export niches within the primary sector. Such niches do in fact exist, a point to which we turn at the end of this chapter.

It is not an indictment of trade theory that African export performance has been so depressed over recent decades. Sub Saharan Africa has experienced a slower rate of growth of exports by volume than other developing regions since 1975 and its share of world trade in primary products fell between 1975 and 1992 (UNCTAD 1994: Tables 1.5 and 1.7).

Many analysts point to depressed international market conditions in primary commodity markets as the root cause, especially the tendency for primary commodity prices to decline over the long term and, by extension, for Africa to experience declining terms of trade. But this does not explain the falling African share of the world market for primary commodities compared to other developing regions.

Accordingly, structural factors, such as weaknesses in infrastructure or poor government policies in relation to trade, are usually held to blame. The social dimension of the structural explanation warrants greater attention. The argument of this chapter is that gender-based factors have contributed to the poor supply response of African agricultural exports, an argument that the mainstream policy debate has not yet taken on board.[4]

Gender asymmetries in African agriculture

This section examines how social relations of gender are manifested in African agriculture and considers their relevance to trade in respect of the distribution of income from trade and the agricultural supply response to international market opportunities.

Gender differences in property rights and access to resources

African farming systems fall into two main types (Koopman 1992). In both there is a strong dualism in men's and women's roles, rights and responsibilities. The first type, 'women's farming system', is found predominantly in West Africa, western and southern Cameroon and Zaire. Under this system, most household food plots are considered women's fields. Women are responsible for the production of most staple foods and for all other food crops. The second type, 'mixed farming systems', is widespread in the Sahel and common also in Eastern and Southern Africa. In this case, staple food crops are grown in household or compound fields with both male and female labour. Only non-staple food crops are women's sole responsibility.

Asymmetries by gender common to the two systems unequivocally favour men over women as productive agents. They relate to property rights in land; capabilities for enhancing agricultural productivity; rights to cash revenues from the market sale of products; and labour commitments. Of these, property rights in land are of prime importance and reinforce asymmetries in other dimensions.

Property rights in land

Social relations of gender confer relatively weak and contingent property rights in land on women compared to men throughout Africa (Joekes et al. 1996: 2; Quisumbing 1994). Women seem to have somewhat greater rights in 'women's farming systems'. Nevertheless they do not in that system own or control the 'women's fields', which comprise land designated to them by men

[4] With the partial exception of UNCTAD (1998). Curiously, many of the elements of the argument that follows have been taken seriously in mainstream institutions (especially the World Bank and International Food Policy Research Institute), in the sense that much of the analysis has been conducted and supporting evidence assembled inside their walls. The answer seems to be that the work was carried out in specialist 'women' or 'gender' units and their findings not incorporated into policy-setting processes at the centre. Analysts of gender in institutions examine the reasons for this phenomenon (see for example Goetz 1997).

(Koopman 1992: 14). In mixed farming systems, women have only sole use rights (for production of non-staple foodstuffs) on a smaller part of the total holding.

Women's access to land accrues to them through male relatives' decisions about land use (Meinzen-Dick et al. 1997b: 1300). A study of property rights in Kenya and Nigeria found that women had lesser rights than men across a whole set of dimensions of rights in property, whether they were heads of their household or members of a farming household of which they were not head. A complex definition of bundles of property rights was used in this study. The definitions used encompassed distinct rights to improve, lend, rent out, sell and mortgage land (Saito et al. cited in Quisumbing 1994). Of these dimensions, the right to sell was the least often open to women. The right to improve land was women's most widespread right (but fewer women than men had this right).

There is an ongoing shift to more formalized private property systems in land throughout Africa. Under customary tenure systems different kinds of rights for a given plot could be given to different persons. By contrast, privatization tends to assign all rights to a single holder, rather than recognizing multiple claimants on a plot. Women have found themselves doubly disadvantaged as a result. The security of their customarily sanctioned 'embedded' or secondary use rights is threatened (MacKenzie 1994; Lastarria-Cornhiel 1997: 1320) and the existence of markets in land can remove the very land on which customary rights can be claimed. There are reports of widowed women's sons selling land on the death of their father, making no alternative provision for their mother to grow her own food (Quisumbung 1994).

Women also have particular difficulty in acquiring ownership rights within a privatized system (Meinzen-Dick et al. 1997a). Title can be acquired by 'sweat equity', (i.e. in exchange for past labour input), inheritance or purchase. The evidence on the extent to which women can acquire rights through sweat equity is mixed (ibid.). Inheritance for women is rare under customary tenure systems[5] and is mostly a recent phenomenon, relating to gifts (by inheritance or inter vivos) of land privately owned by the donor. Purchase of land is very difficult for women. They are caught in a Catch 22 situation, since in rural areas of Africa accumulation of funds is most easily done by offering land as security for loans. Accumulation is easier for urban women and relatively more land purchases by women have been observed in peri-urban locations (Lastarria-Cornhiel 1997: 1329). It is also notable that collective

[5] Note that women do not generally inherit land in matrilineal societies, where the family line is traced through women, but land is passed on from men to men. However, women do have somewhat stronger land rights in matrilineal than in patrilineal societies, e.g. a woman retains cultivation rights on her birth family's land, even after her marriage. Most examples of customary inheritance by women are found in West Africa, where the 'women's farming system' is prevalent (it is not clear to me if this system is correlated with matrilineal organization).

savings made by women's groups are sometimes (in Embu district, Kenya, for example) used to purchase land and property (see also Hamner et al. nd).

A small minority of African farms is managed or owned by women who have either acquired land in one or other of the above ways, or who have been left behind to farm the family holding after out-migration by male kin, or who find themselves in sole charge of a plot through widowhood or divorce. But as well as being few in number, surveys have shown that on average female holdings are of significantly smaller size than male holdings (Quisumbing 1994: 19).

Access to complementary resources

African women farmers have far less access than men to the various resources needed to cultivate land productively (Quisumbing 1994). This relates to many different types of input. Access to credit, which allows purchase of livestock, improved varieties, capital equipment and current inputs, is almost entirely dependent on ownership of land as collateral; few women can offer this, even for land on which they customarily have use rights. Agricultural extension services still target male farmers. Improved plant varieties facilitate increased productivity, better quality production and higher incomes. But they need to be purchased and women have less access to cash than men, and new varieties are in any case generally available only for men's crops, agricultural research having been biased towards cash crops at the expense of subsistence food crops. Last but not least, education is known to boost farmers' productivity (Jamison and Lau 1982). The gender gap in education in rural areas in Africa is very wide, with female enrolment rates and average attainment falling below male rates. The gender gap has widened further in several countries during the 1990s (Bredie and Beeharry 1998).

There is no 'gender' factor as such that explains differences in male and female farmers' output and productivity in Africa. Observed differences are due entirely to differences in the respective endowments, i.e. the complementary factors of labour-saving equipment, technology, and current inputs, which men and women are able to bring to agriculture (for a review of econometric studies see Quisumbing 1996; see also Quisumbing 1994). Once these are allowed for, there is no productivity difference between male and female farmers left to explain.

Rights to returns from production

Women's rights in the crops they grow are also circumscribed compared to men's. In women's farming systems, women derive their personal incomes from the sale of food products that exceed family requirements. In mixed farming systems, the male household head controls jointly produced food output, usually storing it for household consumption, but having the right to sell any surplus. Women and men also in this system have individual fields for foods and/or other crops. In some cases men claim the right to control all the income resulting from their wives' labour, although this is now said to be exceptional (Koopman 1992). But, in what can be an equally effective method of control, men have the right to decide the particular crops that women may grow on their plots, e.g. proscribing women's production of the most remunerative crops. This both limits women's incomes and secures the cultivation of particularly high priced crops to themselves.

Labour commitments

Women are less free to allocate their labour than men are, for two reasons. First, women observe the socially prescribed gender division of labour that puts on them time-consuming 'reproductive' work, i.e. the obligation to provide food and care for others, notably their children and male kin. This is a world-wide phenomenon, which Ingrid Palmer has called the 'reproductive [labour] tax' on women (Palmer 1991). The time requirements this work imposes are considerable.[6] Numerous studies of women's time use in rural Africa attest to it. A general estimate is that on average rural African women may spend two hours a day on childcare, three hours on food preparation, and two hours fetching wood and water (Quisumbing 1994). What is distinctive in Africa is that women's reproductive obligations extend to the requirement to grow as well as to prepare food, which adds enormously to the workload. In a typical example, a study in Cameroon found that women spent 26.9 hours a week on agricultural production, of which 24.1 hours was for food production, and 35.5 hours a week on domestic labour. For comparison, men spent 12.1 hours on agriculture and 19.9 hours on other activities (including four hours in domestic labour) (cited in Koopman 1992: 7).

Second, social relations of gender permit male heads of household to mobilize far greater amounts of family labour for the cultivation and processing of 'male crops' than women are able to mobilize for their individual enterprises (Roberts 1988). Claims on women's labour are enforced more rigorously where production of cash crops is at stake (Lastarria-Cornhiel 1997: 1321). Women are rarely able to commandeer any male labour in support of their own activities. To gain support in their much heavier workload, they have to use the labour of their children to help out with domestic and agricultural work.

Effects of gender asymmetries on the distribution of the gains from trade in smallholder agriculture

Women's lesser rights in land and in access to other resources have damaging distributional and efficiency consequences in the new global context. They lead to the unequal distribution by gender of gains from trade in Africa. By hindering growth in agricultural productivity, they hamper supply response capabilities in general, and response to price incentives in international

[6] Unequal workloads between men and women have been amply documented worldwide.

markets in particular. The distributional effects differ in form but are inequitable in effect in both mixed and women's farming systems. The output effects may, in general, be expected to be more severe in areas where a women's farming system predominates, although they are certainly also manifested elsewhere.

The starkest demonstration of the gender inequitable distribution of income from trade comes from research in Kenya. Kennedy (1989) found that among sugarcane farmers in Kenya producing for export, household income increased with the expansion of export sales. But the income gain was not shared by all members of the household; women and children's economic position in fact deteriorated. Household income increased, in part because of women's labour input into increased production of export crops. But the implicit wage paid to women for their labour input into male-controlled marketed crops was so low that women's extra energy expenditure was not fully compensated for by increased food energy intake. They received a truly less than subsistence wage. As a result their nutritional status – along with that of their children, whose food intake was dependent on what their mothers could provide – declined.[7]

In general, intra-household income distribution arrangements in African smallholder farms result in disproportionately small returns paid to women, in cash or in kind, which are insufficient compensation for extra labour at the margin (Hamner et al. nd). Incremental income gains, notably from trade, go disproportionately to men.

In nearly all African farming systems men control the great bulk of the production and income from major export crops. Women may derive some income from export-oriented production, either as a worker for others or as an own-account producer, but women's average own-account production is invariably far smaller than men's (Koopman 1992: 15). Figure 3.3 is an example of this, illustrating the disproportion in returns and inputs by gender in smallholder export crop production of green beans and snow peas in Kenya.

The dynamics of the distribution of incremental farm income may differ from this in women's farming systems. In this case, men may have lesser powers of allocation over women's labour, and women have some production autonomy over their plot. But women have little access to own-account cash income and new, well-remunerated trading opportunities are likely to be monopolized by men directly. While the distributional outcome also favours men, it is less likely to involve absolute deterioration in women's real income position.

---

[7] Given low (even negative) returns on their labour in cash crop production, it is not surprising that researchers have found instances of women's resistance to the co-optation of their labour into male-controlled cash crop production (Joekes et al. 1996). It may be significant that the most commonly cited studies of this phenomenon were done in West Africa where women's farming systems predominate.

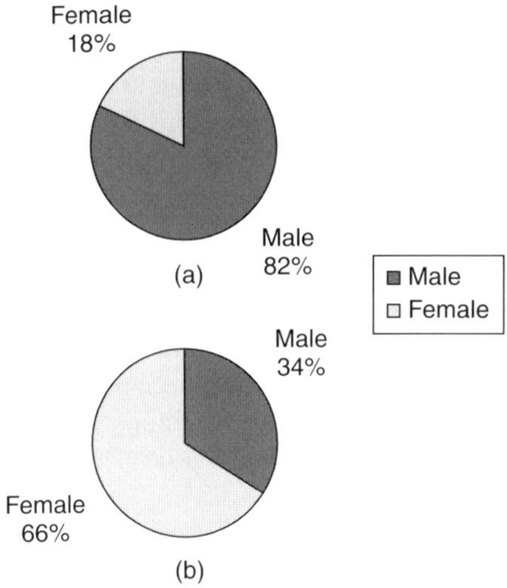

Figure 3.3: *(a) Control of income from selected crops, Meru, Kenya (b) Labour performed*
Source: Dolan (1997).

Effects of gender asymmetries on agricultural output

The impact of gender-based constraints on output is likely to be more severe where the mixed farming system predominates, since women tend to have more managerial authority on a higher proportion of the holding in such settings.[8]

As noted above, in some contexts women have the right to improve the land they work. But they lack both the incentive and the means to do so. The incentive for making sustained improvements is weak, since women's use rights are liable to be overturned at any time. Insecurity of usufruct tenure may be increasing with the opening of new high-value markets for crops. In Kenya, men take back land from women to grow export crops, which offer far higher returns than any other crop (Dolan 1997). Leach and Fairhead (1995) found that land use practices on women's gardens were superior to those on other land, in the sense of sustaining higher soil fertility than elsewhere. Thus women's plots may be targeted specifically for this purpose. Women's relative lack of access to other resources (technical knowledge, finance, own and

[8] It is notable, however, that most of the research showing substantial negative consequences of gender difference seems to have been carried out in East Africa, especially Kenya. The remarks here suggesting that even larger-scale effects may ensue in women's farming system areas are speculative.

others' labour) limits their adoption of measures for enhancing productivity, whether through current purchases of improved varieties and other inputs, or by way of capital or labour-intensive investment in improvement of soil structures and fertility, construction of soil and soil moisture conservation structures, and so on. The incentive to overcome these obstacles and improve land productivity is further undermined for women by the direct and indirect restrictions on the returns that they can realize from production.

In combination, these gender based constraints muddy incentives and impede the aggregate capability of household-farming systems to adapt and expand production. There have been partial estimates of the output effect of one such constraint, the gender gap in educational provision. It has been estimated for Kenya that, among maize farmers, giving female farmers primary education would have increased maize production by 24 per cent (in 1976) and among foodcrop farmers the effect of giving female farmers male farmers' inputs and education levels would have increased food production by 22 per cent (in 1990) (World Bank 1995: 41). A much lower take-up rate of new export cash crops was reported among female-headed than among male-headed farm households in Kenya (World Bank 1995). One general estimate is found in the World Bank's Poverty Assessment for Zambia. This source suggests that the sex division of labour in agriculture (and accompanying asymmetries in resource ownership and control) 'can reduce net returns by up to 60 per cent' (cited in Hamner et al. nd: 5.15).

There are even more generalized effects on accumulation and the dynamism of the rural economy. The gender segregation of agricultural activity distorts many aspects of household expenditure. Parents have little incentive to invest in girls' education, since they will never control the income they generate. Women have no incentive or means to invest in new technologies, and men have no incentive to invest in assets that would be labour saving for women's activities (Hamner et al. nd).

The gains from globalization are highly unevenly spread within the developing world. There is no overall 'gender bias' – there are winners and losers among people of both sexes (Fontana et al. 1998). But if the income from those gains are to be spread more widely, if the gains are to be larger, and if trade is to stimulate the human and economic development which it has the potential to do, policy attention urgently needs to be given to ways of improving the returns from trade to rural women in Africa.

An African agricultural export success story

One primary product category, non-traditional agricultural exports (NTAEs), has in fact achieved – albeit from a very low base – exceptionally rapid growth in export revenues to some African countries. Exports of non-traditional agricultural products, comprising flowers, vegetables and fruits exclusively for export, often supplied on a contract basis for foreign buyers and air-freighted out, fresh or chilled, are a particularly bright spot in Kenyan export performance, but also important in Côte d'Ivoire, Uganda, Zimbabwe and elsewhere.

That African producers should prove internationally competitive in this product category is fully consistent with the prediction of the theory of comparative advantage discussed in the first part of this chapter. NTAEs also seem to have the merit of generating high returns and qualifying as a high value added product niche, breaking out of the primary commodity stereotype in this respect. In Kenya the rapid growth in smallholder supply of NTAEs is clearly attributable to the relatively high returns to farmers from these products (Dolan 1997).

It is also instructive, in terms of the argument of this chapter, that this is a sector which by-passes the problems imposed on agricultural production by gender relations. Although very little information is available about production conditions in NTAEs in Africa, it is known that the sector involves two distinct types of production, i.e. small farm contract growers and large-scale, 'estate' type production in enterprises using high technology pest and disease control methods, fertilizer application, irrigation, and even temperature control under plastic cover. In the latter, which in Kenya is now overtaking smallholder production as the main source of supply, a wage labour force is employed on quasi-industrial terms. All the available evidence suggests that, as in the export manufacturing sector worldwide, and as in the large and important NTAE sector in Latin America, the majority of this workforce are women.

It is easy to understand why African women should, if the chance is available, accept work for cash-in-hand wages, rather than working so hard and long, and for so little reward, within the traditional farming system. Women's willingness to offer labour to NTAEs may also rest on its compatibility with some continued domestic labour obligations, e.g. growing perishable foodstuffs: work in NTAEs is likely to be seasonal and/or sporadic. Another possible benefit is to women's position within the farming system itself. Their engagement in wage labour in NTAEs may, insofar as it gives them an independent source of income, confer some leverage and help women claim better access to resources and returns on their labour in their own-farm agricultural production.

On the other hand, although higher immediate returns to their labour in wage employment in NTAEs may appeal to African women, they may be putting themselves into a particularly hazardous form of employment. The occupational health problems of women working with pesticides and so on in NTAEs in Latin America have been well documented (Thrupp et al. 1993). In the longer run, employment conditions, wage rates, the dynamics of the wage: profit ratio and the characteristics of international contract arrangements in NTAE production will determine how much the value added generated in the sector is retained by the workforce and, indeed, by the exporting country – given that foreign investors may be active and that foreign buyers may have strong market power and the ability to control the division of the revenues along the total value added chain.

In general, therefore, much more information is needed about wages, working conditions and health hazards, and international contract terms in NTAEs in African countries, as well as an appraisal of the prospects for extending NTAE production within Africa to assess the growth potential of this sector. It should become a stronger focus of attention for African policy makers. It is also important, in the new climate of ethical consumerism, that NGO concerns about working conditions in this sector do not provoke a premature reaction against the activity and provide a focus for protectionist interests in the North. NTAE is a branch of primary commodity production which has important potential contributions to make towards gender equality as well as to export-based growth in Africa; the policy challenge is to ensure that the activity generates maximum local returns, supports greater gender equality, and provides maximum developmental benefits.

Part 2
Small and Micro-Enterprises and the Development Agenda

4 MSEs tackle both poverty and growth (but in differing proportions)

DONALD C. MEAD

Introduction

Micro- and small enterprises (MSEs) are receiving increasing attention among policy makers and scholars in developing countries. With fiscal pressures constraining the growth of public sector employment and with large enterprises in turmoil, often in response to the process of market liberalization, many observers see MSEs as a source of economic salvation.

While time-series statistics are weak, it appears that, in many countries, the number of people working in MSEs has increased over the past decade or more. But how should we view that increase? Should the expansion of employment in MSEs be seen as a sign of success, reflecting a response on the part of entrepreneurial individuals to profitable and productive opportunities? Or do the expanding numbers of people establishing MSEs reflect a desperate search on the part of people forced into such activities by the absence of better alternatives, in spite of the low and declining returns they generate?

The discussion of this chapter is based largely on surveys of MSEs done over the period 1990–98 in nine countries of Eastern and Southern Africa. In the course of those surveys, questionnaires were administered to over 50 000 small enterprises. While the questionnaire itself evolved over time, there was a core of similar questions asked that provides an overview of the characteristics of MSEs in all these countries. The upper size cut-off point in these surveys, as in many other similar studies, is defined in terms of numbers of workers, including self-employed, unpaid family members, paid workers and apprentices, whether working on a part-time or a full-time basis. We have generally worked with enterprises with 50 or fewer workers; smaller upper limits can easily be examined as a subset of these. In sectoral terms, the surveys included all enterprises engaged in the production of goods and services. Agriculture was generally excluded, as were mining and fishing. Activities were included where at least 50 per cent of the output was sold (as opposed to production for own consumption).

It may be useful at the outset to emphasize that 'what is' is not necessarily the same as 'what might be'. Survey results tell about the world as it has existed in the recent past. One must be careful about extending that description to what might happen in the future. For example, to say that very few one-person enterprises have grown in the past does not necessarily mean that they are unable to move beyond the subsistence levels. It means only that most have been unable to make this transition in the past; if the future is to be different, some conditions will probably need to be changed. It is helpful to know 'what is', as a background for knowing the need for change to achieve desired outcomes.

Some major findings concerning the characteristics of MSEs

Most MSEs are very small. If the universe of MSEs is defined as all enterprises with 1–50 workers, 64 per cent of these enterprises were made up of one person working alone. Another 33 per cent had 2–5 workers (including working proprietors and unpaid family members). Only 2 per cent had 6–10 workers. If 'micro' means 10 or fewer workers, then 99 per cent of all MSEs with up to 50 workers are micro, with only 1 per cent in the 11–50 worker category. Three-quarters of the enterprises are in rural areas (localities with less than 2000 people). This is important since much of the early work on MSEs focused on urban areas, leading to a substantial underestimation of the magnitude of the small enterprise universe as well as a distorted focus of policies and projects.

Just under half (48%) of all MSEs are owned and operated by women. Since working proprietors are the single largest category of employment, it is not surprising that about 44 per cent of the total labour force in these enterprises is made up of females. About a third of the enterprises in the MSE universe are essentially supplementary activities, in the sense that they provide less than half the household's income. But another third of the enterprises provided the sole source of income for the household. The remaining 30 per cent contributed between 50 per cent and 90 per cent of the household income. These percentages are approximately the same across different size categories, including the one-person enterprises.

Most of the activities captured by the surveys are pretty much full-time activities. Over 80 per cent of the enterprises were active for at least 11 months per year; about three-quarters normally worked at least 24 days in the month. In the two countries where information was collected on normal hours worked per day, the analysis indicates that, on average, people were working somewhat more than the 45 hours a week normally considered to be full-time employment (although about a third of the MSE labour force normally worked less than that number of hours per week). In the aggregate, there were more people working extra-long hours in MSEs in a struggle for more income than there were people who participated only on a part-time basis as a supplement to other primary activities.

Most enterprises that started out very small have not grown subsequently. Among those enterprises that started out very small and that had been in existence for at least five years, fewer than 20 per cent had grown at all in terms of numbers of workers from the time of their start-up to the date of the survey. These figures are not very different for those that started with only one person, compared to those that started somewhat larger; for single-person enterprises, as for larger businesses, growth after start-up by taking on additional workers has overwhelmingly been the exception rather than the rule.

For an economist, one of the most important indicators of the characteristics of an enterprise concerns the income that it generates. The estimation of returns in MSEs is notoriously difficult, but the subject is so important that it constantly returns to challenge us. After some very data-intensive work in the 1970s and early 1980s, the MSU/GEMINI team shied away from income measurements for many years, finally coming back to it with a survey in Kenya in 1995. The approach used in Kenya has since been replicated in a major study of four provinces in Mozambique, and in a simplified version in Zambia. A recent survey in Zimbabwe (the third in the GEMINI series in that country), incorporating some simpler income measures, has recently been completed.

What we learn about MSE income from those studies is first of all the unsurprising fact of wide variability in net returns per person working in MSEs. There are some patterns in those variations, many of which again are not surprising: urban enterprises earn substantially more than do rural ones; those owned by men generate higher incomes than those owned by women.

In all the countries studied, one-person enterprises generated substantially lower returns than those that are even slightly larger. There are some consistent sectoral patterns, with enterprises engaged in commerce generally earning higher average returns than those in manufacturing (although there were exceptions to this generalization for some types of products being traded, such as charcoal, or agricultural produce). But within any one industrial sector, there were also substantial variations in earnings, so income differences by sector were generally not statistically significant.

Moving from the fact of variability to levels of earnings, it is clear that the majority of MSEs generate only limited amounts of income for those who work in them. It is hard to know the best standard of comparison here. In the survey in Kenya, earnings from MSEs were compared with the minimum wage for unskilled workers, which is reported to be set by the government at such low levels that a family would find it very difficult to live solely on such an income. The survey results indicate that, for about two-thirds of the enterprises, the per worker contribution of the enterprise to income was below the minimum wage. For about half of those involved in MSE activities in Kenya, where income per worker from the enterprise was below the minimum wage, the MSE provided less than half the household income. For such households, it appears that the MSE was essentially a supplementary endeavour, to augment income earned in other activities of the household. However, for 20 per cent of those earning very low returns–somewhat over 10 per cent of all MSEs in the country–this activity was the sole source of income for the household. For another quarter of all small enterprises in Kenya (36 per cent of those with low returns), the MSE supplied at least half of the household income, even though the return to the MSE was below the minimum wage. This means that over a third of the people working in MSEs find their welfare heavily dependent on the MSE, but they are very poor.

While the majority of MSEs appear to be earning very low returns, there was also a significant minority that were doing very well. In the Kenya results, about 20 per cent of the enterprises were earning returns that were at least double the minimum wage. Since these were generally enterprises with more than the average number of workers, the share of the total MSE labour force in enterprises generating higher returns is even higher.

Particularly in rural areas, patterns of growth of MSEs are strongly influenced by other things happening in the household. There is a rich literature on rural farm–nonfarm linkages. One of the main points of contention in that literature concerns the degree to which people in rural areas are pushed to operate MSEs by a lack of viable alternatives (e.g. landless households, or people living in unfavourable agro-climatic conditions), or pulled to do so in response to favourable opportunities (e.g. a response to dynamic local markets that open up profitable possibilities; or the presence of other activities in the household that generate funds, enabling the operator to invest in the MSE).

A recent survey in Mozambique makes it possible to say something about these inter-relationships between the performance of an MSE and other characteristics of the owner's household. The Mozambique survey indicates that a significant share of rural households with very little land are engaged in MSEs. For these households, presumably the MSE operator is responding to forces of necessity, especially since the very limited rural labour market leaves them little option in terms of selling their labour to other local employers, whether agricultural or non- agricultural. But an equally important finding may be that households with larger land-holdings and with higher agricultural incomes are even more likely to be engaged in MSE activities. Not only are those households that are richer in terms of their agricultural income more likely to establish an MSE, but the income that they derive from the MSE is also substantially higher. The analysis suggests that, in Mozambique, while both push and pull factors are at work in different households, the percentage of people in more favourable circumstances who are pulled to respond to auspicious MSE opportunities is higher than the percentage of people in unfavourable circumstances who are pushed to start MSEs through a lack of alternative income sources.

Looking across all these survey results, the findings suggest a picture that is perhaps not surprising to anyone who has spent time working with MSEs in the Third World. The majority of such enterprises are very small; the modal category engages only one person, who works long hours to make relatively low returns. Only a minority of enterprises have been able to move beyond the constraints facing such enterprises to earn higher incomes and/or to expand by taking on additional workers. Yet there is also a significant minority of enterprises in the MSE universe that are doing substantially better, both by generating higher incomes and through an expansion that has involved their taking on additional workers.

Some characteristics and determinants of success among MSEs

It would be wrong to think of the universe of MSEs in a bi-polar way, suggesting that each enterprise can be categorized as either a survivalist or a grower. The world is not like that; rather, it must be thought of in terms of continuums. There are several dimensions here, some of which are measures of outcomes, while others are factors that may influence the patterns of outcomes. In terms of outcomes, two indicators might be seen as key measures of success among MSEs: the level of income generated in the enterprise, and the extent to which employment in the enterprise has grown. Judged from this perspective, the preceding discussion suggests that the overall success rate among MSEs has not been high. The majority of enterprises that started out as one-person undertakings have subsequently not grown by adding to their work force, and have produced distressingly low returns for those who work in them. Yet there has also been a significant minority of enterprises that have measured up well in terms of one or both of these success measures. The discussion that follows explores some of the factors that appear to have contributed to success among different groups of entrepreneurs. This is done under two headings: the 'human capital' characteristics of the entrepreneurs; and the macroeconomic context in which the enterprise operates.

Human capital characteristics

Anyone working in this area knows the importance of motivation, enthusiasm, and a whole list of similar personal, entrepreneurial characteristics, as determinants of success in enterprise development. Taking that set of factors as given, what does the research based on GEMINI surveys show about the contribution of experience, education and training to success among MSEs? McPherson (1992 and 1996) looked at survey data from several survey countries, using multiple regression analysis to explore relationships between MSE growth and three human capital measures: years of experience working in similar businesses; levels of education; and training received.

His results indicate that completion of primary school was unrelated to enterprise growth in any country. Completion of secondary school was associated with higher enterprise growth in only one of the three countries with relevant data, while years of experience appeared to matter in only one of the two countries with the requisite data. With regard to training, McPherson found that enterprises in Lesotho with proprietors who had received formal business training grew 68 per cent more rapidly than those with untrained managers. In four other countries that he examined, however, this relationship was either negative (enterprises whose owners had received some business training grew less rapidly) or the relationship was statistically insignificant.

Daniels (1995) used a similar approach to analyse data from the 1993 Zimbabwe survey; she found that neither education nor experience were significantly related to patterns of the growth of employment in MSEs. Parker (1995), focusing her attention on only one country (Kenya), looked at these factors in more detail. Her findings provide important insights into the complexities of these factors as determinants of enterprise success.

Her analysis indicated that MSE owners that had completed primary school were better able to deal with fluctuating economic circumstances, relative to those with less education; they were better able to grow, regardless of the general economic environment, while entrepreneurs with less education were more severely hurt by economic downturns. In general, entrepreneurs with more education were able to follow a smoother growth path, while those with less education showed substantially more fluctuations in the level of employment in the enterprise.

There are significant interactions between education and experience, in that the contribution of either one by itself to growth is much less powerful than in circumstances where they come together. It appears that education makes it possible for people to benefit more from experience, while experience adds to the benefits that people derive from education. Another interesting finding concerns the relationship between schooling and the profitability of the enterprise.

Both the Zambian and Kenyan surveys explored this relationship. Both found that education beyond the primary level was associated with significant increases in enterprise profitability. In Zambia, average hourly profits of those who had completed lower secondary school were more than twice those of enterprises run by people with only upper primary schooling (it is worth noting that the latter was not significantly different from those with no schooling, or those who had completed only lower primary). Those with upper secondary or higher education had even higher returns (Parker 1996). In Kenya, the share of all enterprises generating returns equal to at least twice the minimum wage was twice as high for those whose owners had completed upper primary or more, compared to those with lower primary or less. Similar relationships were found in multiple regression analysis of these data (Daniels and Mead 1998). The surveys in both Zambia and Kenya also found similar positive relationships between training and enterprise profitability.

These findings suggest that, while small amounts of education appear to have made little difference to enterprise profitability, going beyond a certain threshold – lower secondary in Zambia; upper primary in Kenya – was associated with substantial increases in enterprise profitability. In view of the standard problems of associating more education with more productivity (those who get more education are already more able and more highly motivated), these results may be important more for suggesting that a little education makes little difference, rather than as a way of bolstering the stronger but more dubious conclusion that a lot of education makes a lot of difference.

Most of the surveys asked a question about the principal problem facing the enterprise. In most countries, the issue listed in first place was that of markets. Many MSEs find that they are selling a limited range of products in restricted and saturated markets; if they seek to increase their production, they find it difficult to sell the extra output. Enterprises that have done better have found a way of addressing that problem: by selling in niche markets, by being established in favourable locations, by finding more favourable marketing arrangements.

Our interviews and experience in the field indicate that education and training can make their most effective contribution when they are closely linked to this issue of markets: helping enterprises take advantage of market opportunities, to enable them to grasp those opportunities. One area where this approach has been particularly fruitful is in relation to business linkages, where MSEs sell to larger buyers; focused training can strengthen the capacity of small enterprises to operate as reliable partners in such contracts. The more closely education and training can be focused on an approach that starts from identified market opportunities, helping entrepreneurs take advantage of those opportunities, the more effective it is likely to be.

The importance of the broader macro context for enterprise success

Suppose, following the ideas presented in the first paragraph in this section, one could range MSEs along a spectrum. 'Survivalist' activities, reflecting factors pushing people to establish new MSEs, in spite of limited earning opportunities that they offer, would be at one end of this spectrum; at the opposite end would be employment opportunities that emerge as MSE operators identify opportunities to start profitable new businesses, or to expand existing ones, in ways that generate substantially higher incomes. It might be, then, given the number of productive new jobs emerging in other sectors of the economy and given a labour force growing more rapidly than this, that total employment in MSEs would continue to grow, in good times and in bad; it would serve as the reservoir, taking up the excess of people who must support themselves in one way or another.

But there is mounting evidence that the pattern of growth of employment in MSEs is strongly influenced by the macroeconomic circumstances in the country. In good times, a relatively high share of the new MSE jobs are closer to the 'growth' end of the spectrum, reflecting a response by entrepreneurs to profitable business opportunities. When the state of the macroeconomy is less favourable, by contrast, the opportunities for profitable employment expansion in MSEs is limited; people will be forced to seek their living in alternative ways. In such circumstances, a larger proportion of the MSE employment growth would reflect decisions by entrepreneurs to start new enterprises, a higher proportion of which would be closer to the survivalist end of the spectrum.

There are several pieces of evidence that support this view. First, in Kenya, the 1995 survey was able to identify the time patterns of employment growth among respondent enterprises. Analysis of those data indicates that, when the economy was less favourable, a higher proportion of new jobs among MSEs was in newly established enterprises, yielding only relatively low returns. When the overall macroeconomy was growing at a somewhat more robust rate, by contrast, MSEs were able to participate in that more healthy growth by adding to their labour force, often in activities that generated higher incomes.

A second piece of evidence here comes from the recent, third round GEMINI survey in Zimbabwe (McPherson 1998). The data from that survey indicate that, in the five years since the previous survey (in 1993), the total number of MSEs in the country has declined by nearly 9 per cent. This decline in enterprise numbers was confined to enterprises in rural areas; urban enterprise numbers increased by nearly 30 per cent over this period. At the same time that the total number of enterprises was declining in rural areas, many existing enterprises were taking on new workers, so total employment in MSEs increased over this five-year period; again, this employment growth was concentrated in urban areas. One plausible explanation for this pattern is that, in 1993, the country was operating under the shadow of one of the most serious droughts of the twentieth century; particularly in rural areas, many people were scrambling for any source of income, to compensate for their inability to support themselves in agriculture. In the years since then, with more favourable weather and more healthy patterns of growth in the overall economy, many people in rural areas have returned to their traditional pursuits in agriculture, while a more robust economy has created new opportunities for a profitable expansion of existing MSEs, particularly in urban areas.

Analysis of data collected in an earlier (1993) survey in Zimbabwe provides further evidence of the impact of the macroeconomic environment on MSE growth patterns. Using data from that earlier survey, Daniels (1995) found an inverse relationship between the rate of growth of GDP and the birth rate of MSEs in industrial sectors that earn low returns. She interprets this result as reflecting the fact that, in bad times, people turn to MSEs in low-profit industries, while in good times, there is a decline in the numbers of people who are led (pushed?) to start new, low-profit MSEs.

Concluding comments

Many people refer to micro- and small enterprises as 'the informal sector'. Unfortunately, this terminology means different things to different people. Perhaps the most clear dimension here concerns the degree of legality: the extent to which an enterprise is registered, pays taxes and obeys the regulations. In this sense, a goal of 'formalizing the informal sector' is one that deserves low priority. Entrepreneurs consistently say that there are other factors that constrain them more than the legal and regulatory environment (Mead and Morrisson 1996).

Should MSEs be viewed as essentially survivalist activities, enabling people to get by until better opportunities come along? Or are they rather a component of a dynamic growth process, such that one might expect that they will continue to expand and thrive as the economy develops? The evidence presented here makes clear that the answer must be that each is true of some components of the MSE universe. Significant numbers of MSEs make their major contribution by helping people to survive, when nothing better is available. These have the effect of enabling large numbers of very poor people to be somewhat less poor; they are good at poverty alleviation, although they have been much less successful in terms of poverty elimination.

But there are also other MSEs that have been effective in enabling significant numbers of people to move up and out of poverty. The evidence also indicates that the relationship between these different components is not a binary one, such that all enterprises could be classified in one or other of these two categories. Rather, it is a continuum, with plenty of intermediate cases and with no sharp dividing line between one category and another. There is also some movement back and forth along the spectrum. The number of enterprises that graduate from the survivalist end is not as many as we would like, but it is not insignificant and is an important feedstock for today's larger enterprises (Mead 1994).

What this means is that enterprises at different points along this continuum have different contributions to make to the welfare and development of a country. It is also true that different types of projects and policies have their most important impacts on enterprises at different points along this spectrum. Thus, micro-credit programmes are designed primarily to help enterprises closer to the survivalist end of the continuum. Macro-policies leading to stable prices and robust aggregate growth, by contrast, make their principal contribution primarily for somewhat larger enterprises that generate higher incomes; indeed, such policies may reduce the pressures for expansion in employment in enterprises closer to the survivalist end of the spectrum.

A recognition of this diversity in the MSE universe should lead to a parallel recognition of the diversity of needs in terms of projects and policies, to respond to diverse opportunities and constraints facing enterprises at different points along the spectrum. With regard to the contribution of education and training to micro- and small enterprise development, the preceding discussion leads one to ask: for enterprises at various points along the spectrum of enterprise types, what are the opportunities for the enterprises to do better? Then, what types of education and training can be most effective in enabling them to improve their performance? A recognition of the diversity in the MSE universe leads logically to the need for a similar diversity in education and training programmes, to meet the needs of different participants in the system. Only in this way is it possible to enable the complex universe of MSEs to make their full contribution in areas of both poverty alleviation and poverty elimination.

5 Micro-enterprises in West Africa

The need for a follow-up survey of their dynamics and role in job creation within the continuous expansion of the informal sector

JACQUES CHARMES

Following the adoption by the XVth International Conference of Labour Statisticians in 1993 (ILO 1993a and b) of an international definition of the informal sector as a concept of labour force, estimates and figures of the size of this sector and of its contribution to GDP have become available. For a number of countries, and often for a number of years, we have good data for employment and output of the informal sector. This can increasingly be disaggregated by gender, but it is still difficult to identify clearly the trends of the various segments. While family enterprises, home-based work and street vending are of special interest for policies addressing poverty alleviation, micro-enterprises represent a high potential for job creation and are a matter of concern for policy makers and donors.

After a brief reminder of the new international definition of the informal sector and of its main components, recent empirical evidence of its size, contribution and trend will be presented. Finally, methodologies for the follow-up of micro-enterprises will be emphasized, which are currently about to be implemented in several West African countries.

The international definition of the informal sector and its main components

Emerging from more than two decades of surveys, the main features of informal sector economic units are:

- ease of entry
- small scale of the activity
- self-employment, with a high proportion of family workers and apprentices
- little capital and equipment
- labour-intensive technologies
- low skills
- low level of organization with no access to organized markets, to formal credit, to education and training or services and amenities
- cheap provision of goods and services, or provision of goods and services otherwise unavailable
- low productivity and low incomes according to some analysts, or, on the

contrary, incomes that are notably higher than in the public sector, especially during the recent past and in the context of structural adjustment policies, for other observers.

Although these activities are legal, they rarely comply with official and administrative requirements. More specifically, as they are often unregistered, they do not pay relevant taxes. This arises in part from a desire to remain concealed. It is, however, more likely that the principal reason is the inability of governments to enforce often inadequate regulations. Informal sector activities are often tolerated as a kind of recognition that the laws are inadequate. Furthermore, they have become a means for many countries to cope with population growth, rural-urban migrations, economic crises, poverty and indebtedness. In this respect, the informal sector can be seen, rather than reflecting a low stage of development or of maladjustment, more as an adjustment to the inadequacy of the regulations in force. Therefore, the more difficult the economic context, the more extensive the informal sector; and the more dynamic the economic context, the more restricted the informal sector – the growth of micro-enterprises meaning that many of them have attempted to enter the formal sector.

In addition, many formal wage-earners are also engaged in informal businesses as additional jobs in order to compensate for declining wages and purchasing power. Thus, one cannot consider that there is a perfect distinction between participants in the informal sector on the one hand, and people who receive wages and salaries from the formal sector on the other.

The complexity and looseness of the concept explain why it has not been possible until now to reach international agreement on a definition covering the variety of analytical purposes adopted by data users. For this reason labour statisticians distinguish the several definitions which may vary according to the need of users, from the single statistical definition used for the purpose of data collection.

The underlying 'umbrella' concept encompasses the various parts of the economy that are insufficiently reflected in official statistics: it is kept as simple as possible and uses a single criterion, or a small number of operational criteria, yet it is broad enough to cover as many types of enterprise as is conceptually compatible with the notion of the informal sector.

The definition may be summarized as follows: for statistical purposes, the informal sector is regarded as a group of production units which form a part, within the System of National Accounts (SNA), of the household sector as unincorporated enterprises owned by households.

Household enterprises (or unincorporated enterprises owned by households) are distinguished from corporations and quasi-corporations on the basis of their legal status and the type of accounts they hold: accordingly, household enterprises are not constituted as separate legal entities independently of the household or of the household members who own them, and no complete set of accounts is available which could permit a clear distinction between the production activities of the enterprises and the other activities of their owners.

The informal sector is defined, irrespective of the kind of workplace, the extent of fixed capital assets, the duration of the activity of the enterprise or its operation as a main or secondary activity, as comprising:

1 informal self-owned enterprises which may employ family workers, and employees on an occasional basis. In different settings this segment comprises either all self-owned enterprises, or only those which are not registered under specific forms of national legislation.
2 enterprises of informal employers who may employ one or more employees on a continuous basis and who comply with one or both of the following criteria:

   - the size of the establishment is below a specified level of employment (defined on the basis of minimum size requirements embodied in relevant national legislation or other empirical or statistical practices; the choice of the upper size limit taking account of the coverage of statistical enquiries in order to avoid an overlap)
   - non-registration of the enterprise or its employees.

Furthermore, and for practical purposes, the informal sector may be restricted to non-agricultural activities. Professionals and domestic workers are included in the informal sector in so far as they comply with the definitional characteristics or criteria. Home-based workers are included if they are self-employed or subcontracted to other informal sector units. Non-market production is excluded. The value of this definition resides in the fact that it relies on existing practices for estimating informal employment at a national or macroeconomic level.

The statistical definition distinguishes two main components or segments of the informal sector:

- the 'family enterprises' (own-account informal enterprises) without permanent employees
- the 'micro-enterprises' (informal employers) with permanent employees.

An important characteristic of the informal sector – the place of work – is not part of the definition although it plays a major role in the differentiation of the activities. However, for present purposes, it should be stressed that micro-enterprises are defined as those informal sector units that employ salaried employees on a continuous basis, and which are below a given size, be they home-based, street-based or established in fixed premises.

Three points have to be specified:

1 the employment size cut-off point may differ according to national circumstances, but one should not exaggerate the difficulties of making

international comparisons because the size limit usually incorporates legislative or administrative thresholds or, in other words, it corresponds to a natural or national obstacle to entry into the formal sector, or to growth within it.

2 the extent of employment may be calculated on the basis of the number of employees, of workers or of jobs. The number of jobs is to be preferred, but it may be assumed that five employees represent 10 jobs in total.

3 employment size must be calculated on the basis of the establishment rather than the enterprise. This is necessary in order to reveal the 'missing middle' – the intermediate sector comprising enterprises made up of several small establishments.

Recent empirical evidence on size, contribution and trend of the informal sector

The adoption of an international definition of the informal sector which is not too restrictive nor too difficult to apply (as an umbrella concept) has given a great impetus to the implementation of national surveys on the informal sector in several countries, and has allowed researchers to acquire indirect estimates for various periods, including years preceding the adoption of the 1993 definition.

Table 5.1 synthesizes the available comparable data compiled, at national level, on the basis of homogeneous concepts and methods for sub-Saharan Africa.

In sub-Saharan Africa, the population grew more rapidly than output during the 1980s and this trend was forecast to continue during the following decade, resulting from an increase of the population growth rates over improved economic growth rates. Meanwhile, the labour force was steadily increasing, and will continue on the same trend. Consequently, increasing unemployment rates, and especially the expansion of the informal sector, will have to absorb the surplus of labour and ensure the equilibrium of the labour market.

The average size of the informal sector (as a proportion of the non-agricultural labour force) in sub-Saharan Africa (on the basis of seven countries) reached 66.5 per cent in the 1980s (from 1976 to 1984), compared to 38.8 per cent in North Africa and 39 per cent in Latin America. In the following decade (1985–94), this figure rose to 75.9 per cent. For countries where more recent estimates or figures have been made available, the rise of the numbers employed in the informal sector has been even more dramatic: 90.4 per cent in Mali in 1994 and 94.1per cent in 1996; and nearly 90 per cent in Chad in 1995–96.

Growth of employment in the informal sector is observed all over the world: in the mid-1990s, the rate of informal employment had risen to 56.1

Table 5.1: Trends in labour force, unemployment and informal employment

	Annual growth rate		*Urban unemployment rate*	*Employment rate in the informal sector(2)*	
	GNP % *1980–91*	*Labour force %* *1981–90*	*1990* *%*	*1980* *%*	*1990* *%*
North Africa	1.0	3.0	15.8	38.8(1)	43.4(1)
Sub-Saharan Africa	−1.1	2.5	—	66.5(1)	75.9(1)
Mauritania	−1.8	2.8	31.6	69.4	75.3
Senegal	−0.1	1.9	24.4	76.0	—
Mali	−4.1	2.6	9.9	63.1	78.6
Niger	1.2	2.4	—	62.9	—
Burkina Faso	2.0	2.6	—	70.0	77.0
Chad	3.8	1.9	—	—	74.2
Benin	−0.9	2.1	10.1	—	92.8
Guinea	—	1.7	12.3	64.4	71.9
Zaire	—	2.3	—	59.6	—
Kenya	0.3	3.5	16.2	—	61.4

Source: Charmes (1996c).
Notes: (1) Non-weighted arithmetical mean.
(2) As a proportion of total non-agricultural employment.

per cent in Latin America, to nearly 80 per cent in India, and one can guess that the recent financial crises which occurred in the emergent economies of Asia will have had the same impact in a very short period of time.

At the same time, unemployment rates are also growing rapidly. A recent comparative survey undertaken by Afristat (the economic and statistical observatory for sub-Saharan Africa) in the seven capital cities of the West African Economic and Monetary Union showed unemployment rates ranging from 10 to 28 per cent, with an average rate of 16 per cent in 1996.

It has also been asserted, and occasionally demonstrated, that structural adjustment programmes, through the shrinking of the public wage bill, have had a negative impact on the demand addressed to the informal sector, at least at urban or capital levels. However, this impact may have been counterbalanced by an increase in incomes earned by agricultural producers, and this has also been documented occasionally. The fact is that the number of people working in the informal sector has increased much more rapidly than the GDP – and especially the value added generated by the informal sector. This gives credence to the assumption that informal sector activities are less and less productive and generate smaller incomes, leading to a minimum equilibrium in incomes earned by informal sector participants or operators.

Table 5.2 indicates the proportion of GDP generated by the informal sector of various African countries in recent years, giving a better idea and measure of its contribution after several years of continuous methodological efforts. The informal sector currently represents between 20 and 40 per cent of total GDP, and between 40 and 60 per cent of non-agricultural GDP.

Table 5.2: Informal sector as a proportion of non-agricultural employment, and as a proportion of non-agricultural and total GDP in various African countries

Country (years)	*% non-agricultural employment*	*% non-agricultural GDP*	*% total employment*	*% total GDP*
Tunisia (1995)	48.7	22.9	37.8	20.3
Benin (1993)	92.8	42.7	41.0	27.3
Mali (1989)	78.6	41.7	13.3	23.0
Burkina Faso (1992)	77.0	36.2	8.6	24.5
Senegal (1991)	76.0	40.9	—	33.0
Mauritania (1989)	75.3	14.4	—	10.2
Chad (1993)	74.2	44.7	11.5	31.0
Niger (1995)	—	58.5	—	37.6

Sources: Personal compilations of the author on the basis of official National Accounts and Labour Force data. Published in the proceedings of the experts' meeting on Household Satellite Accounts. October 1997: *Handbook of National Accounting. Household Accounting: Experiences in the Use of Concepts and their Compilation. Vol. 1: Household Sector Accounts*. United Nations Statistics Division. New York. 1998.

In contrast to labour force data, figures available on the contribution of the informal sector to GDP are scarcer and, moreover, they are not significant across time, because their trends are only the results of national accountants' assumptions, not properly based on real facts and data.

This means that strenuous efforts have still to be undertaken for the follow-up, in the short term, of the trend of output generated by the informal sector. The increase in the informal sector's contribution to GDP is deserving better than a simple assumption linking its growth to that of the population or to growth rates of overall production. As a result of such an inaccurate registration of its trends by the National Accounts, the general assumption is that the informal sector is globally anti-cyclical.

This global anti-cyclical characteristic of the informal sector (the labour force engaged in the sector is growing when the economy as a whole is depressed and dropping, or even slowing down) has still to be investigated and documented in a more detailed way, especially in order to identify the role of its various components or sub-sectors. Is the segment of 'family enterprises', or the segment of home-based workers or street vendors, anti-cyclical and increasing when economic growth is slowing down?; and is the micro-enterprises sector pro-cyclical, increasing when economic growth starts again?

Tightly linked to this anti-cyclical characteristic of the informal sector is the idea that such a type of growth goes with an increase in the number of women engaged in the sector, in correlation with its tertiarization. Although empirical evidence of such trends is still expected, efforts have recently been made, and are currently in progress (mainly through the WIEGO project – Women in Informal Employment: Globalising and Organising – a coalition initiated by SEWA [the Self-Employed Women's Association], UNIFEM and the Harvard Institute for International Development) better to measure the contribution of women in informal sector employment. Table 5.3 shows recent estimates of women's share in labour force and GDP, derived from this project.

As to the micro-enterprises, it is possible, at the present state of data collection and comparative analysis of sources, to know the approximate size of the subsector, but not its growth or trend. This is precisely why there is an urgent need for a better measurement of the trend and composition of the informal sector in the short run, and especially of its segment of microenterprises which conceals such high potential.

Table 5.4 gives an idea of the size of this sub-sector in various countries.

Table 5.4 shows that the micro-enterprise segment is all the more important as manufacturing activities are extended in the country: the more trade-oriented or tertiary-oriented is the informal sector, the less it is characterized by micro-enterprises. As a matter of fact, the size of this segment of the informal sector is probably underestimated due to the fact that structural adjustment programmes have not encouraged employers and own-account workers to hire employees on a permanent basis, and has rather led them to sub-contract home-based workers on a piece-rate or task-rate basis. This kind of enterprise should be included in the micro-enterprise segment, but questionnaire design and survey methodologies are not yet adequately adapted to capture and measure this type of job. Home-based workers often report that they are independent or self-employed, while the owners of contracting firms do not declare those workers in establishment surveys.

Table 5.3: Proportion and contribution of women in the informal sector in five African countries

Country/statistic	*Benin*	*Mali*	*Chad*	*Burkina Faso*	*Tunisia*
% of women in informal sector employment	59.7	71.9	53.4	41.9	18.1
Informal sector GDP %	51.1	68.2	62.3	61.4	15.7
Total non-agricultural GDP %	21.8	26.1	27.8	28.6	3.6
Total GDP %	14.0	14.8	13.9	19.3	3.2

Sources: Charmes (1998). 'Contribution of women working in the informal sector in Africa: a case study.' Paper prepared for WIEGO and the United Nations Statistics Division 'Umbrella Gender Statistics Programme' and presented at the second meeting of the Delhi Group on Informal Sector Statistics, Ankara, 28–30 April 1998. The estimates are calculated from personal compilations of the author on the basis of official labour force statistics and national accounts.

Table 5.4: The micro-enterprise part of the informal sector of some African countries (as a proportion of total informal employment)

Country (years)	*Micro-enterprises %*	*Manufacturing employment %*
Tunisia (1995)	55.4	47.4
Burkina Faso (1985)	18.5	29.3
(1995)	16.6	31.8
Mali (1989)	18.3	47.4
Chad (1993)	7.3	12.2
Senegal (1980)	5.0	16.9
Benin (1993)	5.0	—
Guinea (1991)	5.0	37.2
Latin America (1990)	20.2	—
(1995)	22.5	—

Sources: Charmes (1996a) and (1997).

Despite the relatively small proportion of micro-enterprises in total informal employment, this subsector is a centre of attention for policy makers because it is rightly supposed to have great potential for job creation, accumulation and growth, which often remain concealed, at least statistically speaking. The thesis of the 'missing middle' has emerged from the observation of a bimodal distribution of employment between small informal firms on the one hand, and medium and large firms on the other. However, I have shown (Charmes 1984) this to be a statistical illusion due to ill-adapted techniques of enumeration and reporting omissions. Nonetheless, it is still being discussed and implies the necessity to improve survey methodologies, observation units and concepts, as well as techniques and methodologies for the follow-up of such a challenging segment of the informal sector.

Finally, the level of educational attainment is increasing in the informal sector: this is the natural result of the general increase of the number of school attenders at country level, despite the recent failures and decrease in the quality of education. All surveys show that, as a result of the generation effect, the educational level of owners is lower than that of the employees, which is again lower than the apprentices'. Gradually, this improvement in the quality of human capital will have an impact on the informal sector, its productivity and output. And even if public interventions naturally tend to formalize the informal sector – although it is not properly a goal of such interventions – some kind of formalization will occur spontaneously. This will be seen in terms of management, accountancy, interest and ability to lean on the institutional framework and to react to policy incentives rather than abiding by the law. Such gradual changes have also to be observed and followed up.

A follow-up survey of micro-enterprises in West Africa

Data presented above show that many gaps have been filled, thanks to the adoption of an agreed international definition and to recent national comprehensive surveys, paving the way to better knowledge of the informal sector and its components. However, a few major gaps are still evident, among which is the unavailability of regular and comparable time-series. As a matter of fact, the estimates presented earlier result from a comparative static process rather than a dynamic study. While these kinds of data are useful, and are essential to take the measure of the growing importance of the informal sector, detailed conclusions cannot be derived from them for at least two reasons:

- From one period to another, concepts and sources may have varied and comparisons are too rough to proceed to in-depth analyses.
- Informal sector growth may find expression in the transformation of informal jobs into formal employment, which is precisely the process opposite to the so-called 'informalization'; and even if it is commonly taken for granted that such changes are rare, it has to be ascertained whether this is not another statistical illusion.

Therefore, during the past few years, there has been an increasing need for longitudinal data concerning informal sector enterprises, micro-enterprises and, more generally, the mechanisms of insertion into the labour market. In order to meet these needs, several recent or on-going programmes or methodologies have been implemented at international, sub-regional or national levels.

The first to be mentioned, in the area with which we are concerned, is certainly the implementation in several West African countries of 'Observatories (or information systems) of Employment and Training' set up under the wing of Ministries of Employment or Manpower and with the support of the ILO, the World Bank, and/or the UNDP (Benin, Burkina Faso, Côte d'Ivoire, Mali, Senegal, Togo). Mali has been one of the most productive until now (the observatory has become the main source of Mali's labour force statistics) and has taken the initiative in creating a network linking several observatories in the region.

But it is in Benin, coming out of a period when statistics were just good enough to confirm the accuracy of designed policies, that, as early as 1990, a regular annual survey was implemented to monitor the social consequences of drastic structural adjustment programmes, especially through labour market and living standard indicators. The 'light' or 'lean' household survey has been designed to understand better the behaviours of households and small entrepreneurs in the difficult context of structural adjustment. Table 5.5 gives some interesting longitudinal results of such an approach.

From a relatively high level during the first year of adjustment, the

Table 5.5: Unemployment and informal employment rates in Cotonou and Parakou (Benin), from 1990 to 1996

	1990	*1992*	*1993*	*1994*	*Mar 1995*	*Sep 1995*	*Mar 1996*	*Sep 1996*
Declared unemployment rate %	24.5	13.0	10.2	12.2	12.0	7.9	7.6	7.5
Real unemployment rate %	13.1	8.4	6.3	1.8	4.6	4.4	4.7	5.0
Informal employment rate %	69.5	84.4	86.3	86.7	87.0	83.4	82.2	82.0

Sources: Charmes (1996b).

declared unemployment rate dropped down to 12–13 per cent until the beginning of 1995, then to 7–8 per cent where it seems to have stabilized. The real unemployment rate (excluding the active persons who spontaneously declared themselves as unemployed, but who, at a further stage of the interview, revealed they were occupied according to international standards) is much lower and has regularly decreased to become stable at around 5 per cent, after reaching a very low minimum immediately after the devaluation of the CFA Franc in 1994. During the same period, the proportion of informal sector employment increased continuously to the peak in March 1995, from which it has now begun to decrease, revealing renewed job creation in the modern sector.

Being available less than two months after data collection in the field, these data are of great interest to policy makers, who can assess the immediate impact of policy measures; they are also of particular interest for the understanding, by economists and researchers, of the role of the informal sector during periods such as the post-devaluation, or the effects of external or internal shocks.

No wonder that the Observatory of Employment in Mali has recently decided to launch such a survey – which has to be clearly distinguished from an ordinary annual labour force survey. Its lightness, its special focus on the labour market, living standards, social solidarity and the informal sector, and the short delay in producing and releasing the results, are essential and distinctive features which make this survey an efficient tool for monitoring economic and social policies in the short run.

Moreover, the survey provides a sound framework and a sampling frame for specific follow-up or tracer surveys devoted to improving the understanding of the functioning of the labour market. For, as useful and accurate as they are, these surveys and time series are not sufficient in themselves to understand how jobs are created in the informal sector, and especially in the micro-enterprise subsector – how young school leavers and young graduates succeed or fail in finding jobs in sectors of activity for which they have not been specially educated and trained; for how long they remain unemployed and what happens during this period which leads them to accept jobs outside the usual opportunities offered by the civil service or the modern sector (where they exist at all).

In Benin, the Observatory of Employment is currently carrying out three follow-up surveys:

- on a sample of the unemployed
- on a sample of young school leavers and university graduates
- on a sample of micro-entrepreneurs.

All of these were selected from the permanent household survey.

It is well known that one of the major weaknesses of follow-up studies is the progressive exit of the sample members and/or the increasing difficulty for the interviewers to trace them. As a matter of fact, the vanishing members are precisely those who are the most interesting, because they are atypical from the point of view of the study. High non-response rates always cast a gloom over the conclusions of such surveys (because the most mobile persons are either those who are the most efficient in seeking work or are those who, on the contrary, are the least efficient in this respect, and it is exactly the reverse for entrepreneurs). In this respect, these surveys have a major advantage compared to others. Biographic surveys are an interesting alternative (consisting of the reconstitution of the work-life of the persons in the sample), but they are better adapted to the follow-up of the entire population in the labour force (or out of it) than for specific segments of this population which would require too large a sample size. The method, which consists in seeking the persons or the enterprises surveyed a few years earlier, interesting and successfully used though it may be (see, for instance, Marniesse 1998) is subject to the same drawbacks as described above.

Therefore, an original approach has been adopted which consists in getting all selected persons standing by the study, namely:

- all the persons declared unemployed during the first round (March) of the 1998 light household survey (more than 200)
- 200 young school leavers and graduates of the school year 1997–98, selected according to several criteria, such as: level or degree, gender, success or drop out
- 200 micro-entrepreneurs, selected through the permanent household survey or, if possible and because the number of units could be insufficient, through a two-stage area sampling method (enumeration areas are selected with a probability proportional to the number of economic units in the 1992 establishment census; then all units are once again enumerated in the selected areas to allow, at the second stage, a random selection of units among those that have permanent employees or more than five workers).

Everyone in the sample will be invited for a first interview, during which the purpose, the objectives and the methodology of the survey (particularly the importance of the follow-up over three to four years) will be explained in depth; the unemployed and the school leavers will be invited to attend a meeting during which they will have to fill the questionnaire and will receive an amount of money equivalent to the monthly legal minimum wage (approximately 20 000 F CFA). It is considered that this method is simultaneously ethical (the money is given to the needy who have not yet got a source of income), cost effective (it will be less expensive than the payment of 40 interviewers for five months) and more efficient (interviewees being financially interested) – all the more so as these interviewees will report changes in their addresses during the year, in order to receive the invitation to attend the second meeting in the following year. Those two categories will be maintained in the sample (and informed of that rule) even if they find a job in the meantime.

For the micro-entrepreneurs, the rules of the game cannot be the same: they will be offered gifts, drawing of lots or placing of orders, so as to keep interest in staying in the sample.

With an expected very low non-response rate, the three follow-up surveys are expected to provide detailed and reliable information on the real functioning of the labour market in economies where the informal sector is reaching more than 90 per cent of the non-agricultural labour force, while the unemployment rate is high and affects a large number of young graduates.

This methodology is expected also to be applied in Mali and, through the network of the 'observatories' and by example and demonstration, extended and duplicated in several other countries of the region.

6 Small enterprise development in post-apartheid South Africa

Gearing up for growth and poverty alleviation

CHRISTIAN M. ROGERSON

Introduction

In post-apartheid South Africa, major policy significance is attached to the promotion and support of the small, medium and micro-enterprise (SMME) sector. A radical policy shift has occurred from the apartheid period when the SMME economy was either largely neglected by policy makers or, in the case of black-owned enterprises, actively discouraged by an arsenal of repressive measures. In the changed policy environment of the 1990s, promotion of the SMME economy is linked to a range of new policy objectives, including poverty alleviation and enhancement of national economic growth. The National Project on Poverty and Inequality highlights the importance of assisting the SMME economy as part of a package of integrated strategies for poverty alleviation in urban and, more especially, in rural areas. Programmes for nurturing the SMME economy are seen as offering a basis for addressing poverty and inherited apartheid inequalities through strengthening existing coping strategies of poor households or by offering alternative livelihoods to those individuals engaged in the survival informal economy (May 1998). By contrast, in South Africa's new macroeconomic strategy, the Growth Employment and Redistribution (GEAR) programme, the strengthening of the SMME economy is identified as one of the core elements for achieving a medium-term improved growth and employment performance as well as for enhancing the long-term competitive capacity of the economy (Republic of South Africa 1996). The task in this chapter is to debate and tease out these differing directions for SMME development in post-apartheid South Africa, presenting an analysis of key policy objectives, constraints and opportunities, and current operational programmes for the SMME economy.

Within the macroeconomic context provided by GEAR, the specific framework for SMME development in post-apartheid South Africa was laid out in the 1995 White Paper on Small Business (Republic of South Africa 1995). At the outset, it is acknowledged that the SMME economy is not a homogeneous entity; rather there exists a continuum of enterprises from those at one end which are essentially survival enterprises, to successful small and medium enterprises, at the other. Officially, the South African SMME economy is divided into three sets of enterprises: (1) survivalist enterprises of the informal economy, (2) a segment of growth-oriented micro-enterprises, and (3) the formal SME economy which is presently dominated by established white-owned enterprises. The group of survivalist enterprises and the micro-enterprise economy form the emergent SMME economy, which is dominated by members of South Africa's historically disadvantaged communities (Ntsika 1997a). Overall, the White Paper observes that the largest component in the South African SMME economy is the survivalist sector, which numbers an estimated 2.5 million as compared to 800 000 in the rest of the SMME economy (micro-enterprise and the formal SME economy).

The White Paper sets forth several policy objectives (Republic of South Africa 1995: 15–16). The primary goal is stated as 'to create an enabling environment' in terms of national, regional and local policy frameworks for SMME development. In addition to this basic objective, several more specific policy objectives are identified. First, is 'to facilitate the greater equalization of income, wealth and economic opportunities' which is inseparable from a strengthening of the labour-absorptive process in the micro-enterprise and survivalist segments, the redressing of discrimination with respect to blacks' as well as women's access to economic opportunities and power, and the facilitation of growth in black and small enterprises in rural areas. Second, is to create long-term jobs, which demands policy interventions designed to upgrade human resource skills and to strengthen the use of appropriate modern technologies. Third, is the goal of stimulating economic growth through addressing the obstacles and constraints that prevent SMMEs from contributing to overall growth. Fourth, is the policy objective of strengthening the cohesion between SMMEs to overcome their isolation or loneliness by facilitating the networking of SMMEs, in an endeavour to build collective efficiency, to address development obstacles and to take up opportunities. The fifth objective is to level the playing fields both between large enterprises and SMMEs and between rural and urban businesses. Lastly, the national strategy targets the goal of enhancing the capacity of small business to comply with the challenges of globalization and an internationally competitive economy.

It is important to understand that the policy interventions undertaken by the South African government for SMME promotion derive from a conceptualization of at least three key roles for SMMEs in the national economy and society. These relate respectively to SMMEs as agents of employment promotion, redistribution, and for the improvement in global competitiveness. As Manning (1996: 68) observes:

> Not only are these very divergent policy objectives, but the policy instruments required to effect them are equally divergent (ranging from technology support, R & D support, to literacy and numeracy training, and access to basic information).

While it must be acknowledged that each of the policy objectives is both valid and critical in relation to issues of poverty eradication or growth enhancement, 'policymakers necessarily have to impose a hierarchy of importance upon them, in order to decide on the distribution of resources' (Manning 1996: 68). In the absence of clear guidelines for resource allocation, the current South African SMME strategy strives to meet this range of different objectives (Rogerson 1997a).

In terms of the existing principles for intervention, a reassessment is needed based upon current research on the South African SMME economy. The first basis for government intervention in the SMME economy is as an instrument for employment promotion. Throughout much of the writings and research in South Africa considerable emphasis is placed upon the ILO's approach to SMMEs which regards them as having considerable potential to enhance labour absorption in the economy. The decline in the labour absorptive capacity of the formal economy is interpreted as a major impelling factor for large numbers of people to be squeezed into both SMME activities in urban areas and the rural non-farm sector out of circumstances of necessity rather than primarily out of choice (World Bank 1993; Rogerson 1996a and b; Rogerson and Reid 1997). Despite this supply-push trigger for SMME births, particularly of survivalist enterprises, most analysts interpret SMMEs as having a potential to play a positive role in employment creation, given the establishment of appropriate enabling conditions.

Manning (1996: 63–64) challenges some of the conventional wisdom surrounding the equation of SMME promotion with employment creation. It is argued that the 'evidence in support of the perception of SMMEs as important sources of employment is somewhat weak'. In the case of manufacturing SMMEs, existing evidence points to SMMEs' share of employment as being substantially lower in South Africa than in other international contexts (Liedholm and Mead 1993; Manning 1996; Rogerson 1997b). Equally important is the question of the quality of the jobs that are generated through the SMME economy. Increasingly, a number of research studies are suggesting that 'the quality of employment in South African micro-enterprises is poor' (Manning 1996: 63–64). In research conducted in metropolitan Cape Town and Durban, poor wage and work conditions were found among groups of primarily women home-based workers (Budlender and Theron 1995a and b). Further confirmation of the vulnerable plight of both entrepreneurs and employees in manufacturing micro-enterprises is available from other studies which reveal that wage and working conditions are uniformly poor for both owners and their employees (Manning 1993a; Manning and Mashego 1993; Rogerson and Rogerson 1997). In the sphere of survivalist SMMEs the quality of jobs in terms of wage and work conditions are most severe; most survival activities 'cannot be idealized or romanticized as opportunities for employment promotion since they are essentially a poverty trap' (Pityana 1997: 8). Overall, such evidence collectively places at least a question mark on 'a development strategy which promotes these (SMME) enterprises as a viable alternative to other forms of employment' (Manning 1996: 64).

The second key function that is associated with SMMEs is in terms of facilitating economic redistribution. Overall, it is evident that an SMME strategy will undoubtedly contribute to redressing severe inequalities inherited from the apartheid period in terms of patterns of economic ownership (Republic of South Africa 1995; May 1998). None the less, it must be cautioned that while SMMEs 'do represent one vehicle for redressing racial income inequalities, it would be dangerous for policy-makers to rely on SMMEs as the main agent for economic redistribution in South Africa' (Manning 1996: 65) for at least three major reasons. First, it must be acknowledged that a reliance on SMMEs to redistribute wealth 'does not tamper with the core economic power of South Africa, most of which is concentrated in the hands of the large white-owned corporations'. Second, as at present the majority of black-owned businesses are very small and yield only limited incomes to their owners, these alone 'cannot be expected to significantly shift the patterns of income distribution'. Lastly, it must be recognized that 'even if SMMEs are a successful channel of wealth to black entrepreneurs, this does not necessarily translate into reduced income inequality'; instead, one likely outcome is the enrichment of a limited number of black South Africans at the expense of the majority of blacks (Manning 1996: 65).

The third key contribution which SMMEs are expected to play in the post-apartheid economy is to augment economic competitiveness of local industry in terms of an increased contribution of SMMEs towards growth and even towards exports. This particular issue has sparked considerable controversy and local debate (Rogerson 1994). In terms of discussions around flexible specialization and the development of industrial districts, it is argued that the introduction of flexible production into South African manufacturing holds considerable promise for renewal of the small-scale industrial sector. More specifically, it is held that through subcontracting arrangements, groups of small-scale producers may experience growth and increased levels of competitiveness as they become more integrated into the mainstream of industrial activity (Rogerson 1995). The other side of flexibilization is, however, the danger of the emergence of the extended 'informalization of formal enterprise' which leads to highly exploitative labour conditions and work relationships under subcontracting (Rogerson 1991). The existing evidence suggests that while out-sourcing by formal enterprise and casualization may be an increasing trend in the South African economy, the actual proportion of home-based workers who are subcontracting is at present very small (Budlender and Theron 1995a and b). Overall, therefore, it is argued that post-apartheid South Africa's programmes for SMME support are being driven by conflicting and sometimes contradictory objectives. In addition, there is a need for some reassessment of current directions in order that transparent guidelines be determined to enable more appropriate targeting of funds and support programming in order to address the manifold constraints upon, and facilitate new opportunities for, the emerging SMME economy.

Constraints and opportunities

In interpreting the constraints on the SMME economy, it is essential at the outset to appreciate that the numerical growth of South Africa's SMME economy is underpinned by different processes. First, is the effects of the demise of the labour-absorptive capacity of the formal economy which accounts for a surge of survivalist enterprise in both urban and rural areas in already over-traded income opportunities, such as the running of retail *spazas* or street hawking (Rogerson 1996a; Rogerson and Reid 1997). Second, is the break-up of formal enterprise and the new opportunities afforded to certain (mainly urban-based) emerging SMMEs to have positive business linkages with large formal enterprise. The net effect of these divergent processes is that the SMME economy becomes stratified into distinct class divisions. Accordingly, it becomes misleading to conceive of all participants in this economy as entrepreneurs with real growth opportunities; while some participants may grow towards micro-enterprise and formal SMEs, the majority will remain poor (Horn 1995: 35). Indeed, the mass of 'entrepreneurs' will be trapped in a range of casual work relationships aligned within the structures of the dominant formal capitalist economy. Forms of casual work include short-term wage work, disguised wage work (e.g. commission sellers and home-workers) and dependent work (common among street traders with dependency based on credit relationships) (Rogerson 1997a). Overall, it must be recognized that the majority of the population working in South Africa's SMME economy are unable and unlikely ever to make a transition away from everyday struggles for meagre survival, 'constrained by a number of factors which constantly reinforce their position at the bottom of the pile' (Horn 1995: 35). Worst affected are women entrepreneurs, constrained by patriarchy and the responsibilities of child care which limits their choice of income options, skills, and their capacity to pursue training opportunities. The inevitable consequence is the feminization of the lowest echelons and least remunerated areas of SMME work in South Africa, namely of survivalist enterprise.

The key constraints facing the different segments of the SMME economy have been extensively investigated across both urban and rural areas in South Africa (World Bank 1993; Rogerson 1996a; 1998a and b; Rogerson and Reid 1997). Historically, the core emphasis was placed upon the problems of SMME entrepreneurs as linked to narrow regulatory restrictions, suggesting that the main source of problems was to be found in excessive patterns of regulation. Nevertheless, it is apparent from a body of recent works that legal restrictions are no longer the major impediment to SMME development in South Africa (World Bank 1993; Rogerson 1996a; 1998a and b). Instead, the key needs of the emerging SMME economy, surround improved access to market opportunities, limitations in finance and credit supplies, inadequate basic infrastructure, and issues of human resources and training. The themes of constrained markets, inadequate provision of credit, poor basic infrastructure and a weak human resource base for entrepreneurship run as common threads through most research on problems of the emerging SMME economy both in urban and rural South Africa. In addition, Manning (1996) stresses that an aggressive SMME policy is also required to address the area of 'competition policy', for an important explanation for the under-representation of emerging SMMEs in the mainstream economy relates to the collusive power and activities of larger enterprises (Rogerson 1998a, 1998b).

Finally, in dealing with constraints, it is necessary to acknowledge the existence of gender-differentiated patterns of SMME development. Some observers point to a need for policies and programmes to transcend the particular environmental constraints that relegate women to the poorest niches in the SMME economy (Horn 1995). What is required is an integrated policy framework which takes into account the set of specific factors which ghettoize women's participation in the SMME economy largely to the area of survivalist enterprise (SEWU 1995 and 1996). Suggested intervention programmes concern the organization and regulation of informal workers, the re-design of social security systems and extended workplace child care provision (SEWU 1995).

In terms of growth opportunities, a key issue is the fostering of closer linkages between South Africa's large white-owned corporate sector and the emerging SMME economy (Rogerson 1995). The expansion of business linkages with large private sector enterprise through subcontracting is seen as a means of boosting the markets of particularly emerging SMME manufacturers (Manning and Mashego 1994; Rogerson 1995). In South Africa's industrial heartland of Gauteng, a number of corporations are now involved in emerging SMME support and promotion through subcontracting and several large enterprises have established corporate small business units with a mandate to expand linkages with the emerging SMME economy. Among the most prominent linkage programmes are those operated by Anglo-American, Eskom and Hoechst.

Historically, however, co-operation between large manufacturing enterprises and SMMEs has not developed to a great extent in South Africa. Indeed, Manning and Mashego (1993: 75) argue that 'serious developmental problems (exist) in the current configurations between small and large businesses' in South African industry. It has been observed that 'big business lacks a culture of co-operating with small firms' and that most corporate responsibility for micro-enterprise development 'remains at the level of rhetoric' (Manning, 1993b: 16). Unlike the situation in countries such as Japan, Germany or Italy, there has never evolved in South Africa an extensive network of subcontracting relations between large and small enterprises in order to facilitate the latter's development in a mutually symbiotic relationship (Manning and Mashego, 1993, 1994). Instead, a pattern has existed in which the highly concentrated structure of the South African economy encourages large manufacturing enterprises to do business mainly among themselves. Indeed, the psychic distance from big business 'is a perennial complaint by SMMEs' in South Africa (Karungu et al.1997: 32).

The limited extent of large firm to emerging SMME subcontracting is a theme emphasized in several studies. Indeed, Tendler (1994) observed that, at present, the majority of the corporate sector is not very interested in outsourcing, notwithstanding the examples of Japan and their knowledge of it. Much of large enterprise support for emerging SMMEs has been seen as part of the private sector's programmes for social upliftment or community outreach; in other words, it was often based more on grounds of philanthropy rather than economics (Bukula et al. 1998). Many linkage programmes and experiments are therefore merely cosmetic and tokenistic, reflecting the desire of large firms to look politically correct *vis-à-vis* the New South Africa (Tendler 1994). The result was that the bulk of large firm–SMME subcontracting was accounted for by service activities (such as cleaning, food services, security, gardening) rather than manufacturing activities.

The new importance of economic considerations for developing subcontracting has emerged, however, in more recent analyses (Tendler 1994). Nevertheless, on present evidence, large firms appear to be creating linkages with emerging SMMEs 'mainly in those particular areas which are in their own interests' (Harrison et al. 1997: 56). Three examples of such linkages would be (1) in the construction and building industry where a recession has caused a shift towards extensive subcontracting, (2) in large firms affected by recession which increases their need to increase flexibility, or in sectors such as clothing where linkages are taking place as a defensive means to reduce costs, and (3) in retailing franchises which enable large enterprises to access, in particular, township markets. As has been shown, the nature of horizontal linkages between large business and the emerging SMME economy remains dominated by 'non-core' and 'non-critical incidental items', which severely limits their potential impact (Clark et al. 1996). Two other unsatisfactory aspects of current linkage or outsourcing initiatives are their frequent associations with union-busting and the strong monopsony power of the large enterprises over their suppliers (Tendler 1994).

Many problems exist in the way of evolving expanded and symbiotic business linkages between large enterprises and the SMME economy (Clark et al. 1996). One important blockage to a more spontaneous and general growth of production subcontracting is the historical legacy of the apartheid education system which has limited the reliability and quality of subcontract work by the emerging SMME economy (Rogerson 1998a). While the political and legal environment has shifted, emerging SMMEs are still at a competitive disadvantage as compared to established SMMEs with respect to their lesser resource base, access to capital and levels of technology (Clark et al. 1996: 31). From the perspective of emerging SMME entrepreneurs, relationships with large enterprise are 'mostly unsatisfactory in that orders were difficult to get, selling prices low and payments delayed' (Clark et al. 1996: 47).

From Gauteng research there are important suggestions that many of the problems earlier noted may not be insurmountable blockages on the emerging SMME manufacturing economy (Rogerson 1998a). Although it is true that many large enterprises entered into linkage arrangements with emerging SMMEs for reasons of social responsibility 'some of them have–through this process learned to their surprise that the result turned out to be a supplier product that was competitive with previous larger firm sources or in-house production in terms of cost, quality and delivery times' (Tendler 1994). Two examples are the supply of protective uniforms to Eskom from emerging garment manufacturers, and the window-kit programme operated by Wispeco. For Tendler (1994) these are examples of the positive outcomes of a demand-driven process of SMME support.

Current programmes and key policy interventions

At the core of SMME programmes are the policy interventions introduced by the new institutions and structures which were set up to implement the national SMME strategy; the key actors are Ntsika Enterprise Promotion Agency and Khula Enterprise Finance. In terms of SMME support services, the responsibility of Ntsika is with non-financial services whereas Khula functions as a wholesale finance institution supporting a range of retail finance intermediaries which would deal directly with the SMME entrepreneurs themselves. In launching the implementation of several programmes as proposed in the White Paper on Small Business, the South African government severely underestimated several vital institutional factors:

- the problems of establishing a whole set of new support institutions
- the capacity of these new support institutions to establish and implement a wide range of new policy initiatives
- the capacity of the existing NGO network in South Africa to become involved in the highly ambitious set of programmes that were implemented both as regards financing and non-financial support for SMMEs in South Africa (Rogerson 1997a).

These institutional problems provide important background to assessing the workings of the SMME programmes launched by Ntsika and Khula. At the heart of NEPA's interventions is the planned establishment and accreditation of a national network of decentralized local business service centres (LBSCs) which are to deliver a package of non-financial business support and 'real services' to emerging SMMEs. In the first round of accreditation, Ntsika funding was given to a total of 27 LBSCs, the majority of which were servicing the needs of urban SMMEs. Initial assessments of the functioning of LBSCs reveal a diverse range of experiences (Rogerson 1997a). None the less, the broad conclusion is that the activities of these LBSCs are making a contribution both towards upgrading of the SMME economy and enhancement of growth opportunities. Although some LBSCs target growing micro-enterprise, a focus on poverty eradication and economic empowerment of historically disadvantaged communities through assistance of survivalist enterprise is a feature of most accredited LBSCs. Certain blockages exist in the network and operations of LBSCs which demand attention as regards fine-tuning the programme; the training programmes of several LBSCs still perpetuate women's concentration in certain traditional activities such as sewing, dressmaking and knitting; skill shortages exist and financial management requires tightening; the outreach of small town LBSCs into surrounding rural areas often is weak; few linkages of LBSCs occur to local government and more widely to Local Economic Development planning initiatives; the existing network is sparse and needs to be extended geographically; and, finally, there is a need to link LBSCs and their non-financing support services to the co-ordinated extension of financial support for SMMEs, especially in cases of those LBSCs situated outside of metropolitan areas where the demand for LBSC services is often restricted by the absence of NGOs operating in the financial sphere (Rogerson 1997a; Rogerson and Reid 1997).

Certain improvements need to be effected in the important activity of expanding access to financing for SMMEs. The Khula lending programme has been in operation only since January 1997; none the less, Khula officials already concede that the volume of loans that have been made to NGOs is currently insufficient to match the enormous funding needs of the SMME community (Rogerson 1997a). Moreover, the present reach of the programme is geographically uneven and must be deepened. Another bias inherent in the present programme is towards funding the more established SMMEs rather than the needs of survivalist enterprises. The major blockages in expanding financing appear to lie in the lack of suitable NGOs or other Retail Financial Intermediaries operating as lenders and that the existing distribution of financing NGOs introduces considerable spatial biases into accessing finance. The establishment by Khula of a credit guarantee facility will be great assistance to more established formal SMEs and some larger micro-enterprises and of lesser significance for survivalist enterprises. Nevertheless, the impact of this credit guarantee programme so far has been reduced by the reluctance of South Africa's major commercial banks to participate actively in the programme, an issue which in future may need to be tackled by government legislative intervention (Rogerson 1997a; Bukula et al. 1998).

A range of other, newer SMME initiatives introduced by NEPA potentially can impact either on promoting growth opportunities or on eradicating poverty. In terms of supporting new growth opportunities for the emerging SMME economy, of greatest importance are a number of sector-specific support interventions designed to promote associations of enterprises or sector partnerships and the initiation of the programme of Manufacturing Advice Centres (MACs), which was inspired by Denmark's highly successful experience of SMME support. The MACs will largely serve growth objectives through seeking to strengthen the competitiveness of more established SMMEs; the programme's mandate is to help 'small to medium sized firms become more productive, more competitive and more profitable'. More specifically, the two pilot MACs in Durban and Port Elizabeth are to serve as regional centres to improve the competitive performance of small manufacturers offering a co-ordinated outreach programme of assistance which includes advisory services, technical support, information support and assistance to SMMEs in coping with quality and product standards. The initial assessments of the MAC pilots show promising results (Steven 1998).

Another area of growing support concerns the enactment of initiatives to expand the access of emerging SMMEs to government tenders. The issue of public procurement is particularly crucial in light of international experience (see Tendler and Amorim 1996) which suggests that 'public procurement policy represents a powerful instrument which governments could use to stimulate inter-firm collaboration' (Manning 1996: 240). In many parts of South Africa, especially in urban townships and in rural areas, much optimism surrounds the potential growth opportunities that may flow to emerging entrepreneurs from the government's new guidelines for public procurement (Rogerson 1997c). The Green Paper on Procurement Reform (Republic of South Africa 1997) offers a 10-point plan towards improving the access of emerging SMMEs to public sector procurement and introduces an affirmative SMME participation programme. Key issues relate, *inter alia*, to the simplification of the tender procedures, to the packaging of tenders into suitably sized segments to target SMMEs, to the setting of appropriate standards, delivery dates and contractual obligations, and the introduction of elements of price preference for targeted SMMEs. Another related policy initiative is the establishment of several Tender Advice Centres, where information about tenders is available and tender advice and counselling support services provided to emerging SMMEs (Ntsika 1997b). The early workings of the new procurement programme, however, suggest that there remain several blockages to be overcome before major changes can occur in the existing patterns of public procurement. Evidence from the experience of both Gauteng and Free State provinces suggests that while national government is committed to changing the rules and operations of public procurement, its executive arm in the area of procurement–the provincial tender boards–have not been doing enough to open opportunities for emerging entrepreneurs (Rogerson and Reid 1997; Rogerson 1998a). Indeed, it is argued that many old attitudes and problems remain in the tender system and that, as a result, the flow of procurement contracts to emerging SMMEs is extremely meagre (Bukula et al. 1998).

It has been argued that current national programmes are weighted towards the support of emergent micro-enterprise and the formal SMME, and offer little in the way of support for survivalist enterprise. Another bias in current interventions is towards support for urban SMMEs with little attempt to deal with the specific needs of disadvantaged rural SMMEs (Rogerson and Reid 1997). For the groups of survivalist enterprise, the most effective level of policy intervention may be at the local level rather than the national scale of government (Rogerson 1997a). Important opportunities exist for local governments to enact a range of measures to support survivalist enterprises as part of local economic development initiatives towards poverty alleviation. In particular, for groups of urban survivalist enterprise, engaged in, for example, the business of street hawking or the running of retail *spazas*, the activities of local government can exert a profound impact upon the economic health of these kinds of enterprise and on the coping strategies of poor households (Rogerson 1997a). The establishment of formal markets, appropriate policies towards land use zoning and improved infrastructure provision, among others, are key areas of local government intervention which can impact positively upon the workings of survivalist informal enterprise. In addition, the local planning and support for the development of periodic markets is seemingly an attractive and inexpensive poverty-redressing policy intervention for SMME upgrading, not only in rural areas but also as components in integrated projects for urban reconstruction. Another set of local interventions can relate to the potential of promoting agriculture as more than a mere safety-net for the urban poor (May and Rogerson 1995). Especially in the peri-urban areas of South Africa's secondary cities and small towns, the potential for promoting the poor's greater access to natural resources and of establishing an active peri-urban agricultural sector requires serious investigation and support measures designed to improve the poor's access to cultivable land (May 1998).

Conclusion

This chapter sought to illustrate the differing objectives, directions and interventions in the SMME economy of South Africa. In post-apartheid South Africa the key contemporary debates relate to balancing the needs for both improving competitiveness and growth as well as facilitating poverty eradication.

The evidence since 1995 is that the prime targets of South Africa's new national programmes for support of the emerging SMME economy are growing micro-enterprise and the formal small or medium-sized enterprise. It is clear that the successful upgrading of SMMEs into the mainstream economy requires the implementation of policy at a range of levels: at the micro-level, policies must be targeted directly at enhancing small-firm capacity; at the sectoral level, policies must be aimed at improving the performance of all enterprises in a sector; and, at the competition level, policies need to challenge the long-established structures of large-firm corporate dominance (and often collusion) in the South African economy.

In the emphasis so far given to issues surrounding the promotion of growth and competitiveness, however, the essential needs of the urban and rural poor engaged in survivalist enterprise have slipped down the national policy agenda. Survivalist enterprises are critical target groups for securing the objectives of poverty alleviation in terms of helping a large number of poor people become a little less poor (Mead and Liedholm 1998). Given the gender differentiation within the South African SMME economy, there is a danger that a growth-biased policy threatens to neglect the large number of women entrepreneurs that function at the survival level. In the final analysis, it must be concluded that the activities of local government rather than national SMME programmes may be the most critical intervention points for poverty reduction and support of survivalist enterprise. Indeed, SMME support in the context of local economic development initiatives for poverty reduction is an emerging critical policy agenda in post-apartheid South Africa.

7 Inherent gender inequities in small and micro-enterprise development in rural Africa

FRA VON MASSOW

'I just remember the silence of the women's stare as we talked to the men'[1]

Introduction

Despite general commitments to poverty reduction, structural adjustment reforms imposed by the IMF and World Bank have locked African nations into growth strategies directed towards debt servicing priorities. This has led to impoverishment, particularly among women and children in rural areas. Pro-poor growth strategies envisage accelerated poverty reduction as 'an economic imperative for global prosperity' (UNDP 1997). 'The leadership of the World Bank is essential for more rapid action on debt relief and restructuring of aid in line with priorities for poverty reduction' (Jolly 1997). Pro-poor growth pertains to the investment in educated, healthy, economically active populations on an equitable basis, with particular emphasis on reducing disparities between women and men. Idriss Jazairy argues: 'Africa needs resources now both to compensate for the volatility of the prices of its exports and to fund pro-poor and gender sensitive policies to consolidate its emergence from conflict' (Jazairy 1996: 3–8). A focus on export/cash crop production, poor investment in diversity, and pressure on land with increasing populations polarizes opportunities and results in persistent rural unemployment and under-employment. Low income households, particularly women being responsible for household food security, seek income in micro-enterprise activity. This chapter focuses on the socio-economic environment, the micro-enterprises themselves, and the different constraints and opportunities faced by the women and men managing them. A gender perspective is used to highlight two areas of concern in micro-enterprise support: the lack of integration between poverty reduction and economic growth approaches, and the apparent lack of recognition of the validity of the different economic and social contribution low-income female and male entrepreneurs make to economic growth.

Given scarce resources, Liedholm and Mead (1987) promote the support of enterprises that invest in productivity-enhancing technologies located in 'dynamic subsectors', often urban. Survivalist enterprises, some argue, characterized by low growth, returns and productivity, do not contribute to economic growth and employment creation. While men tend to seek daily

[1] Male Rural Programme Manager, Ethiopia.

labour employment, or migrate, women manage the majority of survivalist enterprises in rural areas and are marginalized from mainstream enterprise development.

Is there a conflict of interests between poverty reduction and economic growth under structural adjustment? There certainly appears to be one in the allocation of resources to 'the eradication of poverty based on sustained economic growth, social development, environmental protection, and social justice' including gender equity (United Nations 1996). Economic development and social transition in the 'globalisation' era of the 1990s is characterized by 'rising disparities within nations and between nations' (UNDP 1995: iii). Disparities persist along the lines of class, age, ethnicity and gender. Advances in reducing gender disparities in education have been made over the past two decades, despite low public spending on education. Translating improvements in women's education into their economic advancement requires proactive initiatives. Only then will general economic advancement further a reduction in gender disparities and women's increased access to productive resources and mainstream development. Per capita GNP in Zimbabwe was US$580 and adult women's literacy rate was 78 per cent. In Gabon on the other hand, with GNP at US$4220 per capita, women's literacy rate was a mere 48 per cent (1992) (UNDP 1995: 32).

Social institutions involved in economic policy formulation and implementation have an inherent male bias. This, it is argued, is a contributing factor to the misinterpretation and per capita under-resourcing of survival-oriented enterprises, a significant proportion of which are owned by women. The progression of these entrepreneurs into more stable circumstances is also impeded by poor investment in diversification of local markets. Access to more specialist business advice and resources is greater for growth and specialization-oriented entrepreneurs where women are in a minority. Incorporating a gender perspective into the process of supporting micro-enterprise development in Africa will result in the identification of alternative strategies and monitoring indicators which recognize and nurture the different ways in which micro-enterprises can contribute both to economic growth and poverty reduction.

Gender and development

'Gender' is interpreted and applied multifariously: a term evocative of personal and professional experience and prejudices, sceptically referred to as a fashion adding to conditionality on development assistance, or as a Western (feminist) imposition on other cultures. To embrace pragmatism: 'gender awareness and equity are irreversibly on the agenda and increasingly pursued in practice' (Chambers 1998).

A gender approach recognizes that activities undertaken by women and men are not 'natural', but socially constructed, and are contextually specific.

'Gender' refers not to women or men but to the social, economic and political relations between them, relations in which women are often subordinate (DPU 1997). These social relations prescribe women's and men's responsibilities, roles, rights and mobility. They become formalized through custom, legislation, organizational cultures and contextually specific norms, creating differential barriers and opportunities. Gender also refers to the relations between men and between women and cross-cuts other social categories such as age, religion, ethnicity and class. Gender relations are characterized by processes of negotiation around the allocation and distribution of productive and consumption resources, from the household to socio-political institutions. They are power relations in which women are often disadvantaged, having fewer rights to express their reality, their interests and needs, and being under-represented at all levels, influencing their options as economic actors and entrepreneurs.

Gender policy and planning provides a set of tools for gender diagnosis in the context of institutional constraints and opportunities (Moser 1993; Levy forthcoming). These include the analysis of women and men's gender roles.[2] their access to and control over resources and their gender needs. A community water programme targeting women (community managing role) uses time and resources needed to fulfil their other roles: e.g. as entrepreneurs. Targeting women–or inherently male-oriented planning–can have a positive or negative impact on socio-economic and political equity between women and men at household, local and national levels. A gender diagnosis needs as its central pivot 'the web of institutionalization' (Levy 1996). Unless gender is institutionalized, recognizing inequities within organizational practice, mainstreaming a gender perspective in policy, planning and delivery is hard to achieve.

Gender differentials in access to and control over resources perpetuates inequities in SMEs

The household is where the gender division of labour and gender roles are learned and reproduced. In the domestic and public spheres, women and men do not have equal access to and control over resources (Kabeer 1991; Moser 1993; DPU 1997). Inequitable gender relations affect women's ability to manage enterprises successfully, particularly within male-headed households. Women in Malawi have statutory citizenship rights, however: 'most men are inclined to believe marriage gives them an unrestricted right of access to and

---

[2] Definitions: *Reproductive role*: biological reproduction, social reproduction and sustenance. Women engaged in continuous routine reproductive tasks, men only intermittently. *Productive role*: activities earning income in cash or kind. *Community managing role*: voluntary work for provision of services of collective consumption, water, health, schools (increased under SAP efficiency). *Constituency-based politics role*: elected into activities in political, religious or social interest-based groups, men tend to be leaders (DPU 1997).

control of their wives' assets' (NCWID 1993; see also TGNP 1993: 36–61). When women's reproductive and productive roles are undervalued, and men's assumption of control undermines women's and their own potential productivity, the result is poverty and divisive conflict.

Statistics on gender disparities are available. However, a recognition of the value of the reproductive role and subsistence production to economic growth, and the methodology to include it in mainstream statistical records, is missing. Women's contribution is therefore overlooked and lacks support in the economic development process. As long as women's status as second-class citizens, and men's as controllers, is reinforced and persists, poverty reduction strategies which could contribute to socially sustainable and equitable economic growth will remain simply poverty-reduction strategies.

Women and men have different gender needs[3]

The gender roles of women and men are different in content and responsibilities, and there are differentials in women's and men's access to and control over resources. Women and men therefore have different gender needs. With increasing poverty, the potential for conflict and domestic violence in the negotiating process around the allocation of diminishing resources increases. Often, although women may have access to productive resources, including their own labour and income, they do not necessarily have control. All too often men requisition women's labour, income, time and channels of access to external resources. Women in Malawi, for example, increasingly demand their economic independence from men (von Massow 1995). This empowerment approach to enterprise development (Mayoux 1995) meets women's strategic gender need to control their own production and income in a context where men assume control.

Opportunities and choices are prescribed by the gender division of labour

The gender division of labour and gender stereotypes in a particular context tend to prescribe the types of business that women and men are able to engage in. Traditionally women's enterprise was associated with low status and low income. Economic activity was 'culturally mediated with strong gender, class and ethnic association influencing who participated in which kinds

---

[3] *Practical Gender Needs (PGNs)*: needs identified by women and men arising from the customary gender division of labour, a response to immediate perceived necessity such as water, health , employment.
Strategic Gender Needs (SGNs): a challenge to customary gender relations, implies change in power and control relationships between women and men. Women's SGNs challenge their subordinate position in relation to men, e.g.: equal access to resources, legal and human rights. Men's SGNs challenge their exclusion from domains which customary male roles impose and which contribute to the perpetuation of women's subordination. SGNs are context specific (DPU 1997; Moser 1989; Molyneux 1985).

of enterprise' (Gaidzanwa 1993: 282–4). Such prejudices and perceptions persist in influencing policy and planning, and women's and men's choices, today. Women's income generation programmes (in the 1970s) focused on women's reproductive skills, and had low economic value (Buvinic 1986). Women continue to predominate in enterprises that have little economic comparative advantage.

Because of the gender division of labour, in which women have lower status and less access to and control over resources, women tend to manage enterprises with the crudest technologies and lowest income potential (Berger 1989). They have less access to production and marketing resources, including information and training, and to influential socio-economic and political networks beneficial to entrepreneurship.

Adapting a model of entrepreneurial behaviour recognizing stuctural and gender-related constraints and opportunities

The following section is an adaptation of 'a model of entrepreneurial behaviour' developed by Downing (1991) on the basis of research conducted by Grown and Sebstadt (1989). Some characteristics of enterprises, their ability to persist and diversify or graduate from 'survival-oriented' into 'growth-oriented' and 'specialization-oriented' enterprises are analysed with a gender perspective. This is not a linear process and few entrepreneurs graduate from 'survival-oriented' to 'specialization-oriented', where owners are predominantly men. Policy and practice should aim to provide an enabling environment for the majority of entrepreneurs in survival and security-oriented enterprises. A large proportion of these are women who face particular gender-related constraints and have substantial responsibility for household food security and maintenance.

Micro-enterprise activity needs to be analysed in the context of prevailing socio-economic conditions. Historically, rural areas have been characterized by low investment in local health and wealth and by a process of extraction of 'surplus labour' and primary products for export markets. Fluctuating commodity prices (e.g. coffee 1989, 1997) and devaluations create insecurity and undermine local purchasing power. Structural adjustment and export-led growth priorities influence macroeconomic resource allocation and investments, decisions which have a differential impact on women's and men's livelihoods. (Elson 1992; Commonwealth Secretariat 1989). This analysis aims to draw attention to gender equity concerns in the context of socio-economic policy towards:

- creating an equitable environment to increase the number of survivalist women entrepreneurs able to graduate, or diversify, into enterprises with higher returns
- maintaining the 'human economy' (socio-economic relations of 'mutual

obligation'), recognizing the contribution of diversification to economic growth.

Enterprises targeted by poverty reduction programmes or by poverty alleviation components of mainstream agricultural or rural development programmes

Entrepreneurs fall largely into two groups, those (a significant proportion of women) targeted by poverty reduction programmes, and those (the majority men) targeted by mainstream economic growth priorities. The Ministries, expertise, packages and allocation of national resources differ widely between the two 'camps'.

The first group are categorized as: 'survival-oriented', 'security: subsistence-oriented' and 'security: value-oriented', a majority located in the rural and peri-urban areas, often with poor road transport and communication. Markets are thin, local purchasing power is low, and access to health, education, employment and information is minimal. There are high illiteracy rates, particularly among women, poor nutrition and high fertility rates. Men have often migrated for work.

'Survival-oriented' enterprises

These are potentially the largest group of micro-entrepreneurs, producing the lowest value. They diversify depending on seasons and fluctuations in agricultural and natural resource conditions. Because of the gender division of labour and lack of rural investment, unskilled men tend to be under-employed or in search of employment (von Massow 1992; FAO 1988). Women represent an important proportion of survival-oriented entrepreneurs, involved in a combination of farming, crop, spice and fish processing, trading, cotton spinning and basket weaving, for example. Men may be engaged in seasonal farming, basket production, weaving, occasional hunting and trading, charcoal burning and palm wine production for sale. They use family labour, traditional technology and local natural resources. Output and productivity is cumbersomely low. For women in male-headed households successful negotiation around production resources can be paramount for survival. Women's lack of control over their own production and income can create insecurity and affect investment decisions. Women's income is more likely to be used for daily sustenance. There is rarely a surplus.

Skills tend to be passed on along gender lines rather than learned in formal institutions. A by-product is the gender stereotyping of productive roles, men tending towards activities with higher returns. Those men with skills, engaged in enterprise, may reach investment thresholds faster than women. Women with older children, women heads of households and women who customarily trade (e.g. in Ghana) are more likely to reach an investment threshold than, for example, the youngest co-wife in Sierra Leone, with three under-5s and a disproportionate reproductive burden. Men, even those under-employed, do little to share the domestic workload.

The system of mutual obligation (von Massow et al. 1993), or 'human economy' (Tinker 1987) is born of necessity and describes informal networks of support, labour exchange and sharing (including child care), bartering, and credit sales. These are akin to 'uncertainty reducing networks' in 'traditional' sub-sectors described by Barr (this volume, 1999). However, here it is argued that these are survival strategies, as is diversification, which create and support economic activity. There is also a significant difference between women's networks and men's networks: women carry the unpaid responsibility 'for the reproduction and maintenance of human resources' (Elson 1992: 49). Income and turnover is often inextricably linked into household and the wider network's changing patterns of consumption and shortage. The human economy seeks to share access to scarce resources in both the reproductive and productive roles, and enables women's survivalist enterprise to take place. When resources are so scarce that the system of mutual obligation breaks down, health, infant mortality and nutrition statistics describe the result. This human economy absorbs the social costs of structural adjustment and poverty. 'What is regarded by economists as "increased efficiency" may instead be a shifting of costs from the paid economy to the unpaid economy' (Elson 1998: 50). These rather informal, often kin-ship based, networks may form themselves into groups for the purpose of gaining access to credit-plus packages, but this is rather in response to externally imposed conditionalities to form 'solidarity groups'. These groups, often organized by international NGOs, differ in nature, formation and function to the more self-initiated and perpetuated organization of the clusters studied by McCormick (this volume, 1999). The 'human economy' has an unrecorded economic value.

However, a misinterpretation of the human economy can lead to under-valuing women's objectives as entrepreneurs. If planners assume that women's entrepreneurial objectives refer not to their productive role but to their (undervalued) reproductive role, planned interventions are unlikely to result in the higher returns women so badly need. It is generally assumed that men's objectives are economic and focused on increasing productivity of the enterprise, i.e. linked to their productive role. Such assumptions influence research, planning and intervention methodologies, and resource allocation, to the detriment of the development of women's entrepreneurial capacity in particular. For example, the World Bank Microcredit Summit included a proposition to use women's credit solidarity groups as a vehicle for water and family planning programmes. This targets women in their productive role, by providing credit, while assuming their time for additional reproductive and community managing activities, potentially reducing entrepreneurial capacity.

To alter the portfolio of economic activity, therefore, a certain level of decision-making freedom, mobility, and control over productive resources is required. Such entrepreneurs have at least three options:

- diversify laterally into other 'survival-oriented' enterprises
- diversify into more stable 'security subsistence-oriented' enterprises
- diversify into new product or function in 'security value-oriented' enterprises.

Lateral diversification into other 'survival-oriented' enterprises

Typically, resource-poor women and men diversify to spread risk and to meet needs over the year. If an entrepreneur is able to invest, s/he may add another enterprise to her portfolio, perhaps providing opportunities for members of the family or kinship group, rather than investing in an existing enterprise.

Diversification into 'security: subsistence-oriented' enterprise

Enterprises in this category share many of the characteristics described above. They generate low income in cash and kind and barely cover the basic needs of the household. Children's labour contribution, particularly girls' in their reproductive and productive roles, is still required. This possibly continues to affect school persistence rates negatively. 'The structural setting in which children's work is undertaken and contributes to the reproduction of a society, remains heavily under-researched' (Nieuwenhuys 1994: 15).

Women's pursuit of low risk strategies: choice or orchestration?

Schmink (1984) categorizes women entrepreneurs as security orientated. She suggests that 'households tend to engage simultaneously in survival and income-mobility strategies on a gender basis', i.e. women pursue low-risk subsistence strategies to facilitate men's greater risks. However, in the 1950s and 1960s, it was originally orchestrated that women maintaining subsistence would subsidize men's low wages in the 'modern' sector. Schmink's argument seems to assume choice in this risk-taking gender alliance.

Historically, development policy making and planning has been guided by economic growth objectives, targeting resources towards industrialization, and the modernization of agriculture for export. Sir Arthur Lewis expected economic growth and poverty eradication by utilising 'surplus rural labour' to fuel the development of a modern urban industrial structure. Nyerere was among those concerned for the social and human costs of this approach to the majority, rural, under-resourced populations (Hulme and Turner 1990: 58–67).

However, not only did urban–rural disparities grow, gender disparities became apparent too. The Zambian experience demonstrates this deliberate colonial strategy. During the early developments of the copper mines, 'workers were rarely allowed to take their families with them .... women were expected to continue subsistence agricultural production for maintenance of themselves and their families.' (Munachonga 1988: 181). These distinctions have continued to produce inherent systemic inequities until today. Women were/and are often residual, 'invisible', to economic development, sustaining their families with ever diminishing resources, frequently on their own. Men were/and are targeted as the active participants in the modernization process. In rural Zambia today, as in other parts of southern Africa this process has resulted in between 40 and 60 per cent of households being headed by women. Schmink's analysis of gender-based risk partnerships also overlooks the fact that many men marry in the new setting (e.g. tea plantations, Malawi) and do not always remit to the partner they left behind.

Disqualifying customary and statutory legal rights (e.g. inheritance laws, rights to sign contracts, open a bank account, or own land), seriously limited women's ability to transfer into more lucrative entrepreneurial activities. By the 1970s the 'feminization of poverty' was coined, reflecting high infant and maternal mortality rates and malnutrition alongside growing agricultural output, 'of 1.3 billion people in poverty, 70% are women' (UNDP 1995: 4). Women's problems were defined by poverty alleviation programmes 'in terms of the family's basic needs rather than their unequal access to resources' (Kabeer 1994: 7–8), to which can be added 'rather than in terms of their contribution to economic growth'.

Diversification into 'security: value-oriented' enterprise

Entrepreneurs who invest to increase the product range or add a new service graduate from 'survival-oriented' or 'security: subsistence-oriented' into 'security: value-oriented' enterprises.

The characteristics of the entrepreneurial location are important. More opportunities arise in less remote areas with access to transport and communications, denser markets and customers with higher purchasing power and more diverse needs. 'Value-oriented' enterprises may have to register and pay taxes requiring a certain level of literacy and assertiveness. They may employ paid labour in addition to family labour and have access to networks and information in the market economy, to local government and possibly to development aid. Given existing understanding of gender differentials in decision making, mobility, access to resources, and product value, it is likely that more men than women are in this category.

Whether these enterprises are targeted by mainstream programmes or by poverty alleviation (poverty lending) initiatives will depend on the forward and backward linkages that his/her enterprise has with foreign exchange earning production and services.

'Growth-oriented' enterprise

This category is linked, however tenuously, into 'dynamic sub-sectors'. They include formal and informal sector small business and production, and may operate on the fringes of legality and morality. They typically invest in productivity-enhancing and communications technology. They may link into rural infrastructures to access primary products, and local markets. The level of interaction with the market, the small business community and local government increases, as does the level of administration, control and officialdom.

The owners of growth-oriented enterprises are mostly men. They add to the potential for the creation of a lower/middle income middle class, providing employment for skilled workers (mostly men) and unskilled labour (including women). They may have graduated from 'security: value-oriented' enterprises or have established their business through mostly male dominated kinship trades and/or economic–political connections. These enterprises are driven by profit motives, are evaluated on the basis of economic returns and have strong links with export-led trade and the international community. The economic value generated by these enterprises is measurable by traditional evaluation methodologies and appears in national statistics. They aim to achieve economies of scale in production, or improved efficiency in service provision, through investments in technology and the employment of more skilled contracted labour. In the service, textiles or food processing enterprises women are employed as unskilled labour. Women tend to manage small businesses such as cafés, hairdressing salons and clothing production on a small scale.

Currently, there is minimal external investment in Africa (a mere 1 per cent of worldwide investment went to the poorest 48 countries in 1997). Development investments focus on export-oriented economic activity. With lagging economies geared to servicing external debts, there are limited opportunities for both men and women in growth-oriented enterprise.

'Specialization oriented' enterprises

This category functions with more efficient modes of business management and communication, including computers, transport, telephone connection, and access to networks and information, including the Internet. Education, experience and status are required to manage this transition. These are urban enterprises, though not excluding urban–rural links in production, supply and exchange, linked into family, kinship or political relations.

Specialization-oriented enterprises are typified by 'the transformation of raw materials into finished products and increasing the number of steps and participants' (Downing 1991: 6). Included is the service industry, with links into more sophisticated business and leisure markets, such as legal firms, insurance, travel agents, hair and beauty establishments and import/export firms.

These firms link into the formal banking system and have access to national and sometimes international networks, information and markets. Even fewer women manage these enterprises, though many are employed in them. Despite low international investment, these small firms contribute to largely urban employment creation, however superficial relative to the scale of national unemployment. They have some of the attributes of flexible specialization but not sufficient to gain the benefits of sustainable economic activity. Jonathan Dawson, when assessing the existence of flexible specialization in Africa, was able to identify only some engineering industry in Ghana as meeting the criteria. He concluded that flexible specialization 'appears to be of greater relevance to an understanding of the small-scale engineering branch than to the small firm sector as a whole' (Dawson 1992: 38). The criteria include good local technology, highly skilled and flexible workers (between jobs within one firm) and connections with other similar small entrepreneurs within large-scale industry.

Few women entrepreneurs are represented in this category due to substantial gender disparities and the need to access male-dominated spheres. Access to certain skills, technology, finance and networking is dependent on education, financial resources, legal rights, connections and gender. There are significant gender differentials in opportunity and exercising these rights between women and men in Africa.

Conclusion

Structural adjustment priorities inherently divert resources into export-oriented production in industry, mining and plantation agro-industry, rather than into strengthening local markets and purchasing power essential to flourishing enterprise. Conflict in the region has further exacerbated potential and morale. A gender approach enables policy makers and planners to understand how gender inequities contribute to the perpetuation of poverty and the different ways in which low-income women and men are disadvantaged by macroeconomic policies. Current policy priorities perpetuate limitation rather than opening up diversification of the local economy. Women continue to try to maintain production and trading to sustain local consumption with diminishing resources. Relief from unpayable debt, pro-poor and local market-led growth is recommended in addition to export production.

Much of the literature on micro-enterprise and gender focuses on women's experience within the gender division of labour. This is essential in order to increase knowledge about the particular experience and needs of women who make up the majority of the world's poorest. However, under-employed men in rural Africa also have few choices under current development priorities and in post-conflict situations. They collectively perpetuate a myth of power and control within the existing gender division of labour, while sinking into inactivity and grinding poverty. Men have little to gain and women suffer in the extreme. This situation inhibits both women and men from increasing productivity, and their ability to maintain and expand successful enterprises. The gender division of labour prescribes occupational choices open to women and men–stereotypes learnt from an early age. Gender stereotyping locates women in low-value production and trading, with the crudest technology, their activities and access to resources often subject to the control of men. Relative to men, therefore, despite the fact that women are largely responsible for daily household provisioning, they have fewer resources and lower returns to achieve this.

A model for categorizing small and micro-enterprises has been elaborated (adapted from Downing 1991). While a large proportion of low income women entrepreneurs are located in the 'survival-oriented' category, there is a small proportion of women in the 'growth- and specialisation-oriented' categories. The 'survival-oriented' sector is significant in terms of sheer numbers and turnover of produce for local consumption. The potential in the sector is enormous. It is safe to assume, given current abysmal levels of nutrition, health and education, that with increased purchasing power, a huge gap between current levels of consumption and potential demand could be filled. In the meantime a 'human economy' or system of mutual obligation, closely entwined in enterprise activity, subsidizing export growth and the reproduction of society, makes an unrecorded contribution to economic growth.

Monitoring and evaluation and statistical data fail to reflect the contribution made by women. Women's micro-enterprise is associated with meeting basic needs rather than with market-oriented, profit-maximizing objectives. By measuring the contribution to growth of single firms, and not of a portfolio of micro-enterprises, women's contribution to economic growth in particular is potentially underestimated. In addition, interventions aimed at promoting 'the growth of the single firm' may fail to meet the needs of low-income women entrepreneurs–and of men, who diversify to spread risk.

The organizational structures and interlinkages between government and donors and government and transnational corporations predetermine a supportive environment for certain types of trade and production. Enterprises are explicitly or implicitly categorized as falling under economic growth or poverty reduction programmes. The human, material and financial resources differ enormously between the different institutions involved, and therefore to the delivery of resources and benefits among different groups of entrepreneurs. A 'zero sum game' is not in question here (i.e. more resources to women, less to men), but a recognition of, and response to, the differential needs of low-income women and men entrepreneurs needing to increase financial returns for their endeavours. This may be achieved only when resources are also directed to developing and meeting the potential of local markets in Africa.

8 Enterprise development in Africa: strategies for impact and growth

GEORGE MANU

Introduction

Dakota tribal wisdom says that when you discover you are riding a dead horse, the best strategy is to dismount. However, in business generally, and enterprise development in Africa in particular, the tendency has been to try other strategies with dead horses, including the following:

- buy a stronger whip
- change riders
- say things like 'this is the way we have always ridden this horse'
- appoint a committee or field an expert mission to study the horse
- arrange to visit other sites to see how they ride dead horses
- rewrite the standards for dead horse performance
- appoint a tiger team to revive the dead horse
- create a training session to increase riding ability
- compare the state of dead horses in today's environment
- change the requirements declaring that 'this horse is not dead'
- hire consultants to ride the dead horse
- harness several dead horses together to increase speed and pulling power
- declare that 'no horse is too dead to beat'
- provide additional incentive funding to increase the horse's performance
- do a study to see if consultants can ride it cheaper
- purchase a software product to make dead horses run faster
- declare that the horse is 'better, faster and cheaper' dead
- form a quality circle to find uses for dead horses
- revisit the performance requirements for horses
- say this horse was procured with cost as an independent variable
- promote the dead horse to a supervisory position
- shorten the track
- establish a benchmark for industry dead-horse leaders
- gather other dead animals and announce a diversity programme
- put together a spiffy PowerPoint presentation to get planners to double the dead horse's budget
- get the horse a website.

There is little doubt that, with few exceptions, efforts over the past three decades at enterprise development in Africa have not yielded significant impact or growth. Certainly, in terms of creating new enterprises and enabling the survival and growth of existing enterprises, which remain the basic approaches to ensuring a healthy small and medium-sized enterprise (SME) sector in any economy, there is precious little to show in Africa[1] for the bulk of interventions to date.

It would appear that the problem is not merely one of efficiency in terms of input-output ratios and the functioning of support institutions and services but also one of effectiveness in terms of the relevance and appropriateness of the strategies employed. For, even in some cases where support institutions have performed excellently in the organization and delivery of core services, impact and growth have proven to be elusive. Take PRIDE Tanzania as an example.[2] By most indicators, this is a very successful micro-credit institution, if not among the very best by the usual benchmark for performance in this industry, namely loan recovery rate. By 1996, the organization had achieved a loan recovery rate of 100 per cent. Yet, when PRIDE Tanzania commissioned an evaluation in 1996, after five years of operation, it found little or no significant impact in terms of the income levels and growth (employment increase and size of business operations) of clients assisted. Similar findings can be found in Ghana, Kenya and elsewhere in Africa in many institutions and projects working with the informal, micro- and small enterprise sector.

Despite the record, the dead horse syndrome is all too prevalent in Africa and, from the vantage point of an international agency and also of a curious observer of enterprise activity in many countries, shows no sign of abating. It is clear that if the international community is sincere about helping African (and other developing) countries in integrating themselves into the global economy, this and other related issues need to be seriously addressed.

Global challenges

The case for a serious strategic rethink of enterprise development in Africa is heightened by current global trends. The challenges and implications of globalization and liberalization are unfolding everyday and becoming more evident everywhere. While these impact on all countries, the effects are arguably most serious for the weakest. A prime case in point here is competition, with African and other developing countries finding it increasingly difficult to maintain market share in their own backyards, to say nothing of making forays into international markets. McGrath and King (1996) have examined these issues and provided valuable insights not only for education and training, which was their primary concern, but also overall strategy for small

---

[1] By this, we refer in this chapter in the main to sub-Saharan Africa and exclude the Republic of South Africa.

[2] PRIDE is an NGO and stands for Programme for Rural Initiatives and Development Enterprise. This information was collected by George Manu during a study visit to PRIDE Tanzania in Arusha in August 1996.

enterprise development in Africa. The authors pointed out, *inter alia*, that one effect of these phenomena is to change domestic notions of what constitutes a viable firm or industry.

It has been recognized for some time that, on an international scale, Africa is the weakest, with a mere 1per cent of world trade: and most of this from South Africa. However, what globalization and liberalization have highlighted recently is that many apparently successful companies in Africa with long track records in their domestic markets are not strong enough when faced with international competition. The competitive advantage, in essence, appears to lie in the human capital that a firm, industry or country can utilize, if current theories and thinking on the theme are anything to go by (see for example Cullen and Sommerlad 1997; McGrath and King 1996; Senge 1990). 'Brain power' has overtaken sheer 'brawn' in the game of productivity, competitiveness and wealth creation: at enterprise, industry and transnational levels. This is most evident in big business and was perhaps best exemplified the day that Microsoft, with 20 000 employees, overtook General Motors with over 700 000 workers, in terms of market capitalization.

The effects of globalization and liberalization come at a time when the development challenge in Africa is perhaps at its greatest, notwithstanding the positive economic growth rates recorded during the last couple of years in a handful of African countries. Unemployment and underemployment remain on a massive and rising scale (over 50 per cent in places) compounded, in many countries, by unchecked population growth and a high number of new entrants into the labour market (on an annual basis, 500 000 in Kenya, 250 000 in Ghana and Zimbabwe and, according to one estimate, 4 million in Nigeria!).

Clearly, given that the strategies to date have not yielded the desired results and that the development path of most of the continent is now heavily dependent on their SME sector, there is now a pressing need to dismount from the dead horse and search for proven alternative solutions. Just as international comparisons have shown up weak enterprises, so they can shed light on best practices. They can also focus attention on current thinking and cutting-edge concepts. This is, of course, not to suggest that Africa should import wholesale 'models' from the North. The dangers in so doing are well rehearsed and obvious. However, the need for a cautious approach is not to deny either that a great deal can be learnt from what works elsewhere and that some of these practices can be adapted, copied and even improved upon. After all, the development paths of countries and enterprises are strewn with stories of many who did precisely that: i.e. copy, adapt and improve upon what works. Furthermore, while acknowledging that all countries are different and have their peculiarities, the weight of experience, after many years of international experience, points to the conclusion that there are more similarities than differences among countries in respect of the main issues and problems that arise in enterprise development.

Enterprise development strategies: some considerations

Against this background, in search of maximum impact and growth, we present below some strategic considerations and options for enterprise development in Africa, with their obvious implications for development assistance. The central message of this discussion, and indeed of this chapter, is that there is potential to replicate the enterprise development success of other regions, most notably the USA, Europe and, despite the economic turmoil of recent months, East Asia.

Clients

One of the greatest constraints to private sector development in Africa is the 'missing middle', coupled with an acute shortage of fast-growth firms. Experience from Europe, the USA and elsewhere has shown that it is precisely this category that contributes most to job creation and, by implication, incomes. Recent research by the European Commission has shown that a mere 4 per cent of enterprises, characterized as fast-growing SMEs, contribute some 50 per cent of net job creation (Papoutsis 1996). Similar findings were reported 10 years earlier in a study of fast growth small businesses in the north east of England (Storey et al. 1987).

This is in stark contrast to the profile of firms in Africa, including those being promoted by most governments, donors, development agencies and enterprise support institutions. Although small firms make up the majority of the total stock of enterprises in all economies worldwide, in Africa the distribution is too heavily skewed towards informal, micro- and very small enterprises: with precious little in the formal small (20–50 workers) and medium size (50–200 workers) categories. Just recently, Mead and Liedholm (1998) reported, from a study of SMEs, that firms with 10–50 workers constituted less than 2 per cent of the businesses in virtually all the surveyed countries in Africa. In fact, the majority of SMEs in Africa consist of only one person working alone, with the bulk of the remainder employing less than 10 people.

While there is nothing wrong *per se* with micro- and very small enterprises, the evidence so far, including some from Africa itself, suggests that, as a strategy for maximum impact and efficiency, much more could be achieved by promoting 'larger small' and medium enterprises. In particular, studies have shown that enterprises in Africa consisting of one person working alone are considerably less efficient than those employing 2–5 workers and that this increase in economic efficiency continues for the next higher size group (see, for example, Liedholm and Mead 1987; Mead and Liedholm 1998.)

What is worse, there is a distinct dearth of growth among these SMEs in Africa, certainly in terms of employment. Mead and Liedholm (1998) reported that, after start-up, over three-quarters of SMEs remained the same size or even contracted in terms of employment, concluding that SME employment expansion was the exception rather than the rule. In essence, these findings are not different from the PRIDE Tanzania study reported at the beginning of the chapter. They are also in stark contrast to the situation in Europe (see above figures) or the USA, for example, where of the approximately 1.1 million new enterprises launched in 1993, 10 – 15 per cent grew to achieve sales of US$1 million or more. Add to this the generally accepted argument that 80 per cent of new jobs in the USA in recent years have come from small businesses (even if 'small' in the USA is by all other standards rather big) and also the fact that the current unemployment rate in the USA is less than 5 per cent, and a picture emerges of the missed potential of SMEs in Africa. The central argument here is that the experience of countries like the USA and others in Europe carry important lessons for Africa and that there is potential in Africa (and elsewhere) to replicate this kind of success.

In the light of the foregoing, it is clear that the hope and reliance by many countries in Africa on the SME sector for job creation and poverty reduction is, frankly, misplaced. For the kind of enterprises being promoted and supported in Africa simply cannot absorb the massive and growing numbers of unemployed and new job-seekers to which we referred earlier. Nor could the countries afford to place people in SMEs, even if they possessed what it took to compete and succeed in a global economy, given other demands on scarce and dwindling resources. The World Bank has estimated the cost of creating one job in a small firm, through enterprise development interventions, at US$4250. At this rate, it is doubtful if any country in Africa could absorb all its current unemployed, to say nothing of the hundreds of thousands of new entrants into the labour market each year.

So, which clients in Africa should be promoted and supported by enterprise development interventionists? This question always raises notions of equity and fairness. However, the stark reality is that resources are limited, even decreasing and choices must be made in the face of competing demands. At a general level, it is clear that, as a strategy for maximum impact and growth, the focus of attention should shift to the 'larger small' and medium size category as well as fast-growth enterprises and others with growth potential (Manu 1995). This is in no way to suggest that micro- and very small enterprises as well as 'average' or stagnant firms have no contribution to make or that they should be totally ignored. On the contrary, all the target groups in the SME sector have a contribution to make and require support. The argument here is for balance. It is also for viable alternatives to the score of strategies usually tried with the dead horse.

Project

Closely linked to the foregoing is the question of which projects are to be supported, not only at the level of technical co-operation but also in terms of the assignments and cases that the local support agency takes on. Far too many support agencies in Africa have operated on the basis of 'we try to assist whoever comes through the door'. This philosophy runs counter to the best practices of management and enterprise development. It has also not worked. Nor is it strategic in terms of identifying, targeting and engineering a certain kind of enterprise or industry.

A related and important issue to be addressed here is whether to target start-ups or existing enterprises, or both. Given that large numbers of enterprises start each year without any external support and, as Mead and Liedholm (1998) point out, in view of the high attrition rates and the multiple needs of new enterprises, one might legitimately ask whether scarce developmental resources should be devoted to helping more new enterprises get established. Furthermore, given that a significant proportion of start-ups will not survive beyond the first three years and that only a tiny number would grow then or later, one might well ask which part of the existing enterprise spectrum to target. We take the view, as some experts have argued for some time (e.g. Little et al. 1987), that if supply-side measures are to be provided then an effective approach would be one of waiting to spot firms with growth potential with a view to assisting them in concrete terms with their needs and priorities.

A good starting point for supply-side measures and a key question to be addressed here in every country is 'what kind of enterprise do we wish to promote?'. The decision should be informed by broad development policies and plans as well as an analysis of effort–result ratios. However, the general rule is to focus on areas where there is a comparative advantage and on projects with the greatest potential for growth and impact. Furthermore, it goes without saying that support agencies need to place limits on what their services offer.

Support agencies in Africa, on the whole, try to do too much, with the result that they end up doing nothing really well. The typical SIDO or SEDO (Small Industry/Enterprise Development Organisation) in Africa lists over a dozen fields of activity in their portfolio for both start-ups and existing enterprises in all sectors of the economy! Some even deliver credit and non-financial services under the same roof with the same staff. In contrast, many of the best support agencies, including a few in Africa but mostly elsewhere, concentrate on just a handful of services; and often for specific sectors only; and do these well. It is interesting to note that even the 'big five' consultancy firms focus on just a couple of core services, that the majority of banks 'stick to their knitting', that the best business schools concentrate on MBA and executive education, yet the SIDOs and SEDOs in Africa and their accomplices try to do all of these and more in the name of SME development!

Policy development and implementation

Analysis of the sources of growth of countries suggests that policy is a major factor in explaining differences in economic performance. Birdsall and Jaspersen (1998), in comparing East Asia and Latin America, found that policy differences in six critical areas: macroeconomics, human resources, savings, the financial sector, trade, and institutions explained the different growth performance of the two regions. SMEs are no exception to the rule: for years, experts have contended that the policy environment is the most important dimension in the sector's development. Yet, with the exception of Kenya and South Africa, we do not know of any country in sub-Saharan Africa that has elaborated a comprehensive and official set of policies for the promotion of the sector. This is in contrast to the situation in major economic blocs such as the European Union (EU), the USA, Japan and ASEAN countries, where SME policies exist and where enterprises have flourished, poverty has decreased sharply and per capita income has risen over the past three decades (even allowing for the recent crisis in Asia).

There is further food for thought here. We presented research findings earlier from the EU showing that 4 per cent of firms, characterized as fast-growth, contributed some 50 per cent of all net job creation. Now, these fast-growth firms are no accident. For, policies at the community level recognize the importance of such firms and specifically target their promotion through special measures such as the new multi-annual programme. There are important lessons here for Africa. There is also much scope for donors, development agencies and other actors to assist governments here.

Internationalization

With few exceptions, African economies are just too small to sustain their businesses and foster expansion and growth. Many countries in Europe and East Asia discovered this years ago and even today go to great lengths to assist their firms to 'internationalize'. Moreover, even the relatively small domestic markets in Africa are now open to stronger, global competition. Furthermore, in economies like Ghana and Kenya, with high inflation and currency devaluation, exports to other countries to generate hard currencies may be the key to the redemption of ailing companies.

Clearly, in this scenario, African countries have little choice but to organize, become competitive and look for alternative markets. There is no reason why the continent should settle for a mere 1 per cent of world trade. To the extent that they dominate the economic landscape and remain the main source for the development of much of the continent, SMEs must necessarily be involved in efforts at internationalizing enterprises in Africa. Faced with similar global challenges, EU countries are currently engaged in several initiatives to internationalize their firms through projects such as ADAPT and Access to Excellence (ATE);[3] to great advantage. There are important lessons here too for Africa.

[3] For example, the author is currently engaged in one such project in the Piedmont region of Italy, co-financed by the EU. Part of an international programme, with partners from over half a dozen other EU countries, the local project seeks to assist 75 SMEs in the region to internationalize over a period of two years.

Foreign direct investment

In 1996, foreign direct investment (FDI) flows worldwide amounted to US$350 billion, continuing a fast growth trend during the past 15 years.[4] In terms of delivery of goods to foreign markets, FDI has become more important than trade, according to UNCTAD. Moreover, according to the same source, FDI has grown faster than GDP or trade during the last 15 years. The important point of note here, for our purposes, is that in 1996 an estimated 10–15 per cent of FDI flows was between SMEs, i.e. from one SME to another SME. (FDI in this context is defined in terms of at least a 10 per cent equity holding in another firm.) That amounts to a staggering US$35 billion at the lower estimate. The sad aspect to this otherwise remarkable development is that Africa's share is negligible: in terms of both FDI flows to the continent and FDI flows amongst SMEs. Contrast this with Japan, for example, where SMEs contributed 10–20 per cent of the country's FDI flows in 1996.

Here too, there are important lessons for Africa. For net FDI flows to and among SMEs do not happen in a vacuum or by accident. They are the result of deliberate policy and design. For example, we know that globally, 50 – 65 per cent of FDI flows are in services. Thus, service activities represent an important reservoir of FDI that can be tapped. Other policy implications of these trends are that countries need to cast their nets wider to attract FDIs, particularly in non-traditional sectors; that a targeted approach to investors pays off; that a sequential approach can become a cue for others. Furthermore, there is need to improve frameworks for both inward and outward FDI. Countries like Japan, China, Singapore, Hong Kong and Taiwan have done just that and have reaped the benefits.

Inter-firm co-operation, subcontracting and networking

Much has been written in recent years about co-operation between SMEs, networking among small firms, subcontracting between large and small companies in Japan and industrial districts in Italy and elsewhere (see, for example, Piore and Sabel 1984; Pyke 1988; Sengenberger and Pyke 1991). Briefly, these have shown that such linkages and relationships are beneficial, even necessary, for SMEs, in particular enabling small firms to attain economies of scale and compete effectively with their larger counterparts. It has also been shown that SMEs organized in this way, apart from synergistic benefits, are able to withstand recessions and weather storms in economic cycles better than those that are not. Furthermore, such relationships are a great source of innovation and provide strong stimuli for productivity and quality management, thus improving the overall competitiveness of SMEs.

Most importantly, perhaps, inter-firm co-operation, subcontracting and

---

[4] Source: UNCTAD conference on FDI and SMEs, Kunming, China, November 1997.

networking arrangements also create jobs. In Italy, to cite one example, 1000 jobs were created by just 10 joint ventures between the giant ENI and small firms, which is more than the average size of employment in small firms. In an era of global alliances, where even conglomerates are merging and competing airlines are entering into partnerships and sharing routes and passengers, one wonders if SMEs have much alternative but to co-operate too among themselves and with large firms.

Franchising

In the 1980s and early 1990s, franchising played a key role in the economic boom in Europe and the USA. It was and remains a major entry route into business for many would-be entrepreneurs. Today, total sales turnover of franchises amounts to several tens of billions of dollars each year in the USA and in Europe, not to mention other regions. Franchises are also widely held to have lower mortality rates, relative to the average start-up, and are generally much easier to manage, as systems tend to be already developed. Banks and investors also tend to look more favourably on franchises than other kinds of routes into business. Yet, with few exceptions, franchises are conspicuous in Africa by their absence. MacDonalds, for example, which is probably the best known and sets the benchmark for much of the industry, is to date not available in countries like Ghana, Côte d'Ivoire, Senegal, Uganda and Zambia: countries which are held to be spearheading economic growth in the emerging continent. There is much scope for intervention here for enterprise development.

Institutional support, public versus private partnership

Related to inter-firm co-operation is the issue of public and private partnership. One characteristic of many countries with strong economies is this kind of partnership in fostering entrepreneurship and enterprise development. A prime example was the UK during the 1980s and early 1990s through Business In The Community. Today, such partnerships are found throughout the EU. Elsewhere, Japan, Korea and Singapore also provide some good examples: all to very good effect.

It is worth highlighting that 'private' in this context is not restricted to SMEs. Indeed, large companies could have a direct impact in terms of enterprise development, creating jobs and export revenues. Furthermore, on the whole, they have shown their eagerness to assist, given the right initiatives and approach. For example, Coca-Cola has calculated that every job that it created in Poland and Romania generated nine additional jobs. Or take South Africa, where large companies like South African Breweries and ESKOM (the electricity company) are achieving some wonderful results in SME development. Even more spectacular was British Steel in the UK which, with support from local enterprise and development agencies, helped to set up 3500 businesses creating 58 000 jobs with an 80 per cent survival rate and 17 jobs per investment. In case there is a temptation to think that this was a one-off, British Coal helped to achieve a similar feat, again in partnership with local enterprise and development agencies as well as donor funding. Five thousand businesses were established, creating 55 000 jobs, again with an 80 per cent survival rate and 11 jobs per investment. Is there a lesson here for Africa?

Special incentives and assistance programmes

Financial and non-financial assistance institutions and programmes for enterprise development now exist in every country in Africa. In many places, special incentives are also available for business start-up. The issue here is not so much availability as adequacy and effectiveness. We know enough now to suggest that these programmes have to be carefully tailored to the needs of selected target clients to be effective. For the most part, current assistance programmes in Africa cater for start-ups, micro- and very small enterprises (typically self-employment up to five employees). Micro-credit is now well developed and reasonably focused. Non-financial assistance such as management training, however, is typically rather bland and seemingly of no direct application or benefit to enterprises or would-be clients. Furthermore, in most cases, finance and non-financial programmes hardly ever meet.

Quite apart from the frustration and the lack of impact that often result from the status quo, it is also worth remembering that, even at best, all of these programmes, incentives and schemes together reach only a tiny fraction of the potential or even target population. In fact, a recent study for the ILO found that, put together, the SME development assistance programmes throughout the world reached only 1 per cent of the target population! Surely, if that is the case, then there is need to be extremely selective. There is also need for specific and/or additional programmes to implement policy and certain strategies such as those put forward in this chapter. A good starting point would be financial assistance for enterprises with fast-growth potential and others in the 'larger small' and medium category. There is a distinct gap in the market here throughout Africa, despite recent attempts to set up venture capital funds in places like Ghana, Zimbabwe and South Africa.

It must be pointed out here that the spectacular figures quoted above in respect of British Steel and British Coal were the result of a deliberate strategy of financial assistance involving venture capital, credit guarantees and small business loans; besides the formal banking system. Elsewhere, in Korea, it took a similar kind of initiative, with the government playing a proactive but facilitative role at the outset, to spawn high-tech, fast-growth SMEs and, over time, some large enterprises. Could there be a lesson here for enterprise development in Africa?

Innovation, productivity and change

Innovation, productivity and change have proven to be powerful components of strategy for enterprise competitiveness and growth; and not just among large companies. It is well known and accepted that SMEs can be very innovative and achieve high productivity. Italy is a good example of such, although this phenomenon is observable practically everywhere. Change has become the constant factor in our times, fuelled by technology and stiff competition. In this scenario, SMEs have little choice but to adapt, compete or die.

Such considerations are taken very seriously in the North. For example, some of the best SME support institutions in countries like Belgium, Italy and the UK have developed relatively sophisticated benchmarking and quality management programmes and systems to assist their clients stay competitive in the global economy; with encouraging results. There are similar programmes in these and other countries aimed at helping SMEs to cope with and manage change. Contrast this with Africa, where industry on the whole is notorious for performing at under-capacity and with low productivity. Or, where examples of innovation that have proven to be winners in international markets are pretty difficult to come by. Could African enterprises survive and grow in the global economy without innovation, productivity and change? Could there be a role for intermediaries in driving these campaigns?

Some implications for education and training

Several implications can be drawn from the foregoing for education and training. We should like to advocate three in particular: first, the concept of the learning organization, second, benchmarking as a tool and third, the promotion of an enterprise culture through education in entrepreneurship.

Learning organization

In seeking to identify ways of making business more competitive, recent attention in Europe and the USA has focused on how SMEs acquire and diffuse experience and know-how. One strand of enquiry here has involved adapting concepts of 'learning organizations' to the activity structures of SME clusters (Cullen and Sommerlad 1997). Senge (1990) defines the concept as an organization in which

> people continually expand their capacity to create the results they truly desire, where new and expansive patterns are nurtured, where collective aspiration is set free and where people are continually learning how to learn together.

Certainly, in big business, the concept of the learning organization is postulated as a powerful competitive tool, with followers claimed to include diverse champions and household names like 3M, IBM, Federal Express and Levi Strauss. The argument, as indicated earlier, is that competitive advantage and the key to economic and business success, in an era of globalization and flexible specialization, lie in human capital: in this case, the minds of the workforce (Reich 1991; Senge 1990). At national and also international level, this point has been taken up by the European Union and more recently the ILO (1998) which devotes its latest *World Employment Report* entirely to training and lifelong learning, arguing that these are the keys to increasing competitiveness, growth and employment.

In short, for our purpose here, the idea is to enable SMEs to 'learn to learn'; it is to get continuous learning and innovation so deeply ingrained in the culture of enterprises that they become part and parcel of work. Programmes for this purpose, designed specifically for SMEs, are now in place in some areas (e.g. ECIPAR in Emilia-Romagna in Italy) and can be introduced or adapted for use in Africa. As McGrath and King (1996) point out, the gap between such programmes and the African reality appears immense. None the less there are grounds for arguing that important insights can be gained from such ideas for the challenges facing Africa.

Benchmarking

Second, much can be (and has been) done to improve the know-how of SME personnel and business performance through benchmarking. In essence, the idea is to identify critical success factors and learn from the best SMEs in the class/sector/industry, at either national or international level. The level and gap between interested firms, on one hand, and the best, on the other, can be determined and then measures (such as training and learning) put in place to close the gap, typically by setting targets and using a step-by step approach towards a plan. Examples abound in several countries, e.g. Belgium, Italy and the UK, where SME support institutions (or business development services, to employ a term currently in vogue) are using benchmarking for their clients, to good effect.

Enterprise culture

Finally, it has been estimated that, put together, all the enterprise development services and projects in developing countries probably reach about 1 per cent of the target population. While the exact figure could be debated, few would doubt the point that only a fraction of potential clients are reached. Given this, and the need to create job creators rather than job hunters, initiatives aimed at developing in the long term an enterprise culture and capability in Africa would seem sensible.

One way towards this is by providing entrepreneurship education throughout the education and training system. There is nothing new about this idea, nor in the ways of going about it. Many countries have been doing this for some time: for example, in Norway, entrepreneurship education is provided at the primary, secondary and university level. Similar schemes exist in the UK and USA, where entrepreneurship programmes are also found in vocational and technical training. Other, more recent, examples could be cited from India and Malaysia.

Thus, mechanisms, materials and methodologies for entrepreneurship education are available and could be (or have been) adapted with relative ease for use in specific countries in Africa. One such package is the ILO's Know About Business (KAB) programme (Manu et al. 1996).

In Africa, so far, Kenya has made the biggest strides in this area, following a UNDP/ILO project which introduced entrepreneurship education, at a national level, into all the government-controlled vocational and technical training institutes. Having seen the impact of the initiative and its popularity with beneficiaries, all the major universities in the country now also offer entrepreneurship education and there is now talk of introducing the subject in the secondary curriculum. Kenya is the exception, however, rather than the rule as far as national programmes are concerned (notwithstanding the fact that entrepreneurship programmes exist or are being piloted in a few institutions in some countries, e.g. Ghana, South Africa and Zambia).

Clearly, there is much scope here and also great potential for enterprise development in Africa, if the experience of other regions is anything to go by. Richard Branson, Founder/Chairman of the Virgin Group, a leading entrepreneur and reputed by *Business Week* in a recent (October 1998) article to have a personal wealth of US$1.7 billion, should perhaps have the final word here:

> Some may question the idea of teaching entrepreneurship on the basis that you can't learn to be an entrepreneur. However, the important thing about entrepreneurship is that it provides young people with skills which may or may not make them entrepreneurs, but will help them to be more innovative and opportunistic in their future working lives, be it in the public sector, industry or running their own businesses. At Virgin, we have over 11 000 employees in over 100 companies and everybody is encouraged to think of new ideas, new ways of working and ways of improving customer service. This sort of entrepreneurial activity at every level is the key to business survival in the modern world. [Excerpt from acceptance speech, doctoral award ceremony, at Glasgow Caledonian University, Scotland, in November 1995].

Conclusion

We conclude with another quote taken from the beginning of a paper presenting findings of a study on benchmarking for small manufacturing companies in Europe: 'The most powerful process any company can adopt and which delivers immediate, measurable and sustainable productivity improvements is the transfer of Best Practice' (Cagliano et al. nd).

The above statement, although perhaps taken slightly out of context, sums up the central message of this chapter. In short, we are advocating the transfer of best practice for enterprise development in Africa. We are suggesting that there is great potential to replicate the enterprise development success of other regions. We are arguing that in order to ensure a healthy SME sector in Africa, governments, development agencies, donors and other concerned actors need to adopt proven strategies to spawn world class enterprises on the continent. The overall implication of the proposals for the key actors on the ground is fairly obvious: as Nike would put it, 'Just do it'. The starting point is to follow Dakota tribal wisdom and dismount from the dead horse.

Part 3
Collaboration between Enterprises

9 Do SMEs network for growth?

ABIGAIL BARR

Introduction

Many small and medium sized enterprises (SMEs) in sub-Saharan Africa operate not in isolation but within networks that link them to a wider business community (van Dijk 1992; Dawson 1992; Livingstone 1991; Bräutigam 1997; Aeroe 1992; Hansohm 1992; Sverrisson 1992; Rasmussen 1992). It has been argued that such networks can lead to collective efficiencies, collective economies of scale and, as a consequence, to growth (Nadvi and Schmitz 1994; Schmitz 1982, 1995 and 1997). In this chapter I look at the extent to which the networks built by SMEs in the Ghanaian manufacturing sector fulfil these functions and, where they do not, ask whether there is a role for policy intervention.

The analysis is based on the premiss that social networks can be of use to entrepreneurs in sub-Saharan Africa for two reasons: they can help to increase the productivity of, and hence the income derived from, their enterprises (Barr 1997); and they can help to reduce uncertainties relating to the variability of that income. The relative importance of these two objectives to a particular entrepreneur affects both the structure of the network she maintains and the effect that the network has on the current and future performance of her enterprise. Where a network is required to assist in the reduction of uncertainty its structure will be such that it has less impact on enterprise performance.

In an earlier paper I present evidence in support of these propositions (Barr 1998). I show that enterprises with restricted access to formal institutions that in various ways help to reduce uncertainties, build small, homogeneous, cohesive networks, while those with reasonable access to such institutions build large, diverse networks. Further, I show that the effect of small, homogeneous, cohesive networks built to aid in the reduction of uncertainty on enterprise performance is much lower than the effect of larger, more diverse networks. Finally, I show that small, cohesive networks generate positive spillover effects, i.e., the benefits they generate are shared, and that the individual members who incur the costs of building and maintaining the networks are unlikely to see a positive net private return on their efforts. In contrast, large, diverse networks generate high private returns and no significant spillover effects.

Given the tendency for SMEs in sub-Saharan Africa to have more restricted access to formal market-supporting institutions than their larger counterparts, it is appropriate to look specifically at both the type of networks that SMEs build and the effect that those networks have on their performance. To do this I employ econometric techniques, the use of which is uncommon in this field. In general, researchers have employed a case-study methodology to look at particular enterprise clusters. As a consequence, there now exists a very rich and detailed literature on the nature of enterprise networks and the roles they have played in the development of specific enterprise clusters. However, the case-study methodology has its limitations, especially when the aim is to identify general patterns linking enterprise and network characteristics (Schmitz 1995).

The empirical results presented below show that SMEs do indeed tend build the type of networks that have only a marginal impact on their performance. They also highlight the need to distinguish between different types of SME, especially with reference to the subsector within which they operate. In the light of these results, it is appropriate to explore the conditions under which SMEs might be expected to change their networking behaviour and ask whether there is a role for policy intervention in this process.

The chapter is divided into five sections. After this introduction the second section sets out the theory linking a network's structure to its ability to improve enterprise performance and reduce uncertainty, and then looks at the type of enterprise one might expect to find in each type of network. The empirical results are presented in the third section. The fourth section considers the evolution of networks from uncertainty-reducing to performance-enhancing and the fifth section concludes.

Networking to improve enterprise performance and reduce uncertainty

Barr (1998) explains how different types of network are best suited for different purposes, although in almost all cases the underlying function of the network is to allow information to flow. Networks affect enterprise performance directly by providing entrepreneurs with information about technologies and markets. Such information can directly enhance worker productivity, increase capacity utilization, reduce costs and improve output quality. An entrepreneur whose networking objective is to maximize access to such information will be part of a far-reaching network. She will face high returns to maintaining a large, diverse set of contacts. She may also benefit from maintaining contacts who themselves maintain large and diverse sets of contacts as, *ceteris paribus*, they will be better informed. However, this positive spillover effect may be offset by the benefits that follow from being better informed than anyone else. *Ceteris paribus*, an entrepreneur will be better informed than anyone else the higher the level of networking she undertakes herself and the lower the level of networking undertaken by others.

Much of the uncertainty facing enterprises in sub-Saharan Africa is due to a lack of contract discipline that ripples through the system (Fafchamps 1996a). As a result of delayed deliveries, unreliable supply quality, and late payments and repayments by customers and debtors, an entrepreneur may at times be unable to meet her obligations to others in the system. One set of delays leads to another, one bad debt leads to another, and so on. In such an environment, entrepreneurs need to be flexible when dealing with trading partners, creditors and debtors. However, they also need to be able to distinguish between unavoidable poor contractual performance and poor contractual performance due to incompetence or malfeasance. The problem here is one of information asymmetries. In more developed countries, formal market-supporting institutions have emerged that help to reduce such asymmetries and improve contract discipline. However, while many similar institutions exist in sub-Saharan Africa, they tend not to permeate the environment within which most SMEs operate. Instead, entrepreneurs rely on their networks to reduce information asymmetries by facilitating flows of information about the previous conduct, current circumstances and future intentions of their trading partners, debtors and creditors (Fafchamps 1996b). Hence, these networks provide a basis for trade, credit and insurance.

It is in the markets for credit and insurance, both of which are highly vulnerable to problems of information asymmetry, that differences in the institutional environments within which different types of African enterprise operate are most readily observed. Formal lines of credit and insurance are available only to those with collateral and who are operating in environments characterized by well defined property rights. Informal credit and insurance arrangements can work in the absence of well defined property rights, but are just as vulnerable to problems of information asymmetry. However, unlike those formal counterparts, informal arrangements can be supported by networks (Fafchamps 1992).

Ceteris paribus, risk-sharing and informal credit arrangements are more efficient the larger and more diverse the group (Alderman and Paxson 1994). This notwithstanding, as the group and hence the network increases in size, so too does the number of agents about whom each member has to be kept informed. At some finite network size it is likely that the costs associated with the need to assimilate information about an additional network member will outweigh the benefits. Increasing the diversity of the network also increases the cost of collecting the required information as it becomes harder for each member to establish the standing of others based on the observations she can make. The size and diversity of the network may also be restricted by the need for continual interaction if information asymmetries are to be effectively reduced.

An uncertainty-reducing network may enhance enterprise performance indirectly. Lower levels of uncertainty have, for example, been linked to higher levels of investment (Pattillo 1997). However, in general, such networks would be expected to have a positive effect on welfare, while having little or no effect on enterprise performance. This is primarily because of the relative importance of spillover effects within networks of this type. The role of this type of network is to make it hard to keep secrets. But if members are unable to keep secrets about themselves, they will also find it difficult to keep secret information that may enhance enterprise performance. As a result, spillover effects account for a large proportion of the overall effect of the network on enterprise performance. Further, the members of this type of network have difficulty excluding others from the returns to not only their networking activity but to many other activities, including investments and all forms of innovation. This will act as a disincentive, making it less likely that the members of such networks will take steps to improve the current and future performance of their enterprises (Posner 1980).

To establish which types of enterprises are most likely to exist and operate in each of the network types identified above one must look at the associated costs and benefits. The costs associated with maintaining a performance-enhancing network as opposed to an uncertainty-reducing network will be lower for enterprises that have access to formal, market-supporting institutions. It is larger enterprises that have greatest access to such institutions. The returns to maintaining a performance-enhancing network are likely to be higher for enterprises that employ rapidly evolving technologies and serve a potentially diverse set of markets. Again, it is larger enterprises that are most likely to display these characteristics. However, the nature of the sub-sector within which they operate may also be of relevance. The opportunity cost of maintaining an uncertainty-reducing rather than a performance-enhancing network will be lower for enterprises using traditional, static technologies to supply local markets, of primarily end users, while the returns to maintaining an uncertainty-reducing network are likely to be higher for enterprises with restricted access to formal institutions in search of alternative mechanisms for reducing the uncertainty they face. SMEs tend to display these characteristics, although, once again, the nature of the sub-sector within which they operate may also be important.

Empirical analysis

The empirical investigation is based on data from the Ghanaian manufacturing sector. Much of the required data can be drawn from the Ghanaian Regional Program for Enterprise Development (RPED) survey, and its successor, the Ghanaian Manufacturing Enterprise Survey (GMES).[1] While

[1] Both surveys were funded by the British Government. The RPED was a World Bank project under which the Centre for the Study of African Economies (CSAE), University of Oxford, and the Department of Economics, University of Legon, conducted the Ghanaian survey. The GMES was conducted by the CSAE and the Ghanaian Statistical Service.

these surveys contain a wide range of data about manufacturing enterprises, their employees and the environment in which they operate, the original questionnaire did not address the issue of enterprise networks. To remedy this, the author designed a supplementary questionnaire which provided a wide range of indicators relating to enterprise networks. Due to time constraints, however, some important aspects of network composition could not be addressed. In particular, no information on the gender, ethnic and kin group dimensions of the networks was collected. If time allows, this will be remedied in future rounds of the survey. The sample is drawn from the population of manufacturing enterprises that are situated outside the home. It includes all sizes of enterprise operating within this category, from the lone artisan to firms employing several hundreds of workers. Due to the absence of a good frame, the sample cannot be described as random. Larger enterprises are over-represented, while small and micro-enterprises are under-represented. As a result, there is a need for caution when drawing conclusions about the Ghanaian manufacturing sector as a whole. This notwithstanding, the data are ideal for making comparisons between enterprises of different size.

The networking activity of each entrepreneur is captured by the number of contacts they purport to maintain. The respondents were asked how many contacts they maintained in each of nine categories. Six of these related to other business people in the same line of business, in different lines of business, with larger businesses, in other regions of Ghana, non-Ghanaians based in Ghana, and in other countries. The remaining three related to bankers, public servants, and politicians. The number of categories within which a respondent has at least one contact is used as an indicator of contact diversity. For a sub-sample of enterprises we can estimate the frequency of liaison between the respondent and her average contact, an indicator of the level of interaction. Finally, starting with the entire sample of enterprises, for each respondent, a sub-sample corresponding to the description of her contacts can be drawn. The average number of contacts maintained by this sub-sample may then be used as a proxy for the level of networking undertaken by each respondent's co-networkers. The inclusion of this variable in the analysis allows us to separate the private from the spillover effects of networking.

Enterprises with up to 30 employees are classified as SMEs, while those with more than 30 employees are classified as large. In an effort to look more closely at SMEs, the enterprises are further subdivided into those in 'traditional' and those in 'non-traditional' subsectors. Traditional subsectors are defined as those in which traditional, static technologies tend to be used to produce for local markets made up of end users, while non-traditional subsectors are defined as those in which modern, more dynamic technologies are used to supply potentially diverse markets. In Ghana, the furniture, garment and food and beverage subsectors generally correspond to the definition of traditional, while the textiles and metalworking subsectors correspond to the definition of non-traditional. The wood processing sub-sector proved difficult to classify as it uses a well established technology to produce an intermediate product for a diverse market. However, further investigation indicated that all the enterprises sampled from this subsector had modern corporate structures, kept accounts and used elements of modern company law to regulate their dealings with trading partners. Thus, it seemed appropriate to classify the subsector as modern. Classifying subsectors inevitably leads to the misclassification of some enterprises. No attempt was made to reclassify any enterprises, as it seemed desirable to keep the classification process as transparent as possible.

By looking at cross-tabulations one can establish whether expectations concerning SMEs and large enterprises in traditional and non-traditional sub-sectors and their technologies, their relative access to formal institutions, their markets, and the type of networks they maintain, are founded. Table 9.1 shows that there are significant differences between SMEs and large enterprises. Compared to large enterprises, SMEs tend to use more labour-intensive technologies. They are less likely to insure their capital stock formally and are more likely to supply only end users. Their entrepreneurs maintain only one-third of the contacts maintained by those with large enterprise. However, they liaise far more frequently (more than twice rather than less than once a week) with each. As well as being smaller, their networks are less diverse and are made up of co-networkers who also maintain small networks. These patterns in networking behaviour are, without exception, con-

Table 9.1: Characteristics of small and large enterprises and their networks[1]

	SMEs	*Large enterprises*	*All enterprises*
Number of enterprises[2]	90	32	122
Mean capital-labour ratio	1861	6078	2967
Percentage of enterprises that insure their capital stock[2]	0.88%	64.29%	35.25%
Percentage of enterprises supplying to end users only	41.11%	18.75%	25.00%
Mean number of contacts	33.48	92.41	48.93
Mean diversity of contacts	3.53	5.91	4.16
Mean number of liaisons with an average contact per year[2]	106.75	47.33	91.34
Mean number of contacts of the entrepreneurs' co-networkers	38.57	63.03	44.98

[1] The table is based on 1993 data. The capital-labour ratio is reported in thousands of cedi. All the between-group differences are significant at the 1 per cent level, with the exception of the differences in the end user variable and the mean number of contact, both of which are significant at the 5 per cent level.
[2] The number of liaisons with an average contact can be estimated for only 80 small and 28 large enterprises.

sistent with the hypothesis that SMEs network to reduce uncertainty, while larger enterprises network to improve their performance.

Further dividing the sample into traditional and non-traditional sub-sectors adds little to the analysis. The differences in the means tend to conform to our expectations. However, they are generally not significant. For the SMEs the only significant difference between those in traditional and those in non-traditional sub-sectors is that the latter liaise less frequently with each of their contacts.

To look at whether the networks built by SMEs have less effect on current enterprise performance, while generating more spillovers, I analyse worker productivity. The approach I use also facilitates an investigation into whether networks generate collective economies of scale. In this analysis variations in value-added per worker between enterprises are explained with reference to enterprise size, the formal education and work experience of the employees, and the capital-labour ratio. The analysis also takes account of whether the enterprises are corporate or entrepreneurial, the year when the data were collected and the sector in which the enterprises operate. The enterprises' networks are captured by including the number of contacts maintained by the entrepreneur and the average number of contacts maintained by her co-networkers. The results of this analysis provide us with a picture of how the effects of networking vary across SMEs and large enterprises operating in different sub-sectors.

Table 9.2 contains estimated networking effects for SMEs and large enterprises in traditional and non-traditional subsectors. The private and spillover effects are presented in terms of the percentage increase in productivity that would result from a 1 per cent increase in the number of contacts maintained by the entrepreneur in the case of the former, and her co-networkers in the case of the latter. The overall effect indicates the percentage increase in productivity that would result from a 1 per cent increase in the number of contacts maintained by both the entrepreneur and her co-networkers.

The pattern of effects across SMEs and large enterprises in traditional and non-traditional subsectors supports the theories outlined above. The overall effect of networking is positive and significant for all types of enterprise.

Table 9.2. Private and external effects of networking on worker productivity

	SMEs			*Large Enterprises*		
	Private effect	*Spillover effect*	*Overall effect*	*Private effect*	*Spillover effect*	*Overall effect*
Traditional	- 0.05	0.20**	0.14**	0.14	0.01	0.15*
Non-traditional	0.26**	- 0.05	0.20**	0.66***	- 0.24	0.42**

Notes: * – significant at the 10% level, ** – significant at the 5% level, *** – significant at the 1% level.

However, it varies considerably in magnitude. A 1 per cent increase in the overall level of networking is associated with a 0.42 per cent increase in the productivity of large enterprises in non-traditional sub-sectors, but only a 0.14 percent increase for SMEs in traditional subsectors. In addition, the relative importance of the private and spillover effects varies. The private effect of networking for SMEs in traditional subsectors is not significantly different from zero. However, there are significant positive spillover effects; a 1 per cent increase in their co-networkers' networking activity is associated with a 0.20 per cent increase in productivity. The corresponding breakdown for large enterprises in non-traditional sub-sectors reveals an exceptionally large and significant private effect; a 1 per cent increase in the entrepreneurs' own networking activity is associated with a 0.66 percent increase in productivity. In contrast, there are no significant spillover effects.

So far I have focused on the two extreme cases of SMEs in traditional sub-sectors and large enterprises in non-traditional sub-sectors. However, the empirical results also reveal a striking difference between SMEs in traditional sub-sectors on the one hand and those in non-traditional sub-sectors on the other. With respect to the effect that networks have on their performance, the latter tend to resemble large enterprises in the same sub-sectors rather than enterprises of a similar size in traditional sub-sectors. For these enterprises the private effect of networking is significant and quite large, a 1 per cent increase in their own networking activity is associated with a 0.26 per cent increase in productivity, while the spillover effects are insignificant. This is of particular interest given that there are no significant differences in the structure of the networks maintained by SMEs in traditional and non-traditional sub-sectors. What one may be observing here is a class of enterprise that can potentially benefit a great deal from a network designed to improve access to information about technologies and markets, but is at the current time heavily dependent on its networks as a means of reducing uncertainty. One consequence of this dependence shows up as a clear distinction between SMEs and large enterprises in non-traditional sub-sectors. The analysis reveals that, in an environment dominated by constant returns technologies, it is only the large enterprises in non-traditional sub-sectors that experience collective economies of scale as a result of their networking activity. SMEs in non-traditional sub-sectors as well as all enterprises in traditional sub-sectors do not experience collective economies of scale and so do not face incentives to expand.

Changing the type of networks SMEs build

The results of the empirical analysis suggest that SMEs in the Ghanaian manufacturing sector tend to build the type of networks that are best suited to uncertainty reduction. The opportunity cost of so doing is that their networks have very little effect on their current performance in terms of worker productivity and tend not to enhance their future growth potential; they do not generate collective economies of scale and may, as a result of the low levels of privacy and high spillover effects within their bounds, deter investments and innovative activities.

It may be desirable to get SMEs networking for growth, but this should not happen at the expense of their security. Their existing networks are substituting for formal market-supporting institutions, including lending institutions, insurance companies, courts of law and credit bureau. While all of these formal institutions are present in sub-Saharan Africa, access to them is usually restricted to larger, less traditional enterprises. For SMEs, especially in traditional sub-sectors, recourse to these institutions is too costly, so they rely on their networks instead. Any attempt on their part to expand and diversify their networks in order to gain access to more information about technologies and market opportunities will compromise their networks' ability to reduce information asymmetries and, thus, support informal credit and risk-sharing arrangements and will leave them vulnerable to the effects of uncertainty. This need to choose between the two types of network affects individuals undertaking many different activities in different environments. Merchants and civil servants, for example, generally 'remain at the edge of the village solidarity network, preferring to rely on their own extra-village networks' (Fafchamps 1992: 162). One appropriate policy response may be to make formal institutions more accessible, by reducing the cost of the services they provide and informing entrepreneurs of their value.

Once the need to rely on networks to reduce uncertainty has been removed, they would be free to evolve and become growth-enhancing. The likelihood of this evolution actually taking place depends in part on the returns to networking that the individual entrepreneurs face. The analysis shows that enterprises that tend to have access to formal market-supporting institutions face high private returns to building large, diverse sets of contacts. But this does not necessarily imply that if SMEs had similar access they too would face similar returns. SMEs in non-traditional sub-sectors appear to face high private returns to networking. They may respond to a reduction in their need to rely on networks to solve problems of information asymmetry and contract enforcement by expanding and diversifying their networks. However, this is not the case for SMEs in traditional sub-sectors. At present, these enterprises accept very low or possibly even negative net private returns to networking in order to generate positive shared returns. If the need to rely on networks to reduce uncertainty are reduced it is not clear what would happen to the returns to networking as perceived by these SMEs. This is because of the interdependency between network structure, access to information and the perceived and actual returns to networking. Consider, for example, an entrepreneur who employs a traditional technology. She may not, until she starts expanding her network, be aware of alternative technologies. If she is not aware of these technologies she will not perceive the benefits of finding out about them and, as a result, will not take this into account when calculating the returns associated with her networking activity. In short, it may be only those who already have large, diverse sets of contacts who know their true value. Under these circumstances, it may be appropriate for policy makers to demonstrate the value of networking or engineer circumstances in which entrepreneurs discover its value for themselves.

If policy makers are to become involved in the formation of enterprise networks, it is imperative that they proceed with caution. Although poorly defined, some of the elasticities presented above indicate that networking activity, especially in non-traditional sub-sectors, may generate negative spillover effects. Negative spillovers are most likely where enterprises are using networks not only to find out about, but also to capture, particular market opportunities. Such activities are akin to rent-seeking behaviour and would be an unfortunate outcome of efforts to promote networking. Emphasis must be placed on the promotion of information flows and collective action.

Conclusion

The analysis presented in this chapter suggests that networks affect enterprise performance in different ways and to different extents, depending on the function they are designed to perform. These differences arise because alternative network structures suit alternative functions. Entrepreneurs with larger, non-traditional enterprises tend to maintain large, diverse, less cohesive networks that provide access to information about technologies and markets and generate collective economies of scale. In contrast, entrepreneurs with traditional SMEs tend to maintain small, cohesive networks designed primarily to reduce information asymmetries, improve contract discipline and support informal credit and risk-sharing arrangements. These networks have only a marginal effect on current enterprise performance and provide little opportunity for growth. They do not generate collective economies of scale and, because it is very difficult for entrepreneurs within their bounds to exclude others from the returns to their own efforts, may even deter investment and innovative behaviour.

Perhaps one of the most enlightening findings of the chapter is the tendency for SMEs involved in non-traditional activities to resemble large enterprises involved in similar activities rather than other SMEs. SMEs in non-traditional sub-sectors may represent a class of enterprise that has the capacity to benefit from greater access to information about new technologies and markets, even though they remain vulnerable to uncertainties associated with poor contractual performance.

With respect to policy, any attempt to affect the networking practices of SMEs, to encourage them to build networks that will enhance their growth potential, should be preceded by measures to improve their access to formal market-supporting institutions. Only then will they be able to change the nature of their networks without leaving themselves vulnerable to increased levels of uncertainty. Once such measures are in place, there may be a case for demonstrating the value of networking for growth or engineering situations in which the owners of SMEs can discover this for themselves. However, where active steps are to be taken to promote the construction of larger, more diverse networks, policy makers need to be aware of the uses to which the fruits of their labour will be put.

10 Enterprise clusters in Africa: linkages for growth and development

DOROTHY MCCORMICK

Introduction[1]

Clusters of enterprises are a familiar sight in Africa: informal vegetable markets occupying road reserves; groups of carpenters making furniture at the edge of a housing estate; vehicle repairers and metalworkers in giant open-air workshops; and groups of garment makers operating side by side in market stalls. The physical closeness of such enterprises should enable them to share information and gain easy access to suppliers, traders, and customers. Enterprises in clusters should also be better able to co-operate on common problems and issues of concern. In the language of cluster studies, clustering should encourage *joint action.*

Observation of African clusters, both on the ground and through the small but growing literature on the subject, suggests that joint action takes many different forms and varies greatly in its ability to achieve its goals. This in turn raises questions about the importance of joint action for the success of individual firms and for clusters as a whole. What can be achieved through joint action? Is one form of joint action more likely to succeed than another? What are the conditions that lead to joint action? And can positive joint action be facilitated through third-party intervention?

Using material from a detailed study of seven African clusters, this chapter explores these questions and offers some preliminary answers.[2] The chapter is divided into five sections. Following this introduction is a brief theoretical discussion of the relationship of joint action to cluster development. The third section describes the seven clusters, while the fourth examines the form and content of a number of examples of joint action found in the clusters. The final section draws conclusions from the analysis, suggests

[1] This chapter draws heavily on research conducted under the Kenya portion of a larger project on *Collective Efficiency and Small-scale Industry* directed by Hubert Schmitz of the Institute of Development Studies at the University of Sussex, and funded by the Department for International Development, London. I am grateful to Hubert Schmitz for his leadership in the project, and to DFID for its financial support. I also acknowledge with gratitude the work of my colleagues, Mary Kinyanjui and Winnie Mitullah of the Institute for Development Studies, University of Nairobi, whose detailed analyses of the vehicle repair and fish processing clusters provided important insights into the strengths and limitations of enterprise clusters.

[2] The case-study approach taken in this chapter means that its findings may not be generalizable. In particular, because the chapter deals with a subset of joint action – action in which at least one of the collaborating parties is located in a cluster – some of the results may not apply to dispersed firms.

some directions for further research, and offers some ideas for fruitful intervention.

Linkages and joint action in enterprise clusters

Before discussing the theoretical links between joint action and enterprise clusters, we need to specify the meaning of the term *cluster*. The word is used in two somewhat different ways in the industrial development literature. Porter (1990) uses the term to designate a group of firms engaged in similar or related activities within a national economy. Although Porter (1990: 761) believes that the relationships within an industry cluster benefit from firms' being located near one another, he does not consider geographic proximity to be a defining characteristic of clusters.

The second use of the term is explicitly geographic. According to Schmitz (1992), a cluster is 'a group of producers making the same or similar things in close proximity to each other'. It is, in other words, *a geographic and sectoral agglomeration of enterprises*. This approach has its roots in Marshall's (1890) observations on the textile and metalworking regions of England, Germany, and France during the latter half of the nineteenth century, which has recently been elaborated in studies of highly successful industrial districts in various parts of the world (see, for example, Piore and Sabel 1984; Becattini 1989; Storper and Walker 1989; Zeitlin 1989; Sengenberger and Pyke 1992; Humphrey 1995).

Networks and linkages offer benefits for firms' growth and development (Barr 1995; Alila and McCormick 1997). Similarly, geographic proximity has certain advantages even when firms do little to cultivate linkages. Identified as external economies by Marshall (1890), these have also been called the passive benefits of clustering (Nadvi 1997). External economies, especially the access to markets that comes from having many producers in a single location, are extremely important to small enterprise clusters in Africa (McCormick 1998). Schmitz (1997), however, argues that reaping passive benefits is not enough to bring about cluster development. Clusters must also be proactive, consciously pursuing joint action around problems and issues of common concern.

Much of the analysis of joint action has concentrated on its form (Schmitz 1997; McCormick 1998). Using this approach, one can identify four categories of joint action in clusters, based on two dimensions. The first dimension has to do with the number of co-operators; the second, with the direction of co-operation.[3] Thus joint action may be bilateral or multilateral. In bilateral co-operation, two firms work together as, for example, when they

[3] The terms *co-operation* and *joint action* are used interchangeably in this chapter to mean 'working together for the same end', i.e., the active aspect of collective efficiency. *Linkages*, on the other hand, are ties between or among firms that may or may not result in joint action.

share an expensive piece of equipment. In multilateral action, groups of firms join together, often in an association or other organization, for some common purpose. Joint action may also be vertical or horizontal. Vertical co-operation happens when firms involved in different stages of the production–distribution chain work together. Horizontal joint action refers to collaboration between/among competitors. The four types of joint action can be viewed schematically in Table 10.1

Useful as this schema is for analysing the pattern of interaction among firms, it ignores what may be an equally important aspect of joint action: its content.[4] Analysis of joint action among clustered small enterprises suggests that the content falls roughly into three categories. The first category includes actions dealing with supply-side constraints, the second includes action around production, and the third, action addressing markets and marketing. Before embarking on a detailed discussion of the various types of joint action observed, it seems useful to describe the seven clusters (Table 10.2)

The clusters

Five of the clusters are in Kenya, one is in Ghana and one in South Africa. Table 10.2 summarizes their main features. The clusters include two in the garment sector, one in metalwork, three in vehicle repair, and one in fish processing. All three vehicle repair clusters also include some firms manufactur-

Table 10.1: Four types of joint action

DIMENSION	*BILATERAL*	*MULTILATERAL*
Horizontal	Two co-operators at the same level in the production chain, e.g., sharing equipment	More than two co-operators at the same level in the production chain, e.g., a sectoral association
Vertical	Two co-operators at different levels of the production chain, e.g., a producer and user improving components	More than two co-operators at different levels of the production chain, e.g., an association or alliance composed of manufacturers and distributors of a product

Source: Adapted from Schmitz (1997)

[4] Even the direction and content do not exhaust the possibilities for analysing joint action. The salience of ethnicity for industrialization in many African countries suggests that one could fruitfully examine how ethnic factors facilitate or block joint action. Gender is another variable that has been raised as an issue in network formation (see, for example, McCormick 1997). Unfortunately space and data limitations do not permit us to explore either of these here.

Table 10.2: Enterprise clusters in Kenya, Ghana and South Africa

Cluster	*Producing firms*	*Average firm size*	*Products*	*Markets*
Kenya				
Garment markets	600	3.5	Clothing	Domestic: mainly rural and secondary towns
Kamukunji	2000	1–2	Metal products	Domestic: consumers, traders and firms
Thika	337	1.6	Vehicle repair	Thika individuals, especially *matatu* and truck owners[5] firms
Ziwani	506	1.5	Vehicle repair	Nairobi individuals, especially *matatu* & truck owners' firms
Uhanya Beach plus industrial processors	560	Fishing: 3–15 Trading: 1–50 Industrial processors: 35–300	Fresh and processed fish	Mainly export Limited domestic
Ghana				
Suame	8000	6.5	Vehicle repair	Domestic: consumers & firms Passive exports
South Africa				
Western Cape	538	126	Clothing	Large retail chains Domestic: 'fashion' and standard; also some to export market

ing spare parts and other metal products. Although producing firms predominate, all of the clusters have some enterprises selling inputs, trading in final products, and providing various services. The smallest cluster is the Thika vehicle repair cluster with 337 firms; the largest is the Ghanaian cluster with an estimated 8000 producers. Five of the clusters consist entirely of small enterprises, and have average firm sizes ranging from one or two

[5] A *matatu* is a privately owned mini-bus that forms a major part of Kenya's public transport system. In rural areas, many *matatus* are converted pickup trucks; in the city and towns, they are more likely to be vans or small buses seating up to 30 passengers.

workers up to more than six workers. Only the Western Cape clothing cluster and the Lake Victoria fish processing cluster have larger firms. Similarly, most of the clusters serve some part of the domestic market, though the Western Cape exports a small proportion of its output and the Lake Victoria fish processing cluster produces mainly for export.

Three of the Kenyan clusters; the garment markets, Kamukunji, and Ziwani; are located in Nairobi. The Thika *jua kali* cluster is in Thika, a town of 72 000 people, 46 kilometres north-east of Nairobi.[6] The Lake Victoria cluster encompasses industrial processors, most of whom are found in Kisumu, and fishermen, traders, and related activities at Uhanya Beach, a rural community on the shores of Lake Victoria, 65 kilometres from Kisumu. The Ghanaian cluster is in Suame, a northern suburb of Kumasi, Ghana's second largest city. The Western Cape Clothing cluster is centred in Cape Town, but covers a wide area of South Africa's Western Cape.

The clusters were chosen for their regional and sectoral representation as well as to provide an overview of a broad range of clustering issues (see McCormick 1998 for details). Most of the studies on which the analysis is based were carried out in the mid-1990s when markets in Kenya and South Africa were opening up, and more liberal economic policies were being adopted. The Suame study is older; fieldwork was done in 1988; but it also coincided with significant market liberalization in Ghana.

Joint action in the clusters

In these seven clusters, horizontal joint action; both bi-lateral and multilateral; is much more common than vertical joint action. The actions range from informal arrangements such as the borrowing and lending of tools, to formal subcontracting agreements, collaborative marketing of products, and membership in associations. There are several reasons for the prevalence of horizontal joint action, and by implication, the relative scarcity of vertical action. The first and most obvious is the fact that joint action is a common feature of clusters, and since our clusters are all made up largely of producers at the same stage of production, this is where the linkages are likely to be made. The second reason also has to do with the associations that are common in both Kenya and Ghana. By bringing producers together, these associations set the stage for collaboration between and among members. The third reason for the predominance of horizontal action relates to the way in which small producers operate. Many, both in clusters and outside, double as traders and retailers of their own products. This integration of the trading function into producing firms greatly reduces the scope for vertical collabo-

[6] The Swahili words *jua kali*, which literally mean 'harsh sun', were initially used to describe manufacturing and repair enterprises operating out of doors without shelter. Over the years the concept has been expanded to include a wide variety of micro- and small enterprises.

ration on the product market side. Finally, in places like Kenya, where traders and producers are often from different ethnic communities, problems of trust may make them reluctant to enter into anything more than market exchange relationships. Nevertheless, vertical collaboration does take place and, as we shall see below, one of the most important examples of joint action in response to a serious market crisis was vertical, involving an African trader and an Asian industrial fish processor.

The content of joint action centres on three aspects of business operation: obtaining inputs, production, and marketing. Several examples of inter-firm collaboration to secure inputs into the manufacturing process reveal both the limitations and the potential of this type of co-operation. The first example comes from the Nairobi garment markets, but it is replicated in many other small-enterprise clusters. The markets are highly competitive, with no multilateral co-operation and little bilateral action. The most basic form of co-operation involves the borrowing and lending of basic tools, such as scissors or measuring tape, or of assisting one another in cases of machine breakdown or shortage of a specific raw material (McCormick 1997: 117). Such co-operation is generally *ad hoc* and irregular. A few businesses provide services to others more regularly. Producers with specialized machines such as electric cutting shears or a buttonholer undertake certain tasks for neighbouring firms, usually for a fee. Similar forms of co-operation were also observed in metalworking and vehicle repair clusters. Borrowing and lending tools is probably the most common form of bilateral co-operation in clusters. October (1996) reports that even in the more sophisticated Western Cape clothing cluster, lending machinery is a common occurrence. In metalwork, as in textiles, the minority of firms with specialized machines will often provide cutting, punching, or bending services to others.

The second example of supply-side co-operation involves acquiring business premises. In Kenya, obtaining a secure site from which to do business is a major problem. A programme initiated by the Kenya Government in 1985 provides work sites to groups of *jua kali* artisans, but even when land has been allocated by the government, there may be no guarantee of long-term tenure. Both the Thika and Ziwani clusters faced this problem. In both cases, multilateral joint action was taken through the association. The Thika Welfare *Jua Kali* Association entered into intensive negotiations with the Thika municipality, which resulted in the transfer of the site to the association. The Ziwani *Jua Kali* Association purchased its site from the Nairobi City Council, but later found itself embroiled in a dispute over what types of businesses had a right to locate within the site. The Ziwani Association is also grappling with the implications of land ownership vested in the association for members who want to retire or move elsewhere (Kinyanjui 1998).

The final example, which concerns co-operation in the procurement of raw materials, comes from Kamukunji, though similar efforts exist elsewhere. The Kamukunji *Jua Kali* Association tried a system of consolidated purchasing of raw materials from the large companies (Hart 1994). By selling the items to the artisans with no mark-up, the association gave members a significant cost break. The effort broke down when, following complaints by the middlemen who had previously supplied the artisans, the large companies made it more difficult for the association to make direct purchases.

The cases offer four different types of inter-firm collaboration in production. The first, from Ghana, has been termed 'joint production' and involves linkages between small engineering workshops and vehicle repairers (Dawson 1988). Before market liberalization allowed free importation of spare parts, the Suame cluster was known for being able to supply whatever might be needed. Sometimes the item was a black market spare, but just as often it was made locally. A mechanic in need of a part would go to an engineering workshop carrying the old part. The workshop would either rework the item or make a new one using the old one as a model. The mechanic would then fit the part and continue with the rest of the repair job. Such bilateral production linkages were crucial to both firms, and helped to establish the reputation of the entire cluster as a place where almost any repair was possible. Although liberalization of markets in the mid-1980s made it less necessary for Suame to be able to produce its own spare parts, the skills that had been developed in the engineering workshops enabled them to compete favourably with imported spares.

Subcontracting is an important feature of production in certain sectors. In subcontracting, a main contractor who is hired to do a job contracts parts of the work to others. The reasons for subcontracting, as well as its mechanisms, vary. Lack of capacity, especially at peak periods, lack of specialized skills or equipment, or a desire to cut costs by contracting labour-intensive tasks to low-wage producers usually motivates subcontracting. The cases offer examples of all three types. Vehicle repair is often organized around specialized subcontracting. The Ziwani cluster provides a specific example, but the pattern is essentially the same in Suame and Thika. Work spaces within the Ziwani cluster are allocated on the basis of specializations (Kinyanjui 1997). General mechanics are the most numerous (22.4 per cent of the businesses), followed closely by panel beaters (20.2 per cent), spray painters (18.2 per cent), vehicle wiring specialists (18.2 per cent) and gas and electrical welders (8.1 per cent). Five other specializations account for the remaining 12.9 per cent of the enterprises. The general mechanic is often the lead contractor, who subcontracts specialized work to others. The Western Cape clothing cluster has skill-based, cost-reducing and capacity subcontracting (October 1996). The cluster has given rise to design houses and to firms specializing in particular production functions such as cutting or pleating. Because such activities require highly specialized equipment and skilled labour, many producers are happy to subcontract them out to others. Large garment manufacturers also subcontract what are called 'cut-make-and-trim' (CMT) activities. Such subcontracting enables firms to smooth production and meet peak season demand. In this sense it can be called capacity subcontracting. Use of CMT firms also reduces costs, both of labour and overheads.

The Lake Victoria fish cluster offers one of the few examples of effective vertical joint action. The action was spurred by a crisis in the industry that occurred when salmonella poisoning, traced to fish exported from Uganda, claimed the lives of two people in Spain. Spain immediately imposed a ban on imports of East African Nile perch, other European countries quickly followed suit, and the European Union sent inspectors to review fish handling procedures. The effect on Kenya's fish industry was immediate and devastating. Factories that had been supplying the European market had to cut production drastically. Fish prices at the beaches fell by 50 per cent almost overnight. Clearly something had to be done or Kenya would lose access to the fish industry's most lucrative export market. The industrial processors responded when called by government health officials to meetings in preparation for the EU inspection visit, but these *ad hoc* meetings did not lead to longer-lasting institutionalized co-operation. Perhaps more interesting is the response in Uhanya (Mitullah 1998). The beach's most prominent trader, who is estimated to control 70 per cent of Uhanya's Nile perch sales, worked with one of the industrial processors to effect a dramatic change in fish handling at the beach. Together they constructed a new weighing shed close to the water's edge, complete with supplies of chlorinated water for washing the fish, and initiated new procedures designed to eliminate the possibility of contamination as the fish is moved from the lake to the processors' refrigerated trucks.

The final example relates both to production technology and to marketing. Since about 1990 Kenya has been importing large numbers of second-hand cars. The first arrivals were reconditioned in Japan and, although many were unsuited to Kenyan road conditions, they were in good condition. With full market liberalization in the mid-1990s, a second group of vehicles began to arrive. These used cars, trucks and vans, nicknamed the 'Dubai cars' because they generally pass through the free port of Dubai, have barely been serviced prior to shipment, and many quickly develop problems requiring the attention of a mechanic. The Ziwani *Jua Kali* Association identified the Dubai cars as a market opportunity, but recognized that many of these vehicles are qualitatively different from the old models they have been accustomed to repairing (Kinyanjui 1998). To tap this market they would need training, diagnostic equipment, and access to a different range of replacement parts. Since the projected investment is beyond the means of individual repairers, the association applied for a bank loan. The application was refused on the grounds that the association had no legal standing to borrow. Officials then turned to the Government for help, but were again rebuffed. Undaunted, the association is continuing to look for ways to get the technology it needs to move into a higher-level market.

Several of the examples already cited have clear marketing dimensions. The following three cases complement these by illustrating how clustered firms can work together to tap new markets. The Kamukunji cluster is home to a group of 12 firms engaged in manufacturing wheelbarrows. Wheelbarrow-making started at Kamukunji in 1984 when artisans copied a wheelbarrow that they purchased from a Nairobi shop, and then modified the design to make it stronger and easier to produce (McCormick 1998). All 12 producers use the 1984 design to make the wheelbarrow in three different sizes. There is no job specialization among the wheelbarrow makers. Each firm makes the product from beginning to end. The workshops attempt to standardize parts for their own wheelbarrows, but there is no standardization across producers. Like other Kamukunji goods, the wheelbarrows have mostly been sold to individuals and traders who visit the site. This may be changing, however, because firms are beginning to join together to market their product, targeting supermarkets that have hardware departments. It remains to be seen whether the lack of standardization across producing firms will be an issue for the retail chains.

As suggested by the discussion of Ziwani's need for technological upgrading, the cluster is attempting to reach new markets (Kinyanjui 1998). Although firms reported repairing all types of vehicles, a casual look around the cluster suggests that heavy lorries and *matatus* predominate. Association officials recognize that the cluster has had a bad reputation. The neighbourhood around the cluster is known for harbouring thugs, and many Nairobians believe that *jua kali* mechanics, if left to themselves, would not only cut corners in repairing, but might actually leave the car in a worse condition than they found it. To counter such beliefs, the association is attempting to improve the cluster's image by strengthening general discipline within and around the site and by taking measures to control theft and the sale of stolen vehicle parts. The purpose of the action, according to association officials, is to make the cluster more attractive to potential customers.

The Western Cape clothing cluster has both horizontal and vertical marketing linkages. One of the ways firms at similar stages of the production process co-operate in marketing is by presenting joint clothing ranges (October 1996: 13–15). For example, manufacturers who produce complementary products; say one who makes shirts and another who specializes in jeans; will present retailers with a colour co-ordinated line drawn from both factories. Vertical co-operation between producers and traders is also present. According to October (1996: 15), agents for German importers are playing an important role in transferring information and design techniques, and in ensuring that quality standards are met.

Action for cluster development

What is striking about the descriptions of joint action in these seven clusters is the variety of both form and content. Co-operation among clustered firms is vertical and horizontal, bilateral and multilateral. Enterprises collaborate to obtain needed inputs, to carry out their production, and to market the final products. A closer look suggests that some types of collaboration may be more beneficial for cluster development than others.

Most of the collaboration in these clusters is horizontal between small firms. Bilateral collaboration includes the ubiquitous borrowing and lending of tools, the provision of specialized services, 'joint production', and the variety of subcontracting relationships. Only in CMT subcontracting do we see a large–small firm horizontal relationship. The most common multilateral horizontal collaboration is the association. Because five of the seven clusters include only small firms, most of these associations have small enterprises only. Even the Western Cape cluster, which has both large and small firms, associational activity tends to divide according to firm size. Kamukunji has another type of multilateral collaboration among small firms: the producers' group.

Small firm joint action can be very useful. The examples have documented some of its achievements. Nevertheless, it may not be sufficient to raise clusters to higher levels of development. A recent donor strategy document argues that in Kenya, one of the constraints to the development of micro-, small- and medium-scale enterprises has been that their existing linkages are predominantly backward, into agriculture and the rural economy, rather than forward to the modern, larger-scale private sector (British Aid to Small Enterprise 1998: 10). This position has been supported by at least one study that found that, in Kenya's tourism industry, enterprises that collaborate with large firms increased employment while those linking with small firms registered no change over the same period (Alila and McCormick 1997).

The examples also provide evidence of the positive benefits of vertical linkages. Collaboration between industrial fish processors and Uhanya's main trader enabled the fish cluster to survive a serious threat to its export markets. In the Western Cape, the link between agents and factories promises to bring the design and quality assistance that could enable firms to establish themselves in export markets.

The content of the observed linkages is as varied as the form. Supply-side joint action appears to be especially important in small-enterprise clusters, but is present in the more diverse fish and clothing clusters as well. The supply-side examples also illustrate the mixed results of joint action. Thika and Ziwani got the land they needed, but now see new problems requiring new responses. Kamukunji's effort at consolidated purchasing worked for a while, but then fell victim to forces with more power.

Production joint action is similarly varied. Two examples raise issues that need further follow-up. The joint production between Suame's engineering workshops and its vehicle repairers suggests another dimension to collaboration that could be critical for cluster development, at least in some sectors. Linking enterprises to leading firms with higher-level technology should raise the quality of final products and ultimately allow the entire cluster to prosper. Sometimes these leading firms are larger, and the technology-based linkage becomes identical with large–small firm linkages. As the Suame example shows, however, size differences between higher technology and lower technology firms may not be great, making it necessary to examine technology as a separate linkage dimension. A second issue that emerges from the discussion of production linkages is subcontracting. Subcontracting offers a number of benefits both to the main contractor and the subcontractor (McCormick and Atieno 1997). It can also result in loss of small-firm autonomy, especially in cases where the partner is a larger, stronger enterprise. Closer examination of the types of subcontracting found in these clusters suggests that the impacts of the different types of subcontracting may not be the same. The type of specialized subcontracting between firms of similar sizes that is characteristic of vehicle repair appears to be unambiguously positive for the partners and the clusters. The case seems less clear for capacity- or cost-reducing subcontracting.

Finally, firms in at least some of the clusters co-operate on marketing. This in itself is striking because African micro-enterprises are often accused of failing to market their products. Yet in both Ziwani and Kamukunji we see clear efforts to tap new markets. The Western Cape's practice of presenting joint clothing lines is of interest, not just for that cluster, but also as a strategy that might be applicable elsewhere.

Most of the examples of inter-firm collaboration reported here have taken place with little or no assistance from persons or organizations outside of the partners to the action. In some cases, government or donors prepared the way by assisting with the establishment of institutions. The Kenya Government, for example, mandated the formation of *jua kali* associations. Suame's engineering workshops originally obtained their technology with assistance from the Technology Consultancy Centre, a small-enterprise support organization within the cluster operated with donor funding. Such institutions provided mechanisms for action, but such action was the response of the firms themselves to a perceived need or problem.

Is there, then, a place for intervention? Or should clusters be left to themselves to act or not, as they see fit? The cases seem to suggest that, while the primary responsibility for joint action lies with the enterprises concerned, a boost from government, a donor, or another interested party could make a difference. This seems especially likely in cases where the cluster consists entirely of small enterprises. Interventions may be substantive or facilitative. They may offer direct inputs such as training, credit, technology transfer, or they may facilitate potentially beneficial linkages. Box 10.1 lists a few examples, mostly taken from the cases, of promising interventions.

The list is not exhaustive, nor will every intervention bear the desired fruit. Some, such as improving infrastructure, organizing trade fairs, or funding technology development, address well-known constraints to enterprise devel-

Box 10.1: Examples of interventions for cluster development

- Strengthening a cluster's physical and/or financial infrastructure
- Organizing local trade fairs
- Underwriting the development of local technology
- Disseminating information about potential subcontracting partners, providers of specialized services, new technologies, market opportunities
- Supporting the upgrading of the 'earning by doing' that is taking place spontaneously in small-enterprise clusters
- Facilitating exchange visits to other enterprises to enable entrepreneurs to see better technology, management practices, or marketing
- Facilitating contacts between small and larger firms, especially when the larger firm is not within the cluster
- Promoting association formation.

opment. The needed interventions can be costly, but they can be expected to produce benefits in terms of efficiency, increased sales, and technology upgrading. Some of the information-based services are clear responses to the lack of free-flowing information that characterizes the African business environment. They can be put in place fairly easily and should yield positive results. Other interventions need to be framed as experiments that allow for trial and error. The issue of 'learning by doing' is a case in point. Many small enterprises undertake both production and training. Most of the training involves a great deal of observation and practice, and very little formal instruction (Abuodha and King 1991). 'Learning by doing' happens, not only in the training, but also as producers work together and show each other what works and what does not (Kinyanjui 1998). The process is efficient and generally results in the quick transmission of very basic skills. The trouble is that, in the African context at least, learning by doing is less efficient for transmitting higher-level skills (Jones and Barr 1996). This suggests a need to complement the current spontaneous learning by doing and informal training with a theoretical component that will promote technological advancement. A fair amount of experimentation in different settings may be needed to find the mix of theory and practice that best suits different learners and subject areas.

In all cases, it is important to stress that an intervention is the result of another kind of linkage, a linkage between the cluster and an outside organization. Just as enterprise linkages thrive on good communication and mutuality of interests, so too do these links. Hammering out the details will take time and effort, but if the result is a stronger small-enterprise sector, the effort will surely have been worthwhile.

11 Trading agents and other producer services in African industrialization and globalization

POUL OVE PEDERSEN

The role of producer services in economic development

In the era of post-isms trade and services are ascribed increasing importance. Where both neo-classical and Marxist theory focused on production and saw trade and services as derived activities of secondary importance, consumption and the feed-back from trade and distribution are now seen as determinants of production. At the same time, vertical and horizontal specialization of production has led to increased inter-industry trade, while internationalization and globalizaation of the economy has increased the importance of trade over long distances. As a consequence, trading companies and other producer services have become increasingly important, because they help enterprises to improve their access to markets: output markets as well as input markets, financial markets, labour markets and markets for new technology.

Producer services are also becoming important in their own right. They make up a large and growing share of world trade and foreign direct investment, and an important part of the expanding global economic and urban networks (see e.g. Dicken 1994; Sassen 1994).

However, the role of trading agents and other producer services is double-edged. Because producer services play an important positive role in economic development by improving the access to markets and scarce resources, they are often able to control and monopolize the access to the same markets and scarce resources, if they are not held in check institutionally or organizationally. That is the reason why both colonial and post-colonial governments in Africa often nationalized wholesale trade and other producer services, and it is the reason why rent-seeking and monopolistic practices often centre on trade and producer services, which therefore have traditionally had a bad image in any developing countries.

In Africa, trading agents and producer services do not seem to have had the same catalytic effect on economic development as elsewhere; and the current debate on globalization tends to see the global economic networks as largely by-passing Africa. However, although the small African economies may not be important for the global networks, the networks are clearly important to the African economies. One need just look at the skyline of office towers coming up in the capital cities of even the poorest African countries to realize that producer services are also growing rapidly in Africa.

The hypothesis advanced in this chapter is that the wholesalers, trading agents and other producer services, and the way they are organized, are an integral part of the organizational and institutional setting in which production and distribution takes place, and that the fragmentation between the global economy, the 'modern' formal African economies and the traditional, more or less informal, small enterprise sectors is a result of what Ferrand (1997) calls organizational or institutional discontinuities.

These discontinuities developed during the import-substitution period when the national economy was protected against competition from the global, at the same time as the traditional economy was to a large extent denied access to state resources. However, the segmentation of the African economies did not mean that the segments were completely isolated from each other. On the contrary, all the time there have been businesspeople and politicians who have been able to benefit from the advantages of operating in more than one segment, while others have been denied that possibility.

The purpose of this chapter is to discuss the changing interface between the traditional, the modern and the global production and distribution systems. We shall look especially at the effect of globalization processes and structural adjustment policies on these interfaces, and the role that trading agents and other producer services play by bridging or widening the gap between the market segments.

The traditional exchange system

The traditional exchange system, corresponding to the small-scale informal sector, consists of three elements very similar to what North (1990) characterizes as the tribal organization, the *suq*, and the caravan, namely:

- the simple exchange between the producer of a good or service and the consumer of that good or service.

Information on market prices and qualities of the good will often be limited and skewed, but cheating and unfair deals will be held at bay because buyer and seller mostly belong to the same social group and the exchange is frequently repeated, so that unfair deals are likely to incur a large social cost. Except in periods of scarcity, when monopoly pricing becomes possible, bargaining will often be limited to the difference between what the seller could achieve at the formal market, and what the buyer would have to pay there;

- a concentration of traders in a market place or of small-scale producers in a cluster of enterprises often producing and selling the same or similar things.

Market exchange is also here a simple exchange between the producer and the consumer, but the advantage to the traders and producers in the cluster is that by concentrating they attract more customers. Market information in such markets and clusters will be larger because prices and qualities of goods can be compared. But exchanges are likely to be more impersonal, and the social retaliation on unfair deals much smaller, than in the simple exchange.

- Long-distance traders attempt to profit from spatial differences in prices and product availability.

But, due to lack of product standardization and trustable transport and money transfer systems, long-distance traders are forced to buy and sell in person or through a trusted agent and follow the goods between their origin and destination. Apart from limitations in capital, it is therefore very limited as to how many goods he can trade with, and the costs incurred are high. Due to the high costs and usually small amounts involved, it requires fairly large price differences to be profitable.

The modern exchange system

Most accounts of industrial development in Africa ascribe the stagnation and inefficiency of African industry to import-substitution policies which have led to involution of the manufacturing industries rather than evolution, and presently make their transformation to a global economy difficult.

A combination of over-valued currencies, unrealistically low interest rates and easily available donor support led to the introduction of complex, capital-intensive production technologies which could not be maintained, sustained or developed locally, and therefore could not be modified to a changing environment (Biggs et al. 1995; Mwamadzingo 1997). It also led to enterprises which were very dependent on imported inputs and therefore on state allocations of foreign currencies and other scarce resources.

The introduction of mass production technologies based on hierarchical management and work organization fitted well with both the hierarchical social structures inherited from the colonial period and the scarcity of skilled labour in the post-independence period. But it has resulted in the perpetuation of education and training policies which saw a need for improved training of managers, but little need for training at the shop-floor level. This has slowed down learning processes in the enterprises and is one of the major hindrances for transformation of the enterprises towards world-class technology (Kaplinsky 1995).

Industrial firms have tended to grow through both vertical and horizontal integration of activities. This has been a natural response to poor infrastructure and an environment that could not deliver (Trulsson 1997). It has resulted in industrial monoliths with few links and externalities and very little diffusion of new knowledge to the environment. It has also resulted in very inefficient use of scarce resources and low productivity, and has been a hindrance to the development of producer services for the smaller enterprises that could not afford to develop the services themselves.

Finally, lack of efficient infrastructure and distribution systems has often resulted in large mark-ups from the factory gate to the consumer, which has reduced the national market still further and often limited it to the larger towns. Lack of product standardization, quality control and trademarks have further increased the cost of distribution. Thus the inefficiency of the modern system of industrial production and distribution is a major reason for the survival and expansion of the traditional exchange system.

The global exchange system

The literature on the global exchange system has especially focused on the growth of four dimensions of the system:

- foreign direct investment (FDI)
- international trade
- international financial transactions
- inter-governmental organizations, international non-governmental organizations and donor organizations.

However, in the literature, Africa is often claimed to be increasingly marginalized in the process of globalization, because Africa receives only a very small and falling share of the world's FDI, and African trade makes up a very small and falling share of both the world's foreign trade and financial transactions (see e.g. Shafaeddin 1996).

This increasing marginalization is seen as a major problem for African development and some of the main purposes of the structural adjustment policies in Africa have been to increase African foreign trade in order to earn more foreign currencies, and to make Africa more attractive for FDI, which is now seen as the major source of new technology. However, measured relative to GDP, sub-Saharan Africa as a whole is not under-supplied with FDI in comparison with Asia and Latin America (McCormick and Pedersen 1997). At the same time, Africa receives about 10 times as much aid per GDP as Asia and Latin America, and one can question whether Africa has in fact the capacity to receive and benefit from more FDI. It requires a considerable technological, commercial and administrative capacity to receive and utilize new technology, and especially to adapt it to a changing environment different from that in which it was invented. In Africa such capacities are scarce. The purpose of much of the development aid has been to create such new capacities. However, to receive and benefit from aid is in itself a transfer process that requires capacities, and the recent literature on aid indicates that donors in Africa compete heavily among themselves for the limited capacities available, and may in fact exploit more capacity than they create and thus also compete with FDI for the scarce technological, commercial and administrative capacities (Pedersen 1997b).

This process of competition for scarce capacities results on the one hand in rising costs, or what economists call 'Dutch disease', and on the other hand in reduced national savings and investments because aid tends to substitute for national expenditures and investments rather than complement them (Paldam 1997).

The interface between the traditional and the modern exchange systems

Due to the monolithic characteristics of the enterprises in the modern exchange system, there are few process links between firms in the modern and the traditional exchange systems. Instead, they compete for market shares in the retail market. The balance between the traditional and the modern exchange systems, developed during the import-substitution era, depended to a large extent on the distribution of state resources and monopolies. With trade liberalization and privatization this is now slowly changing. Whether the traditional exchange system will be able to make in-roads in the modern exchange system depends on its ability to gain access to finance, skills and improved technology. Whether the modern exchange system will be able to gain in-roads in the traditional system depends on its ability to reduce the price of low-income consumer goods in both urban and rural areas.

The capital market

Almost all the investments in small enterprises in the traditional exchange system are based on the entrepreneur's own savings or, to a more limited extent, on loans from family or friends which do not bear interests and often have flexible return payment conditions. Loans from the formal banks and credit institutions are rare.

On the other hand, in most African countries the formal credit institutions also make very little effort to absorb savings from the low-income groups. The interest rate is often very low, and the minimum amount that can be deposited and drawn on savings accounts is high compared to the savings of most people. It is therefore often more attractive to invest small savings in a cow or a small business than to place them in a savings account. The liberalization of the financial systems in general has not changed this. In most countries, the new banks created have not been savings banks, but rather are based on foreign currency speculation.

Although there is undoubtedly a large need for capital to develop the small enterprises in the traditional economy, it is doubtful whether easier access to the formal capital market in itself would lead to dramatically increased borrowing. Most small entrepreneurs are, for good reason, afraid of borrowing at high interest rates and against security. They often operate in rural markets under conditions that are extremely unstable and unpredictable, and where, without any social security, personal risks in the form of illness, theft and fire are high, and may at any time prevent the entrepreneur from repaying his or her loan.

Therefore, the many credit schemes for micro-enterprises established by NGOs and donors could be a double-edged sword. For instance, von Bülow et al. (1995) show in an analysis of a credit scheme for women in Tanzania that although the scheme had a very high rate of return payment, and was therefore seen as a success by the donor, many of the women who had borrowed money were worse off after the loan because they had been forced to sell their cow or some other asset to repay the loan.

Skills and the learning system

The level of general education in the traditional exchange system has increased rapidly in the last 10 to 20 years. A rapidly increasing proportion of the micro-entrepreneurs have secondary education or higher. This is due partly to the general increase in the level of education since independence, and partly to redundancies and voluntary exit from the formal economy.

How this is changing the structure of enterprises in the informal sector is not clear, but the effect may have been limited because relevant technical and commercial skills have not increased at the same speed. Although many of those who come from the formal sector have vocational skills, they are often less relevant in the micro-enterprise. Informal apprenticeship training is therefore still the most common way of achieving skills. Apprenticeship training is a good, and societally cheap, way of learning the ways of a trade, but if it stands alone it cannot bring the apprentice to a higher level of training than the master and therefore does not lead to innovation and change. Therefore, apprenticeship training should be combined with vocational schooling (Sverrisson 1997). However, until recently most vocational schools have catered primarily for the formal sector, and distanced themselves from the micro-enterprises.

A major problem for development of the traditional exchange system is that apprenticeship training for the commercial sector is little developed or non-existent. In many African countries it often appears to have been assumed that trade and commerce do not require qualifications.

The distribution system

Many commodities produced by modern industry are, especially in the rural areas, distributed by traders in the traditional exchange system, while the modern retail trade plays a larger role in the urban areas. This is true, not least in Zimbabwe where large retail chains before independence in 1980 distributed a large proportion of consumer goods, especially clothing and hardware, in the urban areas. Prompted by the government, a number of the retail chains decided in the late 1980s to extend their network of stores to the larger district service centres in the communal areas. As the chains operate with fixed national prices, this led to a reduction in the price differences between rural and urban areas. As a result, trade in the larger district service centres increased rapidly, because people who used to buy their consumer goods in Harare or other large towns now bought them locally.

The arrival of the chain stores meant that most of the local traders, who used to operate as general dealers, were reduced to grocery stores, because they could no longer sell consumer goods at competitive prices. Others attempted to specialize in niches in the consumer goods market that were not served by the chain stores. However, although the chains conquered a very large share of the clothing and hardware markets, and forced the local traders to restructure, the total market expanded so much that the market left to the local traders expanded as well.

African governments have also attempted to spread modern industry to the smaller towns and rural areas through regional industrial development policies and SME programmes. The small industrial enterprises that Pedersen (1997b) describes in Gutu district service centre in Zimbabwe, and which Trulsson (1997) found in Northwestern Tanzania, are examples of such enterprises created in the formal sector by highly educated entrepreneurs with access to credit and aspirations to be part of the formal sector. However, forced by circumstances, many of them appear to retreat to the ways of the traditional local exchange system.

Thus in Zimbabwe, the dominance of the retail chains, which have their own internal wholesale functions, means that the market left for specialized clothing wholesalers has been limited, and open clothing wholesale is therefore little developed. The small clothing industries in Gutu, which were too small to serve the needs of the large chains, therefore had limited access to the market, and were forced to open their own retail stores, or concentrate on market niches, such as work clothes for the enterprise market, where they could obtain small wholesale orders.

The traditional exchange system, which is rural in origin, has also made in-roads into the modern exchange system in the form of the urban informal sector. Thus the GEMINI surveys show that about a third of all the micro-enterprises in Kenya (Daniels et al. 1995), and more than a quarter in Zimbabwe, are urban (Daniels 1994). The urban informal sector is, like the rural, geared primarily towards the local market, but it has often retained strong social links to the rural areas, and especially the larger enterprises in the traditional exchange system often have long-distance trading links to the rural areas. In a study of small metal, furniture and clothing producers in Nairobi, Kinyanjui (1997) found that 6 per cent of the enterprises distributed their products to the rural areas; and in rural and small-town shops in Zimbabwe, Pedersen (1997a) found consumer goods for sale which, through family relations, had been supplied from small workshops in the larger towns.

The interface between the global and the modern exchange systems

The literature on the global exchange system has especially focused on the transnational corporations and the role of their foreign direct investments (FDI) in technology transfer and the changing division of labour in the main international commodity chains (see e.g. Humphrey 1995).

A commodity chain is a set of activities involved in the production and commercialization of a particular commodity. These activities form a series of often hierarchically organized networks concerned with raw materials supply, production, export and marketing. Gereffi (1994) distinguishes between producer-driven and buyer-driven production chains:

> In producer-driven commodity chains large transnational manufacturers play the central role in coordinating production networks including their backward and forward linkages. This is characteristic of capital- and technology-intensive industries such as automobiles, aircrafts, computers, semiconductors and heavy machinery. In buyer-driven commodity chains, on the other hand, large retailers, brand-named marketers, and trading companies play the pivotal role in setting up decentralized production networks. This pattern of trade led industrialization is common in more labour-intensive consumer goods industries such as garment, footwear, toys, housewares and consumer electronics. (Gereffi 1994: 17)

Under the impact of the new Japanese management techniques, the production networks in both producer- and buyer-driven commodity chains have tended to internationalize in the search for lower production costs. However, whereas the buyer-driven chains have been able to spread over most of the globe in search of cheap labour, the producer-driven chains have been more dependent on high-technology suppliers and good infrastructure and have therefore not spread much beyond the industrialized countries within the same world region. It is therefore especially the decentralization of the buyer-driven commodity chains which has benefited developing countries; but in Africa they play only a limited role.

The FDI which has accrued to Africa has been in raw materials production and in marketing in the form of trading agents and services promoting imports of industrial goods. The last is due not least to a rapid internationalization of many small and medium-sized enterprises in both industrialized and industrializing countries, and often supported by donor funds and export promotion schemes in the industrialized countries.

However, the old multinational firms play a larger role in African manufacturing industries than the current level of FDI indicates because in most African countries multinationals own a large share of the manufacturing industries established during the import-substitution era. These branch plants were originally established in order to gain access to the closed national markets. Although they have usually been operated more efficiently than locally owned industries, they have generally not been competitive in international markets and are now rapidly being restructured, but often on the basis of local capital. As a result of trade liberalization they tend to concentrate their production in fewer countries, which will then supply the others. In East Africa, Kenya appears to benefit from this concentration of multinationals (McCormick and Pedersen 1997). A similar process is probably ongoing in the Asian-owned enterprises in Kenya, many of which are owned by entrepreneurs with close family and social ties to the other East African countries. As a result of this industrial concentration, Kenya's export to the rest of Africa (and especially East Africa) has increased from 9 per cent of Kenya's total exports in the mid-1980s to more than 40 per cent in the mid-1990s. However, this pattern is not typical, as only 10 per cent of Africa's foreign trade takes place between the African countries, and almost half of this trade relates to South Africa.

Also, South African investments are provoking African industries to restructure. Thus South African Breweries' recent takeover of Tanzanian Breweries and the establishment of a new plant in Kenya has forced Kenyan Breweries into a collaboration with Guinness and to close its plant in Mombasa and open a new one in Arusha, in order to defend the East African market which until now it has dominated.

South African investments are also likely to have an important impact on the East African distribution system. In Southern Africa, South African retail and wholesale chains today play an important role in the consumer goods distribution, and it appears likely that they will extend their network of stores to other African countries. Thus a South African chain of consumer goods wholesalers presently contemplates setting up three large wholesale stores in Uganda to serve local retailers. This may rapidly change the structure of both formal and informal retail and wholesale trade, as the expansion of retail chains has done in Zimbabwe.

The interface between the global and the traditional exchange systems

The purpose of buyer-driven decentralization of production for the buyer is to reduce costs. However, at the same time the trading agents often play an important role not only in securing a market for the produce of developing countries but also in providing a feed-back of market information, product design and production technology which is necessary for the transformation of local production. In all the small enterprise clusters in developing countries discussed in the literature during recent years, external trading agents appear to have played an important role as catalysts for change (see e.g. Nadvi and Schmitz 1994). It is therefore problematic that trading agents apparently have not been able to play that catalytic role in Africa.

Recent literature on small enterprise clusters has focused on what Schmitz (1995) calls the turning points of development where growth takes off and transformation starts. A review of studies of relatively successful small enterprise clusters in Africa (McCormick 1997) indicates that the first turning point of a cluster often coincides with some windfall gain which permits the cluster to supply the market at competitive prices and therefore leads to increased production and sales. That windfall gain can, for instance, be import restrictions, collapse of the formal sector enterprises, low fuel costs which lower the cost of long-distance trade, or the discovery of the cluster by an external trading agent.

However, such a windfall gain does not last for ever. After some time, other clusters or large enterprises are likely to become cheaper, and traders will leave again unless the cluster has been able to utilize the windfall gain to increase its productivity, improve its products, diversify production, and make itself less dependent on external traders. This is the second turning point. The successful clusters described in the literature were all able to make the transformation out of the crisis and into a new phase. None of the clusters in sub-Saharan Africa reviewed by McCormick have so far been able to make the transformation from the traditional to the modern exchange system.

In some enterprises technological change does take place in the form of acquisition of new machinery, but because the market is unstable this leads to neither reorganization of production within the enterprise nor to vertical specialization between enterprises (Sverisson 1997). Lack of product standardization and quality control is a major hindrance here. Many clusters operating in the traditional exchange system, therefore, hardly develop at all.

After the first turning point, growth of the African clusters is due mostly to 'passive' trade organized by external traders, while active local trading strategies are not pursued. This lead to what Knorringa (1997) calls the *satellite trajectory* of development, which is seldom sustainable in the long-run.

Take-off from the crisis of the second turning point of a small enterprise cluster would require either collaboration and joint action by the enterprises, or that one or a few of the enterprises are resourceful enough to grow and themselves organize the external trade and take the lead in the process of technological change. In the first case the cluster would develop along what Knorringa calls the *Italianate trajectory*, after the Italian prototype industrial district based on small and medium-sized enterprises; in the second case it would develop along a *hub-and-spoke trajectory*, based on a more hierarchical enterprise structure.

None of these trajectories, however, appear to be stable in the long run and most of the clusters studied over long periods of time have shifted trajectory in the course of their development. The Italianate trajectory is seen by most authors as the most beneficial for development, but also the most difficult to achieve and sustain, If it is not permanently and actively pursued by the small enterprises, it tends to shift into either a hub-and-spoke or a satellite trajectory.

In some of the African clusters reviewed by McCormick (1997), some of the larger enterprises have apparently been able to overcome the crisis successfully, but they have not been able to extend their success to other enterprises in the cluster and take the lead in a process of technological change, but rather, the large enterprises attempt to integrate vertically and horizontally in order to free themselves from dependency on the undependable environment.

Collaboration in the form of small-enterprise organizations and capacity subcontracting do take place in many African clusters, but there are few examples of joint action in the form of product development, standardization, quality control, labour training or a common sales organization which could lead to technological upgrading and extended markets.

Trust, producer services and infrastructure in the process of structural change in a context of globalization

The picture we have painted above of the African production system is one where the large enterprises, and also those small ones that are growing, integrate as many functions as possible (input supplies, services and even infrastructure) in their own organization in order to free themselves from an undependable environment. The result is that their productivity remains low, and they therefore are unable to link up with the global economy. At the same time, the small enterprises are kept back in the traditional exchange system, unable to collaborate on stategies to extend their markets and upgrade their technology.

To change this process of involution the large enterprises must open up and the small must collaborate with each other and with the large enterprises. There seems to be increasing agreement that one of the main reasons why inter-firm collaboration and vertical specialization do not take place is the high transaction costs due to lack of trust and poor infrastructure.

In the traditional exchange system, interaction is based on individual trust, because the formal legal system does not work or is out of reach for the small business person. Individual trust can either be *ascribed* or *earned* (Humphrey and Schmitz 1996). Ascribed trust is trust among family or clan members. In many African societies, trust in family members is very important. However, it is also problematic, because family members often feel they are entitled to a share of the business person's profit and therefore cannot always be trusted to return borrowed resources. Many business people therefore do not want to employ family members in their enterprise, but use much time and effort to develop and test earned trust in their employees and collaborators (Sørensen 1997).

However, in unstable, risky environments without social security, insurance and the possibility of legal regress, individual trust has its limitations. It does not help the businessman that his business partner is honest, if there is a large probability that he will be hit by illness, theft, a bad harvest, or some other incident that will make it impossible for him to satisfy his obligations. There are therefore clear limitations to social networks of equals. Such networks may be a safeguard against individual accidents but not against drought or general economic crises which hit everybody at the same time (Fafchamps 1992). In the absence of state social security or large-scale insurance schemes the only alternative is to rely on a rich patron to support you through the crises. Hierarchical patron–client relations therefore play a large role in developing societies, in spite of their high costs.

Thus, in the unstable economic environment of low-income countries, businessmen tend to rely on what Granovetter (1985) calls the *strong ties* based on ascribed or earned trust developed over long periods of time. However, the development of dynamic enterprise structures, where entrepreneurs search continuously for new market opportunities and shifting alliances, to a large extent depends on what Granovetter calls the *weak ties*. Such weak ties develop only where there is a basis for extended or systemic trust guaranteed by the state, large organizations or large collectives. They require effective infrastructures and a legal system which is enforced by and accessible to both small and large enterprises.

Specialized trading agents and producer services are important because they serve as brokers of weak ties. Without systemic trust, however, trading agents and producer services also have difficulties bridging the gaps between the small, the large and the multinational enterprises. As a result they have developed into a three-tier system, where multinational service firms serve the multinationals, and the local private-sector services address the needs of the large national enterprises, while the donors and the NGOs serve the SMER's, if they are served at all. This may widen the gaps rather than close them.

12 MSE associations and enterprise promotion in Africa

HANS CHRISTIAAN HAAN

Introduction

In Africa, as elsewhere, the continued and at times worsening (un)employment crisis, has led policy makers to bank on the *micro- and small enterprises sector* (MSEs) to absorb huge numbers of redeployed civil servants and laid-off workers from the industrial sector, as well as providing jobs for the backlog of unemployed and new entrants to the labour market. In Kenya, for instance, over half a million jobs need to created every year, and the government is banking on the *jua kali* sector to create some 128 000 workers per annum. Similar expectations with regard to the MSE sector are found in other African countries.

A positive aspect of this is that the appreciation of the MSE sector has drastically changed. From the 'informal sector' denoting semi-legal activities of the working poor, which was not recognized and often not even tolerated by national and local governments, when the sector was first discussed in the early 1970s (ILO 1972), it has been upgraded to become the 'micro- and small *enterprise* sector'. In the formulation of economic policies the needs of small producers are more and more (even if often still insufficiently) taken into consideration, and almost all countries have initiated programmes to support them.

It is not certain, however, if the fate of those working in the MSE sector has improved much in the past 25 years. The sector is still facing major challenges. MSEs are characterized by the limited managerial and entrepreneurial competence of the owners of the firms, limited technical skills of the workers, difficulties in obtaining raw materials, limited access to credit and finance, and inappropriate laws and regulations. In recent years, the opening up of national markets under IMF and World Bank policies mean that MSEs are faced with even stiffer competition from imported industrial goods, which in most developing countries carry a premium.

For the MSE sector, it is thus imperative to increase its productivity (i.e. to produce more efficiently to reduce the costs of materials, labour, fuel/electricity, transport), and to enhance the quality of its products, together with making its product designs more attractive. All this requires the infusion of new technologies into the MSE sector, and *technological development should therefore be at the heart of the debate on the role of the MSE sector*. MSE technologies should be 'improved-but-still-appropriate', which means that care needs to be taken that the improved technology to be introduced is compatible with both 'internal' and 'external' conditions. The former concern the restrictions posed by the available skills of the workforce, workshop layout and infrastructure (e.g. power supply), enterprise organization and management capacity, and, most importantly, (access to) capital; the latter refer to market opportunities that follow from the availability of inputs (raw materials and relevant equipment-plus-spare parts), as well as conditions on product markets (e.g. consumer preferences, purchasing power and relative prices): 'appropriate technologies' should thus also lead to 'appropriate products' (Zoomers 1995).

At present most MSEs are characterized by a limited technological capacity: the low level of capital resources available tends to lead to the a small range of tools and equipment, often second-hand or even self-constructed; the variety of items produced is low and the design and the quality is often rather modest; and there is a continuous lack of technological information on products, equipment and production processes. In fact, it can be argued that low capital/labour ratios and a corresponding partial use of technological progress, is a fundamental characteristic of 'informal' enterprises (Haan 1989). This is not to say that the micro- and small producers are technologically stagnating. An ILO study concludes that many small producers show technological progress, because they are actively engaged (in Asia) in adapting industrial equipment for their own use, and (in Africa) self-constructing tools and equipment (Maldonado and Sethuraman 1992: 225). But MSEs were found to face various constraints to their technological development, for instance in the form of locational factors, lack of access to credit, relative prices of labour and capital, shortage of raw materials and equipment, which are imposed by market inefficiency, especially in technology and capital.

A role for informal sector associations

Many micro- and small enterprises are not aware of, or fail to tap into, opportunities to obtain new technologies on their own (e.g. because they cannot afford them); nor do they have resources to participate in R&D programmes that would provide them with new technologies or link them with suitable technology partners (cf. Kyerematen 1993: 7). It has been suggested that associations of MSEs (or ISAs for 'informal sector associations') could play a distinct role in this (Haan 1995). In fact, in recent years a number of donors (e.g. World Bank, ILO, UN-ECA, GTZ, SDC, KAF and FES)[1] have initiated a number of programmes to channel support to the MSE sector in Africa through such organizations.

---

[1] International Labour Office; United Nations Economic Commission for Africa; German Agency for Technical Cooperation; Swiss Agency for Development and Cooperation; Konrad Adenauer Foundation; Friedrich Ebert Stiftung.

The Farm Implements and Tools (FIT) Programme also actively investigated the role that groupings of small metal workers and food-processors could assume in fostering the development of the MSE sector. In reporting on these efforts, this chapter aims to contribute to a growing body of literature on MSE associations (e.g. Levitsky 1992 and 1994; Hossenmamode 1993; Gibson and Havers 1994). A primary conclusion with regard to the existing literature is that in spite of increased attention to MSE associations, not much is known about the origin and actual functioning of ISAs in Africa and the services they provide to their members. A considerable number of the programmes to channel support to the MSE sector through small producers' associations would appear to have been less successful, possibly because donors lack adequate information on the potential of ISAs, while at the same time they, together with national governments, tend to overestimate the role ISAs can play and, in particular, underestimate the time and effort required to achieve results.

Interest in working with informal sector associations led the FIT Programme to commission a number of studies to investigate the actual role and functioning of ISAs in Ghana and Kenya (see Aryetee and Appiah 1995; Njagi 1994; Livingstone 1996; and Mathuva 1996). The extensive field research was meant to get better insights in the background, history and internal dynamics of both semi-formalized and informal groups of small producers, in rural as well as urban areas. The studies noted a number of similarities with regard to ISAs in Ghana and Kenya, while a number of interesting differences were also found. The most important ones are summarized below.

General characteristics

Both in Ghana and Kenya, informal sector associations seem to be mainly an urban phenomenon (Mathuva 1996). It is obvious that rural MSEs face more handicaps to form groupings, such as the fact that they are more spread out. In Ghana there are, however, a large number of small food-processing ISAs, especially of women engaged in *gari* processing, palm oil processing, etc., while in Kenya there are large numbers of women's self-help groups involved in food-processing activities.

While many of the associations in Ghana are sectoral-based, in Kenya 95 per cent of the associations are area-based and are made up of MSEs engaged in different economic activities (Mathuva 1996: 12). Membership of the MSE groups in Kenya would therefore appear to be generally larger, even though in Ghana there are a number of ISAs, such as the National Association of Garages, which have thousands of members. The studies seem to confirm the notion that the smaller MSE groupings tend to have a more active membership.

The MSE groups in Ghana and Kenya have surprisingly similar structures:

chairman, secretary, treasurer, and committee members without portfolio, even though in Kenya they would appear to be somewhat more formal with their intra-ISA relations. It was observed in Kenya that although most MSE groups hold regular elections (two-thirds once every year), the top officials rarely change.

All the studies point out that the ISAs studied have a very weak financial base: incomes from entry and membership fees are low. It would seem that in Kenya a considerable number of members do pay the US$0.50–1.00 monthly contribution more or less regularly, while 'recognized' ISAs in Ghana appear to rely on the commission received for the collection of government taxes (see below), while some get sponsorship, for instance the Association of Wood Workers which is sponsored by the National Timber Export Board.

Origin and history

One of the aspects at which the FIT studies on ISAs were especially directed, concerns the questions: where do small producers' associations come from, how do they get started, how do they grow, why and when are they formalized (or not)? Although on the whole the studies had considerable difficulty in answering these questions, some working conclusions can be drawn.

The main conclusion is that the majority of the ISAs studied in Ghana and Kenya give the impression that they were formed in response to (actual or perceived) opportunities for external assistance. In both countries government agencies and, to a lesser degree, international donors, have been instrumental in the formation of ISAs by encouraging small producers to band together by holding out promises of various types of assistance that would be channelled through MSE associations. In Ghana, the suggestion for small producers (both in and outside agriculture) to group themselves goes back to the early years after independence, and is reflected in the enormous number of registered (but largely inactive?) groupings of small farmers, producers and traders: over 3000 registered associations and 11 000 societies (with a total membership of one million). More recently, the government was instrumental in creating the Council of Indigenous Business Associations (CIBA), which has a political background as it was enacted on the part of the government to strengthen its political base in populous small business sectors. Also, the National Board for Small Scale Industries, the Ghanaian government agency to promote the MSE sector, is actively involved in promoting the cause of ISAs.

In Kenya the encouragement of the government for *jua kali* producers to form associations, which started in the mid-1980s, was possibly even stronger. Initially the government perceived *jua kali* associations mainly as a channel to allocate plots to small producers, and it was therefore interested to stimulate geographical or site associations. As such, ISAs tend to have a large membership; the number of registered MSE associations is in Kenya much lower. The top-down character of many of the government interventions, it has been suggested, provides an immediate explanation for the massive failure of the resulting MSE groupings (Mathuva 1996: 11). While on the whole to be applauded, the active role of the government has led to a distinct politicization of the ISAs, especially in Kenya.

Furthermore, in general, the propelling role of external assistance would appear to have a negative effect on MSE associations (Aryetee and Appiah 1995: 33):

> in the case of associations 'created by' external agencies . . . . there is the high likelihood that they will last as long as externally-supported projects last. If they hang on any longer than that, they are likely to be a dormant association.

According to Aryetee, such ISAs are characterized by a cyclic existence:
1–3 'formative years' with little real activity as the ISA is planning its approach to potential donors;
3–5 years of intense activity during the implementation of an externally supported project;
2–3 years of reduced activity as the project winds up and the members reassess future activities.

Since additional funding is unlikely, most of the ISAs wind up their activities within three years after the end of their projects or simply maintain an 'association' in name only, with little activity.

The studies did not come up with a clear answer as to why certain MSE groupings register, while others do not. Again, it might be that the formalization process is closely linked with the prospects of external assistance, which provides a compelling reason to operate a bank account (Aryetee and Appiah 1995: 6). The studies confirm the notion that smaller and more homogenous ISAs are more likely to have an active membership (Njagi 1994: 29; Aryetee and Appiah 1995: 33).

ISA services to their members

In Africa, associations of small producers and traders have a long history, with some dating back to the 1970s, when many farmers' co-operatives were also formed. However, the majority of present MSE associations emerged in the 1980s. In both Kenya and Ghana, small producers associations would appear to follow closely from the tradition of mutual aid, known in Kenya as *Harambee* and in Ghana as *nnoboa* (farmers pooling their resources to work on each other's land) and *susu* (informal savings groups). In fact, the research carried out on behalf of FIT indicates that the core activities of many associations are welfare and mutual insurance activities:

> [In Ghana] associations may have their own specific goals, but the main purpose they appear to serve is for mutual aid; . . . the majority of the groups, both registered cooperatives and informal groups, are unable to provide any tangible services to their members, . . . most associations exist only for members to . . . provide a collective insurance, assisting each other in times of need or bereavement. (Gyeke and Chinbuah, quoted in Livingstone 1996: 8)

> [In Kenya] 92% of them [i.e. the associations studied] are active in welfare and social activities, such as fundraising for burials, and social objectives: dowry and weddings, communal farming (Mathuva 1996: viii).

Most of the MSE associations in FIT studies on Ghana and Kenya were found to be too weak to provide any tangible services. Lobbying and advocacy would appear to be the main activity of the MSE groups in Ghana and Kenya after the welfare and mutual insurance activities. In Kenya this lobbying centres on securing title deeds for workshop sites, and it has been suggested that associations are indeed formed for the sole purpose of lobbying for the acquisition of workshop sites and sheds (cf. Njagi 1994: 20). In Ghana the larger associations play a curious role: they collect taxes from their members on behalf of the Internal Revenue Service of the government (for which they receive a commission of 1 per cent of the total amount collected).

Only a few examples of actual business support services provided by ISAs were found: small internal credit schemes; purchase of production inputs for the members; organization of marketing events; and provision of secretarial services (e.g. typing of letters); and even legal support.

Examples of fit pilot activities involving MSE associations

The FIT Programme aims to develop innovative mechanisms to support the MSE sector, and especially metal-working and food-processing. Such MSE support mechanisms should be demand-driven, low cost, and potentially self-sustainable (i.e. offer opportunities for increasing cost-recovery). FIT adopted an action-research approach, in which research studies were first carried out to identify problems, after which the solutions that were elaborated were tested in pilot activities. Part of the FIT pilot activities that were undertaken involved informal sector associations. They sought to assist MSEs in the areas of product differentiation, information and networking, and marketing. FIT also carried out some more general activities to strengthen ISAs.

Product differentiation

Even though most micro-producers will indicate that lack of finance is their main constraint, there are strong indications that for many of them a lack of (effective) demand for their goods and services is the prime obstacle to their growth and development. With the opening of markets for imports in developing countries, they will become more and more squeezed between low (and in some countries even declining) purchasing power of their clients and increased competition from industrial goods, especially from liberalized imports.

This demand problem is frequently compounded by a lack of market sensitivity on the part of the small producers themselves, a large number of whom appear to operate within a limited horizon, largely determined by their production conditions, while lacking a 'feel' for the market. Market research is normally not considered an important area, in part because small producers are fully occupied in the production process and are often hesitant to leave their workshop (except to search for raw materials) or feel that they already have a secured market, i.e. among family, friends, and members of their social group. As a result, micro-entrepreneurs often give the impression that they 'sit and wait for customers', while it is of vital importance for small producers to get feedback on the quality of their products, and to be keenly aware of the changing consumer tastes and interesting market niches. Product differentiation is badly needed to escape from the competition from other MSEs in the same subsector, who tend to produce identical items.

Rapid market appraisal

The FIT Programme pilot-tested a 'rapid market appraisal' (RMA) which aims to bring MSEs into closer and more frequent contact with the users of their products instead of relying on middlemen, particularly with the objective of product diversification in the informal sector. Many of the small producers tend to be mainly reactive, waiting for customers to come, and imitating goods and services available from a large number of other firms. RMA concerns a training programme in which micro-entrepreneurs are shown the importance of a more outward-looking market orientation and are given guidelines on how to approach potential clients and assess market opportunities to produce improved or new items (see Burger and Haan 1996). RMA can be applied to any group of small producers, but is also an interesting instrument to strengthen MSE associations, or as an input to capacity-building for MSE support organizations.

Impact evaluations carried out to study the results of the RMA training found small producers unanimously positive about the course. They seem particularly enthusiastic about the relative ease with which they have learned to gather relevant market information for themselves. In Ghana, almost half of the participants reported that the training course had made them more aware of the need to advertise their products and that they had started to produce new items. In Kenya the evaluation showed that, as a result of the training, MSEs had adopted new marketing strategies and accessed more customers, had improved customer relations, were making new products, and had actually increased sales volume.

The RMA courses were also found to be an interesting instrument to strengthen MSE associations. Both the leaders of ASSI in Tamale (Ghana) and the Kamukunji association in Nairobi (Kenya) were of the opinion that the training has contributed to the strengthening of their associations. Very interestingly, the members of the Kamukunji Metal Workers Association, who had not participated in the training, requested the board to organize a repeat course; this took place without further involvement of the FIT Programme.

Information and networking

It is gradually becoming realized that a lack of reliable and pertinent information is possibly one of the most the important problems faced by MSEs. Research shows that they tend to rely for their information on family, friends and, to a lesser extent, on suppliers and colleagues (see e.g. ILO/TOOL 1994).

Exchange visits

An interesting and apparently very cost-effective modality to improve access to information for MSEs, is formed by so-called enterprise 'exchange' visits. This refers to an organized way in which small producers pay a visit to preselected peers to exchange information on technologies and equipment in use, suppliers of equipment and materials, market prices, marketing channels, etc. The visits take place during the MSE workshops, which provide a hands-on context for discussions on various topics and the direct exchange of experiences. In others, this support mechanism relies on the internal resources of the MSE sector in fostering technological progress.

Enterprise exchange visits can be organized on an individual basis, but it has been found more (cost) effective to form groups of MSEs, e.g. of 5–10 small producers, on a sectoral basis. FIT has gained interesting experiences in this area in both East and West Africa involving ISAs and other formal and informal groupings of metal workers and food processors. 'Enterprise visits' do not need to be limited to peer visits. FIT also organized 'host visits' for MSEs to visit medium and large enterprises.

Evaluations of the FIT enterprise exchange visits (see e.g. Craig and Oneko 1994; Hileman 1995; Afenyadu 1996a and b) clearly indicate the positive effects that these visits had on the participating MSEs. The studies indicate that the benefits were mainly related to the areas of technology, management and marketing. The exchange visits clearly contributed to the introduction of new products, transfer of production techniques, purchase and repair of relevant equipment, improved group dynamics and (collective) enterprise management, new ideas on marketing, and generally an increased self-confidence among (especially the female) small producers. A major element in the enterprise exchange visits was found to be the opportunity for MSEs to extend their business networks: new contacts were established with peer producers (who are apparently producing under similar arduous conditions), and also with equipment suppliers and repairers and various MSE support organizations. MSEs were found to benefit greatly from such initial networking on their behalf.

Exchange visits are a prime example of a low-cost MSE support mechanism, which at the same time offers good potential for cost-recovery through contributions from the participants. During the pilot activities, the small producers were found to be willing to pay for all the operational costs (including: transport, food and accommodation in the case of larger exchange visits). A most interesting experiment is about to be undertaken through FIT Uganda, in which a market-based organization, Business Travel, will organize exchange visits on a regular basis, linked to visits to trade fairs and other events that have relevance for small producers. It is expected that by offering such 'packages' a margin can be made over the cost of such visits to cover the operational cost of the agency.

Marketing

An area in which MSEs can possibly benefit most from forming an informal group or more formal association, lies (together with the purchase of their production inputs) in the marketing of their (semi-) finished products. The demand side is overlooked as a determining factor for MSE development. In fact, it has been found that the technological development of the MSE sector is in the end largely dependent on external demand conditions:

> the capability of microenterprises to adapt their technology depends less on any ability to innovate that the individual entrepreneur may possess than on opportunities and constraints in the local market, which act as a lever on both supply and demand: an increase in final demand offers informal sector enterprises an incentive to acquire better equipment and adopt more productive methods. (Maldonado and Sethuraman 1992: 225)

There are various ways in which ISAs can set up marketing services for their MSE members, including joint transport of finished products to sales outlets; dissemination of market information; establishing initial contacts with traders and commercial firms; quality control; and the organization of showrooms and fairs to exhibit finished products.

MSE shows

Small producers can benefit enormously from exposure to (new) markets. For this purpose, in Kenya every year a *Jua Kali* Show is organized to enable small producers to exhibit their products for a national audience, while permitting the participants to establish contacts and get acquainted with other technologies and products. A study shows that the participants have enjoyed considerable benefits from participating in the show (see Esbin 1994). Associations could support informal sector firms to participate in such events and even, on a smaller scale, mount their own shows. Already in Kenya, as in other countries, especially in Latin America, groups of MSEs, at times stimulated and assisted by local MSE consultants, already have experience of the organization of such MSE shows.

FIT has sponsored metal workers to participate in regional agricultural shows and organized 'mini fairs' in rural district towns. On the basis of these experiences, a manual was prepared which can assist informal sector associations to organize their own trade show for members to expose their products (Nzioka 1994).

Support to MSE associations

The FIT Programme has also in other ways worked together with informal sector associations in the countries in which it is working. The overall conclusion from these activities is that it is often difficult to work with ISAs. Representing international donor funding, it was hard for FIT to escape the fate of becoming the driving force of activities which would obviously be unsustainable in the long run. When trying to determine in a participatory manner the services that the ISA would initiate, the (members of the) association would eye first of all some kind of credit programme, and if that turned out not to be possible, at least some scheme to obtain equipment. In a similar way the board members would inquire about possibilities for the association to receive funding for an office (or at least a photocopier).

Interest in setting up business services for which the members would need to pay was found to be rather low. Moreover, there was very little imagination on what needed to be done and how such goals could be achieved. Board and ordinary members would seem to be trapped in a vicious circle in which the lack of funds means that no services can be initiated, and the lack of activities means that very little is invested in the ISA in terms of fees and time. More innovative ideas, such as publishing a catalogue with the names and locations and products of the members, were not embraced.

A notable exception was the Glass Jar Users Association (GJUA), which was formed in Ghana almost as a by-product of FIT activities to assist small food processors in obtaining packaging materials. The main role that was played by the external organization (i.e. FIT) was really to bring in its networking capacity which, together with the felt needs and the commitment of the MSEs to find a solution, provided the momentum which in the end led to the formation of the Glass Jar Users Association. The main reasons for the emergence of GJUA as a well-functioning association would seem to be (see Kordylas 1997):

- the acute need for small processors to solve a common problem (i.e. the inadequate supply of glass jars)
- the significant advantages and economic benefits of working together to

solve this problem and the relatively simple solution (i.e. collective ordering of glass jars to be imported by container)

- the higher than average level of education and the motivation of some of the members (who were elected to the board).

Some conclusions

Groupings of small producers are a common phenomenon in Ghana and Kenya, both within and outside agriculture. Some of them, like agricultural co-operatives, date back to the colonial times or the 1970s, when the government actively promoted groupings of small producers. Others are of more recent origin, again often stimulated by government agencies. From the research that was carried out within the framework of the FIT Programme, and the experiences with the pilot activities in which informal sector associations were involved, a number of conclusions can be drawn.

A first conclusion is that more in-depth research is needed, especially with regard to some fundamental questions concerning the origin, growth, formalization process and functioning of associations of small producers which have still not been exhaustively answered. It would be particularly interesting to have more information on small, non-formalized MSE groupings, and also self-help and other groupings in the rural areas. Even though all the researchers contracted by FIT were requested to focus specifically on genuine bottom-up associations and pay particular attention to informal groups, most of the associations profiled were rather urban and assistance-driven, and the impression remains that there may be other forms of collaboration in existence between small producers.

Second, from the research it would appear that in Ghana and Kenya solid and well-functioning associations are few and far between. Most of them remain small and lead an erratic existence with long periods in which they are dormant. Upsurges in activity seem often to be related to (perceived) prospects for external assistance. In the words of the conclusion of one of the FIT studies on associations in Ghana:

> There is some misconception that groups would generally begin as small informal associations and then ultimately grow to become larger formalized associations. There is no guarantee of that happening and there is indeed very little evidence of that occurring as most associations seldom change significantly in stature and level of activity. They often stabilize after a few years in operation, but at a rather low level of activity. It is important to note that all kinds of groups (registered or not) have been inclined towards a more cyclic existence rather than steady progressive existence. In other words, many groups tend to be *ad hoc* and are characterised by frequent periods in which they are dormant. This might be linked to the pattern of resource flow to the

groups. There are indeed very few situations of small associations growing large and formal on their own resources. Usually, when they have become large formal associations, such transformation has been encouraged from outside the association through some resource transfer (Aryetee and Appiah 1995: 6). It would seem that the role of ISAs in Africa is easily overrated. Donors especially tend to perceive structural forms of cooperation among MSEs whereas neighbouring small producers out of self-interest possibly merely maintain relations of incidental collaboration.

Second it is often rather difficult to work with MSE associations in Africa. Most of them have generally inactive memberships and a rather small financial base. Only a minority of them have set up regular services to support members in their production and marketing. At best they are involved in lobbying activities with national and local governments. Few are businesslike in their approach to the delivery of services to their members. It appears that there is little creativity when it comes to defining their own role and finding ways to 'get going'. They tend to wait for others (government agencies and donor projects) to provide funding for their organization and activities. On the basis of the available information it seems doubtful if informal sector associations in Africa are ready for interventions aimed at flexible specialization (see Schmitz 1998 and Pedersen et al. 1994).

All this probably means that intermediary organizations, and especially external donors, should be careful in using informal sector associations as an instrument to change the MSE sector. General strengthening of associations would appear to be less cost efficient; against the needs for substantial inputs in terms of funds and technical assistance, tend to stand disappointing rewards, especially when it comes to the sustainable delivery of services to the rank and file. ISAs that receive external support often concentrate on the form of the collaboration (e.g. registration, election of office bearers, opening of an office, establishing relations with authorities, participation in forums, etc.). It has been suggested (Aryetee and Appiah 1995: 6) that the simple need to operate a bank account to receive external funding is often the most compelling reason for MSE groupings to register. The results seem to lie more in the area of lobbying with government agencies for their attention and support (and of course, with donors for continued assistance to the ISA), and far less in the organization and delivery of packages of business development services to the members. Moreover, there would appear to be a serious danger that donor-funded programmes to strengthen an ISA will render it ineffective as the result of infighting (e.g. which seems to have been the case for ASSI in Ghana), sometimes even of a political nature (e.g. KNFJKA in Kenya).

FIT experiences suggest that the emphasis should be on activities that are needs-based and demand-driven, and therefore be of an *ad hoc* nature. FIT tried to come up with more innovative activities of support for non-formalized groups of small producers, which seek to stimulate the technological progress of the sector by assisting MSEs to obtain relevant information and to build up their networks. Essentially, their success seems to lie in bringing together micro-entrepreneurs with their peers, as well as with others related to their subsector (e.g. suppliers of inputs and equipment, traders) and representative of relevant organizations. Some of these MSE support mechanisms appear to be quite promising, not only for the metal and food-processing sectors for which they were field tested, but also for other MSE activities. They are low cost and provide good opportunities for cost-recovery. It is hoped that in the end they will be taken up by informal sector associations or by small entrepreneurs themselves.

Part 4
Learning to Grow: SMEs, Skills and Technology

13 Technology, NGOs and small enterprise: securing livelihoods through technical change

ANDY JEANS

Background

A glance at the status of entrepreneurship in countries of the South would show that for those with access to capital and technology, the process of globalization can promise rich rewards. But those without, in the 'excluded' portion of the world economy, are in danger of getting left ever further behind. With the global economy being driven by the needs of industry and consumers in its richer segment, 'the form and direction of technical change is racing off at a trajectory that is further and further away from the needs and capabilities of the excluded majority' (Barnett 1995).

This is the world with limited access to financial capital, modern technology and external markets where the dominant form of production is at the micro- and small scale. It is where most basic needs – for food, shelter, domestic and production equipment and many services – are met not by the trade-driven global economy, but by local small-scale producers. It is where a growing proportion of the world's population, and especially of its poor, will live.

For several decades, governments and international aid agencies have recognized the importance of directing their attention towards this segment of the economy. Support to small producers has been seen as a key element of policies to alleviate poverty. In recent years, there has also been growing interest in, and evidence of, their potential for stimulating economic growth. The opening up of market space, as a result of deregulation, devaluation and the contraction of the state sector, has created myriad market niches which small producers have the potential to penetrate.

Despite some successes, however, this potential remains largely unrealized. All too often, small producers, especially women, continue to operate in saturated, low value-added, low-income markets with few opportunities for qualitative enhancement. The image of small farmers and artisans producing identical goods and competing for market space on the basis of price is all too familiar to practitioners in the field (Dawson and Jeans 1997).

NGOs and small enterprise

Traditionally, NGOs have as their target poorer and marginalized people, those who are excluded from the benefits of assistance programmes by host governments and international aid. Such men, women and children are, with the advent of globalization and the implementation of structural adjustment policies in many countries, also often excluded from any beneficial opportunities that may arise from those processes. NGOs have generally been more concerned with the alleviation of poverty for the excluded and much less concerned with economic growth at any level. The spectacular growth and success (in terms of outreach and cost-recovery) of micro-credit programmes over the last decade has led to many more NGOs becoming actively involved in enterprise promotion and development. A significant proportion of those supported are women and those already engaged in, or wishing to initiate, self-employment.

The dominant instrument of small producer support has come to be minimalist credit: that is where credit is the only service provided. However, recent evidence suggests that minimalist credit often has only a marginal impact on the productivity and capacity of small producers. This is because loans are often used to increase the volume of existing activities rather than to move into new, more sophisticated and high-value markets. There is growing recognition that for innovation of this type to take place, credit is often a necessary but not sufficient requirement: small producers also need improved access both to other productive assets, including enhanced equipment, skilled labour and raw materials and to markets. Such non-financial services for small enterprise development have come to be known as business development services (BDS).

Increasingly, NGOs and other development agencies are acknowledging this fact and are seeking guidance on the design and implementation of such services. In particular they are interested in learning how to design programmes that are cost effective, that maximize impact and that ensure sustainability of both impact and services. There are a number of promising leads and this is an area of research receiving considerable attention at this time.

What is appropriate technology?

Appropriate (or Intermediate) Technology was originally developed as a concept involving the application or adaptation of technology to fit a particular context. The AT movement now also embraces an approach to the management of technical change which is participative and intensive in the use of the resources, knowledge and skills of the people involved.

More recently, the movement has tended to stress appropriate technology more as an approach to technical change rather than a decision about the hardware ('technology choice'). This reflects a more sophisticated view of technology which is now considered to comprise at least four components:

- technique: the specific configuration of machines and equipment required to produce a good or service (often thought of as the 'hardware' component of physical capital)
- knowledge: comprising knowledge of science and technology, skills, experience, know-how, attitudes, (often popularly thought of as the 'software')
- organization: the institutional arrangements by which the technique and knowledge are combined, and the means by which they are managed (again seen as part of the software)
- product: the good or service resulting from the above process.

The essentials of this approach are that it enables the skills and experience of the 'outsider' to be combined with the skills, experience and needs of the 'insider': the excluded small-scale producer. As Schumacher said: 'Find out what people do and help them do it better'. The trick is to combine the strengths of insiders and outsiders in an effective way, that is genuinely 'participative', and creates a capacity to manage the processes of technical change in the future, not just in a single one-off event. Work on hardware is still required, but what is now required tends to be adaptive and evaluative, rather than basic and fundamentally novel (Bush 1997).

The place of appropriate technology in the current context

Most of Africa's poorest people are (and will increasingly be) earning their incomes from small-scale and micro-enterprises in households, fields or workshops. The term 'livelihoods' is now used to emphasize the informal nature of this work rather than the simpler terms of 'jobs' and 'employment'. Sustainable small-scale enterprises are dependent on small-scale technologies.

Much of the existing technology available to small and micro-enterprises is either insufficiently productive to create a secure livelihood with the available resources, or cannot produce goods of a quality or type that enables them to break into new, expanding or more demanding markets. Careful management of technical change in small-scale enterprises can make a real difference to their ability to compete with larger-scale production and to survive rapid economic change.

Experience over at least the past 30 years shows that the existing forces of both state and market have not worked well for small-scale producers. Neither has made available the necessary technology in appropriate forms and in sufficient quantities to prevent the gap between rich and poor from widening. The current debate has moved on from a choice between states or markets, to questions of how governments and markets can work best together to serve the people.

Almost all the new technology being developed in the world today is designed to meet the demands of industrialized countries. Much of this technology cannot be used by the majority of the world's population because of the relatively large scale of Northern production technologies, the complexity of their operation and maintenance, and the exacting specification of inputs and finished products, which make them ill-suited to the market structures and needs of resource-poor people, particularly in the South. Much of the technical expertise around the world is no longer familiar with the technological problems of small and micro-business.

Many of the technological options that are available therefore do not meet the needs or knowledge of particular groups within developing countries. This is generally so for resource-poor people who have little purchasing power, but it is particularly so for women. Furthermore, in a comparative study of technological capabilities in three African countries most firms were observed to operate in an information-poor environment (Biggs et al. 1995).

NGOs and technology

For those NGOs concerned with appropriate technology, enterprise development has always been an important focus of their activities. They have been involved in the provision of technological services (information, training, R&D, etc.) of relevance to sustainable enterprise activities which can be managed by the poor. While the target groups of such NGOs have also been individuals and communities with limited resources, three factors have led to their projects gaining some experience of working with somewhat larger or better resourced enterprises in the pursuit of that goal.

First, the use of targeted interventions at strategically placed enterprise 'nodes' which can facilitate the development of upstream and downstream enterprises. Because technologically-focused NGOs tend to specialize in certain productive sectors, they can readily adopt the subsector approach. In short, this approach requires that the focus of study, and of intervention, be not the individual small producer, but the system (or subsector) in which he operates. This permits the identification of: (1) bottlenecks constraining the economic activity; (2) niches in which small producers can have a comparative advantage; and (3) specific interventions which can ease the bottlenecks and facilitate the exploitation of niche opportunities. This approach can permit the identification of systemic interventions that can benefit large numbers of small producers at the same time.

Some particularly effective examples of this approach are in the manufacture, repair and maintenance of tools and equipment used by other producers. For example, specialized support to tens of blacksmiths who now provide an improved service to hundreds of farmers. Similarly, support to the development of decentralized oil mills which provide not only employment at the mills and a local supply of affordable cooking oil, but also offer a market outlet for small-scale producers of oil seeds.

Second, the use of leaders (dynamic and relatively successful enterprises in the community) to pioneer or pilot the introduction of new technologies. It has been the experience of the Intermediate Technology Development Group (ITDG) and other agencies involved in the introduction of new products or processes that, while spontaneous replication can take place once a critical mass has been achieved, there is first a need for an effective demonstration by those respected in the enterprise community. This approach has been found to have a lower risk of failure (from unrelated constraints facing the entrepreneur) and to permit a greater degree of cost-sharing from the enterprise itself, at the development stage.

Third, the work with already existing (rather than start-ups) and larger enterprises, or clusters, that have the capacity for adopting a greater range of new or innovative technologies, to meet the challenge of new market opportunities. Such enterprises already have some of the important attributes of a successful enterprise, such as a (limited) range of tools and equipment, some skilled labour, business ability and contacts. The owners of such enterprises are clearly not from among the poorest, but the projects offer services that can enable the enterprises to expand, creating new jobs for poorer people.[1]

The rationale for these approaches relates to the achievement of a wide scale of impact on poverty through raised incomes and new jobs, both inside and outside the enterprise. But, observers of such activities – both donors and from within the NGOs themselves – are sometimes critical as they perceive that the projects are supporting better-off enterprises and neglecting the poorer members of the community. The approaches may be viewed as depending upon the discredited notion of 'trickle down'. Clearly, a fair assessment of such approaches needs to look at the benefits to the ultimate beneficiaries (rather than the immediate clients only) and the costs of the intervention when compared with other approaches. In recent years there have been a number of exciting initiatives in Africa and elsewhere which are showing that such approaches can become much more cost effective than previously thought possible (Dawson and Jeans 1997).

Between poverty and growth

There is a growing debate around the apparent dichotomy between addressing, on one hand, the issue of poverty and survival for the most marginalized, and on the other, economic growth. Clearly, the development of small

---

[1] This approach may at first glance appear to be the same as the more traditional 'income-generation projects' (IGPs) initiated by agencies to provide gainful employment for the most needy. But there are significant differences because sustainability of the IGP depends upon many inputs from the agency, such as management, capital, raw materials and marketing.

enterprises that are improving livelihoods (creating jobs and enhancing incomes) for the poor will have a positive effect on both the lives of poor people and the economy as a whole; provided that they are not merely displacing the jobs and incomes of others. If intervening agencies are concerned with achieving a positive impact upon the level of poverty in a community through enterprise promotion, then this issue of displacement is important.

This section examines the links between poverty alleviation and growth of the small and micro-enterprise sectors, and argues that technological interventions by NGOs and others have a key role to play in the achievement of both. (The issue of national economic growth is not discussed here. However, it may be assumed that a growth in the small enterprise sector would contribute to economic development at the national level.)

NGOs are keen that their efforts lead to improved livelihoods for poor people, which are sustainable and that contribute to their ability to survive and thrive amid the changing opportunities and threats that may present themselves in the future. There would appear to be two targets that could guide the enterprise development activities of NGOs. First, the reduction of poverty among the most marginalized and vulnerable; and second the promotion of mechanisms to enable wider take-up, to enable the benefits to be shared.

As mentioned above, a substantial proportion of the support that NGOs provide to small enterprise development is aimed at self-employment for women. It has been argued at the Micro-Credit Summit (Washington DC, February 1997) and elsewhere that the opportunity for self-employment should be open to all. This seems an admirable aim, and indeed for many women, their other responsibilities, including the raising of children, make home-based self-employment almost the only option for earning a livelihood. However, when considering the sustainable development of livelihoods for the mass of poor people – men and women of all ages – there are a number of practical factors that should also be given consideration.

First, is the issue of market saturation mentioned earlier. Many of the markets in which marginalized people are forced to secure their livelihoods are already 'saturated' with too many people trying to sell goods and services to too few people. New entrants to these markets merely displace existing producers or reduce prices to levels that provide incomes below subsistence level, through 'pathological' forms of competition. But technology enables small-scale producers to increase their productivity (by 'doing more with less'), to do old things better, and to widen the range of goods and services that they can sell.

Second, it is often easy to forget that even in the micro-enterprise sector the majority of those who are gainfully employed are not the owners of the enterprise. For each successful micro-entrepreneur there are usually one or more workers. Those workers are almost invariably from among the poor. We cannot assume that all men and women (whether poor or not) would prefer to be self-employed, even if they had the resources to do so. For many, particularly youth without work experience, the difficulties they would face in dealing with customers and suppliers are particularly daunting. Whereas employment within an existing micro- or small enterprise offers some sustainability, as well as the opportunity to gain experience and to develop both technical and business skills which would help in future employment or self-employment.

Third, it is evident from several surveys and studies that the incidence of failure of new self-employment start-ups is very high in the first two years, while both the survival rates and potential for growth are higher among the more mature and slightly larger enterprises.

These considerations, together with the discussion in the earlier sections, lead us to certain conclusions:

- whereas for some of the poor there may be opportunities for the development of self-employment, the potential for very low incomes, or failure of the enterprise, can be high
- many of the poor are unable or unwilling for a variety of reasons to enter self-employment, but could be employed in existing small or micro-enterprises (a lower risk strategy)
- in order to address the issues of widespread poverty, some intervention to support the expansion of existing enterprises is a valid activity. This can create new jobs, provide opportunities for human resource development, and be cost effective[2]
- by targeting support to those enterprises and subsectors with greatest potential for job creation, the goal of growth of the small enterprise sector can also be achieved.

What does technology support offer?

Appropriate technological support can provide the required complementary services both to enable improved livelihoods from self-employment activities, and to stimulate the growth of the small and micro-enterprise sectors, in the following ways:

- by raising productivity, product quality and diversity, reducing the costs of raw material and energy requirements, leading to increased sales and incomes (Jeans et al. 1990)
- by developing the capability, within the small enterprise sector and supporting institutions, to respond to the changing needs and opportunities as they arise, leading to sustainable development of the sector

---

[2] This also raises the related issue of human resource development; there may need to be attention given to raising the skills needed to expand an enterprise.

- through raising the quality and diversity of products and services and catalysing appropriate linkages, expanding the market to include more formal higher-value markets such as exports and subcontracting for large firms, leading to increased production, sales and capacity within the sector
- by developing the local capacity to maintain, repair and, where appropriate, manufacture the tools and equipment needed to operate a wide range of small enterprises efficiently, leading to a increased diversity of successful small and micro-enterprises.

There is no blueprint for delivering such technical services, but recent studies of best practices point to some emerging principles for maximizing benefit/cost ratios, financial sustainability and scale of impact. These include: the adoption of subsector analysis and delivering services through strategically placed enterprises; tailoring interventions for a particular situation or target group; greater attention to replication, and greater use of market mechanisms such as using and strengthening existing private sector production and marketing channels; and charging fees for services offered (Barton 1997; Dawson and Jeans 1997; Gibson 1997).

One area of particular potential for stimulating the development of the small enterprise sector is small-scale manufacturing workshops. A wide range of small-scale producers; from farmers to grain millers, from fishermen to builders, from carpenters to textile weavers, and those running a variety of transport services, depend upon local workshops to repair, maintain and often supply them with the tools, equipment, and components that their businesses need. Those who do well can provide a responsive service tailored to the specific requirements of the businesses in their location. Thus they can be a critical element in the development of a diverse and dynamic small and micro-enterprise sector.

Small-scale manufacturing workshops represent a small sector of many African economies, but it is one of the fastest growing and one of the most promising for further expansion. These small businesses range from village blacksmiths producing agricultural tools and animal-drawn ploughs, to small foundries and machine shops producing water pumps, grain mills, welding machines and oil presses.

I have chosen to use the subsector of small-scale manufacturing (of which there has been considerable experience of new forms of intervention developed in Africa) to illustrate a number of concepts linking the role of technology promoting simultaneously the growth of the small enterprise sector and poverty alleviation. No doubt such concepts can be adapted and applied in different ways to other subsectors.

Recent experience of working in this sector has shown the importance of interaction between producers and consumers which can be catalysed by NGOs through trade fairs, assistance with market appraisal, and other techniques to promote 'user-led innovation'. This has been the focus of the FIT programme in Kenya (Farm Implements and Tools; a collaboration between ILO and TOOL in Amsterdam), and some of the work of ITDG. This work has led to increased dynamism, responsiveness and improved livelihoods among artisans, as well as improving their customers' ability to work productively (Jeans 1997; Tanburn and Osumba 1997).

Another important aspect has been the links to the formal or larger-scale sectors of the economy. Increased capacity, and importantly the recognition of that capacity, to produce goods and services to the more exacting demands of timeliness, quality and volumes required by larger retail outlets, government and larger commercial firms, opens the door to a potentially large and lucrative market for medium-scale enterprises. The situation varies between countries in Africa, some of which have a thriving small to medium enterprise sector (e.g. Ghana and Sudan) and others that are characterized by a 'missing middle' (such as Zimbabwe). To date, there have been few examples of effective interventions to promote such links where they have been found to be weak or non-existent. However, some subcontracting and service contracts have been won by emerging entrepreneurs, through their own personal contacts, and assistance with technical services.

As a long-term strategy, the sustainable growth of the small enterprise sector (and the resultant significant improvement in livelihoods for the poor) is likely to depend upon their being more connected with the mainstream economy through greater interaction between the micro- and the larger enterprises. The medium enterprises (or clusters of small enterprises acting together (Schmitz 1995)) can facilitate those links, and enable those engaged in micro- and small-scale production to capture a greater share of the market.

Human resource development

A further point that may be illustrated through the small manufacturing sector is the role that the private sector can play in the development of skills within the sector. Formal training institutions provide a valuable service for basic skills, but are often less appropriate to those already engaged in small enterprises. The cost of running such institutions in many countries in Africa is also a problem. Studies of the way in which skills are acquired by successful enterprises and a range of innovative programmes to find alternatives to formal state- or NGO-run training programmes provide some useful pointers.

Various forms of apprenticeship traditionally exist in small enterprises, and activities for sharing skills among existing artisans have proved to be a low-cost and effective approach. The links between different parts of the enterprise sector: large, medium, and small manufacturers, retailers etc., can lead to quality requirements being understood and skills and knowledge transferred as part of the trading transaction. Skills in the selection and operation of certain tools can be acquired as part of a commercial transaction to hire a tool from a hire centre. 'Downsizing' and 'retrenchment' from large industry and government has led to a new cadre of entrants to the small enterprise sector who have developed their skills elsewhere.

Finally, the comments raised in the earlier sections identify the critical importance of growth enterprises: of supporting the development of existing enterprises with a potential to employ more. There has been considerable effort placed on developing training packages for aspiring entrepreneurs but more attention could be placed on human resource development for those with good prospects for growth.

Conclusion

Small-scale producers rely on small-scale technology. They often use their scarce capital very efficiently, use local resources wisely and provide livelihoods that are part of the local way of life. Even though there is much more to achieving sustainable livelihoods than technology alone, there are no quick technical fixes; careful improvement of technology in small-scale enterprises can make a real difference to people's ability to compete in more demanding markets and to make their livelihoods more secure.

With the opening up of economies to imports from the world's most powerful monopolies, and the cutting back of services provided by government, there has never been more need for, or indeed more opportunity for, securing livelihoods by using 'technology as if people mattered'.

Technical change on the small scale is likely to provide a crucial input to the livelihoods of the mass of the world's population. But, left to existing forces of both state and market, it is unlikely that the necessary technology will be there in appropriate forms and in sufficient quantities that it can be absorbed quickly enough to prevent the gap between the included and the excluded from widening.

Carefully targeted technical inputs to enterprise development offer particular opportunities for reversing the trend of saturated markets with low-value products and low incomes. This is through promoting innovation, and the growth of both existing enterprises and the small enterprise sector as a whole. The development of capability within the sector, and stronger links with the mainstream economy can also contribute to its future sustainability and growth, with prospects of new job opportunities for many.

14 Competences and other factors affecting the small enterprise sector in Ibadan, Nigeria

SUSANNA ADAM

The primary focus of this chapter is to identify and illuminate factors that affected the survival and development of informal,[1] small-scale businesses in Ibadan, Nigeria, in particular vocational competences as gained through apprenticeship. After a preliminary perusal of relevant literature the following generally, but by no means universally, supported hypotheses were elaborated:

1) The informal sector has inherent characteristic dynamics and independent development potential.
2) Due to its separate status and dynamic character, the informal sector can foster national economic growth and create employment.
3) Unlike the specialized vocational trades in Germany and other industrialized societies, a small-scale, informal tradesman in Nigeria must master a broad range of technical and entrepreneurial competences.
4) The informal sector is inherently flexible and innovative with regard to the application of available technology and the exploitation of changing market environments.
5) The number and complexity of competences in use will correlate with the extent to which a given trade is integrated into technologically industrialized means and methods of production.
6) The divergent levels of complexity among the trades studied will be reflected in the corresponding divergence in means of competence transfer.
7) Informal apprenticeship in its present form, is an efficient vector for the transfer of a relevant breadth and depth of trade-related competences in the broadest sense, encompassing technical, economic and social competences.

For our concrete investigation in Ibadan, Nigeria, a study sample group[2] was chosen, consisting of small businesses, run by self-employed individuals, employing less than five paid workers,[3] and utilizing a limited number of tools and techniques to produce a limited range of goods and services in trades where we assumed an apprenticeship was common. The eight trades studied fell into four natural categories on the basis of several determining

[1] Meaning micro scale and unregulated by the formal institutions of society where similar activities are otherwise regulated.
[2] 310 entrepreneurs, 104 apprentices, 18 chairmen of related trade associations.
[3] However, some masters employed a number of apprentices, in individual cases as many as 40 who themselves paid the master for their apprenticeship.

factors, such as technological complexity, the degree of integration of the competences employed in everyday life, the extent to which imported materials or techniques are used and intra-professional variation:

- caterers
- semi-skilled production trades (tinkers and builders)
- personalized service trades (furniture makers, tailors, and hairdressers)
- industrial service trades (roadside mechanics and radionics).[4]

The enterprise dimention

The first hypothesis, *The informal sector has inherent, characteristic dynamics and independent development potential,* can be divided into two parts, the first of which, the inherent, characteristic dynamics, is in keeping with our choice of definition. Our analysis of the historical background and our field observations lead us, however, to reject the second part of the hypothesis. It appears that the informal sector in Nigeria is qualitatively different from, and yet dependent upon, the formal sector. Periods of prosperity and recession in the informal sector have generally followed those of the formal sector with some delay. A boom in the formal sector thus results in an initial recession in the informal sector, due to the competition of mass-produced wares, followed by an upswing as the generally prosperous environment creates new niches. This upswing is then accentuated as the formal sector recession forces customers to look farther afield for goods and services, but as the materials and competence vital to the functioning of the informal sector stem ultimately from the formal sector the initial growth is finite and self-limiting. It is absolutely essential to abandon romantic notions of the informal sector moving into or replacing the formal sector. At the same time, it must be recognized that the informal sector serves important socio-economic functions that the formal sector cannot. It provides goods and services to marginalized population groups and a survival basis for large numbers of self-employed tradesmen who are unable to find other employment. We hope that future policy plans will work to strengthen both sectors by enhancing the purchasing power of the populace, the general educational competence level and providing a reliable infrastructure.

The informal sector and economic growth

The hope that the informal sector could provide the missing creative force was central to major portions of the Structural Adjustment Programme (SAP). Our observations were less optimistic. While others have seen the growing numbers of apprentices as a sign of growth in the informal sector, we note that few of the apprentices start their own businesses. Interviews with masters and

[4] Nigerian term for those engaged in repairing electrical household equipment, radios and TVs.

statistics on average business age reveal falling income and growing economic insecurity. The growing number of apprentices in a stagnating number of businesses indicates that the sector is not growing as claimed. What is growing is the proportion of unpaid labourers, as both production and the number of people with gainful employment fall. While the informal sector is effectively keeping existing resources in circulation, it is quite unable to create a basis for expansion. The money still in the hands of the consuming populace, as well as limited hoards of spare parts and the finite collective expertise left over from the formal sector's heyday, create livelihoods as they circulate. The influx of competence from rationalized formal enterprises predicted by the SAP has not really materialized. On the contrary, the quality consciousness of producers and consumers alike is falling in the present atmosphere, where getting by becomes the paramount criterion in any acquisition of goods or services. We thus feel justified in rejecting hypothesis (2), *Due to its separate status and dynamic character the informal sector can foster national economic growth and create employment,* at least in its most literal interpretation.

Competence: definition and classification

Competence is defined as the sum of the related and overlapping aspects of ability, behaviour, skills and knowledge. In the context of this chapter, ability is the capacity for self-reliance and innovation; behaviour is the set of social strategies necessary to do business; knowledge is business-related background information; and skills are the set of business-related methods and techniques. As the tradesmen/women under study must generally both produce and market their wares, it has been practical to subdivide the subject of competence into two major categories: craft-related and entrepreneurial competences. We use the expression 'market savviness' to denote the special class of intuitive entrepreneurial competences necessary for business success in the unique market environment in Ibadan. The distinction between craft-related and entrepreneurial skills thus often has a diminished importance in practice, as both producers and consumers will include an assessment of an entrepreneur's status, relations, and other personal characteristics, such as honesty and reliability in the assessment of his wares.

Craft-related competences

The craft-related competences in use were all of an immediate practical nature. Theoretical aspects of the trades were observed only in concrete applications, such as using wiring diagrams or reading instructions for the job at hand. Theoretical preparation for novel types of work not yet encountered, or developing optimal ways of solving conventional problems, were not practised. The abstract planning that was observed, such as how many helpers to employ for a building project or how much food to cook for a large celebration, was apparently undertaken intuitively on the basis of practical experience. We found that practical, applied competences were sufficient to satisfy the demands of market niches, but generally insufficient to satisfy objective needs for resource utilization, worker and consumer safety, and to ensure optimal usefulness of the goods and services provided. The reason for this apparent discrepancy was that consumers and tradesmen were equally naive with regard to industrial standards. A handful of individual tailors, hairdressers, and radionics catered to an élite, sophisticated clientele with standards that approached international standards, but this limited niche was apparently filled. The market that most masters must satisfy is characterized by the lack of both money and technological sophistication on the part of masters and consumers alike. Short-term monetary savings are thus given more importance than the long-term savings that quality goods and services can bring. The low product expectations are reinforced by the products produced, with the result that technical competence level is not at present as great a determining factor for business success as one might objectively expect. In the long term, a higher competence level in most of these trades would be advantageous for society, but this can probably be effected only in tandem with an increase in the competence level of the populace as consumers.

Entrepreneurial competences

Although modular competence categories, such as bookkeeping, advertising, budget projection, etc., are necessary analytical points of departure, it is vitally important to recognize that neither the problems of doing business in Ibadan nor the competences possessed by entrepreneurs strictly match these imported concepts. The essential quality of a successful entrepreneur is a composite sense of a general, multifactorial atmosphere and the accompanying ability to react intuitively and appropriately to a bewildering gestalt of mercantile and social circumstances; he or she must, in short, possess a considerable degree of market savviness. Some of these decisions can appear logical in the light of Western conventional wisdom while others, equally successful in context, may seem counter-intuitive in the logic of classical economics.

Certain skills were given a surprisingly low value by masters, or were used to a lesser extent than the complexity of business might lead one to expect. Arithmetical skills, bookkeeping, knowledge of credit applications, and reinvestment were virtually non-existent in most businesses. There may be two reasons for this. On the one hand, many masters actually do possess competences which they neither use nor consider useful under current economic conditions, e.g. stockpiling, applying for loans. On the other hand, masters are part and parcel of the society which they both adapt to and create. Long-term budgeting competences would give limited benefits in a society where bills, bribes and other expenses such as input prices are utterly unpredictable, but the fact remains that most masters would not be able to plan finances effectively even if the macroeconomy were to stabilize. Masters who do not distinguish between profit and turnover, personal and business expenses, or current and average monetary earnings, are generally quite proficient at long-term planning on other levels. They anticipate future production and sale possibilities by acquiring relevant inputs when possible, maintaining contacts with potential customers and helpers, and by acquainting themselves with general market trends–even in times when none of these activities have immediate use.

The Nigerian market place has always been highly competitive, but in a characteristic permutation rather different from that which externally imposed planning often hopes to encourage. Successful masters were proficient at bargaining, associating themselves with influential people and radiating personal charisma to gain a competitive edge. Subterfuge is generally considered to be a respectable way of doing business, while breaking openly with the solidarity of price-fixing agreements is considered unethical and the idea of increasing competitiveness by increasing product range or quality is novel enough not to occur to many masters.

Didactic competences

Hardly any of the masters had pedagogical backgrounds. The teaching method in practice was essentially demonstration and reproduction, reinforced by corporal punishment. There are no effective measures to ensure that an optimal 'curriculum' is pursued or to evaluate apprentices' proficiency. Masters are generally attentive to apprentices' performance, but as the quantity and types of jobs have shrunk and numbers of apprentices swollen, apprentices are acquainted with a narrower variety of tasks and masters attend to them less. In this system of imitation, the masters' most important asset is the possession of competences to convey, but due to the general lack of business some competences are disappearing. Masters are generally highly motivated as teachers and take pride in the role in principle, but in practice present conditions hinder them in living up to the standards they espouse. The didactic qualities observed and the level of competences conveyed generally correspond well to the requirements of the present market conditions. They are quite certainly not sufficient to prepare for a future in which different market conditions present greater demands and opportunities.

General competence level, range and utilisation and the trade associations

As laid out in hypothesis (3), . . . *a small-scale, informal tradesman in Nigeria must master a broad range of technical and entrepreneurial competences.* We did find that the masters investigated were generalists directly involved in both production and marketing, in one way or another. Hypothesis (4), however, constitutes a more complex problem. It states that *the informal sector is inherently flexible and innovative with regard to the application of available technology and the exploitation of changing market environments*, and, as we have noted, craft-related and entrepreneurial competences must be treated as separate cases. A large battery of complex and often subtle business practices were used creatively to optimize the opportunities of sometimes momentarily changing conditions. While the great majority of masters were extremely dextrous in their intuitive improvisations in response to short-term market variations, adaptations to long-term structural alterations were slower and less nuanced. Despite the robustness displayed in the face of prevailing hardships, informal businesses are sensitive to sudden, massive changes in the foundations of the commercial environment.

Long-term planning, however, is not altogether lacking. The trade associations are a forum in which changing conditions and possibilities are consciously assessed and collective strategies developed. Different trades have developed different strategies in response to the same conditions, which demonstrates that truly active judgements are being formed on the basis of the sets of values and perceptions of the individual trades. These initiatives include measures to guarantee minimal incomes for the rank-and-file tinkers, development of opportunities for the relatively élite tailors, specialized, trade-run markets to ensure the availability and quality of inputs for tailors, radionics and mechanics, as well as varied saving club models in most of the trade associations.

The technological level was low, and creative adaptation of the existing technology was at a still lower level. Work was, by and large, performed as memorized without modification. These limitations can be explained at least partly by the lack of practically oriented theoretical training and the extremely low level of contact between colleagues who might otherwise have exchanged skills and knowledge. The expected gradient of technical complexity and competence predicted in hypothesis (5), *The number and complexity of competences in use will correlate with the extent to which a given trade is integrated into technologically industrialized means and methods of production*, could not be confirmed without major caveats. While the radionic trade did indeed include some of the most competent professionals, these were clearly in the minority, and the roadside mechanics definitely did not in general demonstrate a more complex range of competences than did the other trades; indeed many seemed to have less insight into their trade than masters from other, apparently more primitive, trades. There were, to be sure, especially among the personalized service trades and the radionics, remarkable exceptions to the general low technical standard.

The more successful hairdressers and tailors developed new fashions, and certain radionics studied hard to increase their competence level. But these were only a handful of individuals, although their influence and the potential for future development could be disproportionately great in the context of the trade associations. These organizations function, among other things, as repositories for the collective competences of the trades as a whole, and often (particularly the tailors', hairdressers', and radionics' organizations) as clearing houses for the propagation of new ideas. The most active and dynamic members tend to have a major, positive impact on the collective standard. If these organizations continue to develop, they may represent the source of the flexibility which most of their members lack and so desperately need.

Background, training, and business strategy

While there was a tendency for certain trades to correspond to rough categories of formal educational level, various factors combined to prevent any conclusion as regards causal or even factual relationships. In many cases, the correlation between trade, on the one hand, and factors such as class and geographical background, on the other, was so strong that educational level could be construed as just one of many indicators of social status. A number of trades displayed not one unified qualification profile, but rather consisted of two more or less distinct groups which could be differentiated on the basis of several factors, including education, background, and income. In addition, there was no demonstrable relationship between duration of apprenticeship and a trade's complexity. The available data thus fail to confirm the assumption that the complexity of a given trade will be reflected in the duration of the training and level of educational backgrounds. Similarly, the complexity of a trade as such says very little about the complexity of an individual apprentice's training experiences or an individual master's level of competence. While recognizing that more specialized competences are involved in repairing an automobile than in preparing a meal, we must also recognize that there is not a consistent difference between individuals in different trades, nor a consistent uniformity between individuals within the same trade. In other words, average differences between trades can be described more easily than an average individual member of a trade. What we witness, instead, throughout the trades studied, is a general clumping into two groups.

One group can be characterized by low status, low education, low personal utilization of technology and often rural background. The other group has generally higher education and status, consists mostly of native urbanites, and generally exhibits a relatively dynamic business development potential. The trades studied can to a certain extent be categorized in relationship to these groups, but this relationship is most pronounced at the two ends of the spectrum. The tinkering trade belongs essentially to the first group while the majority of the radionics belong to the latter. Between these extremes, though, we see the pattern continue within the individual trades, some of which are in the process of differentiating into separate classes.

This dichotomy of business strategies based on survival and on development must be seen as at least as important as the multitude of professional categories in any analysis of the training requirements and social potentials of informal sector activities. Some individuals enter a trade ill equipped to compete as high-powered capitalists and desiring only a niche in which they can survive with a reasonable level of comfort and security, while others desire the opportunity to develop and prosper. It is possible, at least in principle, for an individual to change strategy in the course of a career, but the two strategies remain distinct none the less. Both are assets to society by generating employment, on the one hand, and by creating material values, on the other, albeit to limited extents. The prospect of the developers forcing the survivors out of business would be just as undesirable as conditions that could force the developers to get by as survivors. Therefore, future intervention programmes must take the special needs of both groups into account.

Competence transfer mechanisms

Trade-related competences were generally found to be acquired from three sources: the home and social environment, formal schooling, and informal apprenticeship. Wage employment was rare and thus correspondingly rarely contributed to masters' competence. Classes of competence had a tendency to overlap, with a corresponding ambiguity as to the source from which a given competence was obtained. Roughly, though, competences can be categorized on the basis of acquisition. Basic literacy, numeracy, and English skills, as well as a conceptual picture of the ideal society, were conveyed through formal schooling. The concrete, specialized tools and techniques of a trade, and specialized techniques of negotiating, pricing, etc., were acquired in the course of informal apprenticeship. The practical application of these above mentioned competences, as well as the standards of quality, function and ethics, which gave the guidelines for the concrete production process or commercial transaction at hand, were principally acquired more or less subliminally through the home and social environment. The competences in the third category were generally transferred effectively and uniformly, while there was a pronounced divergence in the range and quality of competences acquired through the first two channels. We found, for example, school graduates who could neither read nor write and craftsmen who were ignorant of basic technical applications of their trades, but hardly any who could not compensate for such deficits with an impressive, intuitive sense of how to negotiate a deal with a customer.

The methods of competence transfer in informal settings are essentially the same from trade to trade and are confined, for most practical purposes, to demonstration and imitation. Oral, theoretical instruction, which consists largely of a presentation of tools and description of their use, is offered by only a few masters. There has been a noteworthy decrease in the total duration of apprenticeship, despite the objective increase in the complexity of the trades to be learned in the same period. Thus, we can reject hypothesis (6): *The divergent levels of complexity among the trades studied will be reflected in the corresponding divergence in means of competence transfer.* This tendency was not observable to any major extent in the training of apprentices, but developments in certain trade associations may justify hopes that the hypothesis' optimistic prediction may be vindicated in the future.

The one area in which a differentiation of content and methods of upbringing can be correlated to the professional career is that of the social and home background. The mores, morals and intellectual milieu of different class environments do tend to be reflected in the choice and utilization of business strategy. As discussed, business strategy does not absolutely determine choice of trade, as many trades have sub-populations of haves and have-nots, and the tendency is most clear-cut in the semi-skilled production trades, which consist uniformly of survival entrepreneurs from uniformly 'have-not' backgrounds.

Apprenticeship and the general transfer of basic competence

The basic transfer of specialized technical and entrepreneurial competences is, at present, exclusively the domain of informal apprenticeship. The National Directorate of Employment (NDE) training programme has not lived up to expectations. The many obvious, objective shortcomings in the competence levels of informally trained masters led us to modify hypothesis (7): *Informal apprenticeship, in its present form, is an efficient vector for transfer of a relevant breadth and depth of trade-related competences in the broadest sense, encompassing both technical, economic and social competences.*

If the 'relevant breadth and depth of competences' is considered in the light of the perceived needs of consumers, and thus the demands of the present market conditions, then the trades as practised and, hence, the apprenticeship from which they derive their competence, are satisfactory and even successful. If we, on the other hand, consider objective requirements of safety and product reliability and applicability, then we must conclude that present conditions fall far short of the ideal. While both standards are important for evaluating the complexity of the situation, the all-important problem for many Nigerians today is the lack of purchasing power for goods and services at all. Future development planning must pay due respect to the presently functioning system, that by and large succeeds in providing the competences necessary for the provision of a wide range of goods and services. The ultimately important and undeniable virtue of the existing system of apprenticeship is that it exists and functions. For this reason, if for no other, it provides the most logical and realistic basis for improvement.

Future perspectives

Most earlier researchers and planners have stressed the importance of the recruitment and training of apprentices with the intention of establishing more and more businesses. Our data indicate strongly that the employment potential in the Nigerian informal sector production trades has reached its limits and that the general level of competence has been falling since the connection to a skilled formal sector was broken, long before the SAP. Both problems are exacerbated by the large numbers of unpaid, poorly trained apprentices and trainees who provide damaging competition without having any positive possibility of establishing professional niches for themselves. Although the informal sector provides both survival and development potentials, the issue of the day is survival. The condition for the continued existence of the trades under study is that the masters who currently possess and preserve the trades' competences survive and prosper to the greatest extent possible. Only then can they pass their varied competences on to the next, growing, generation of tradesmen whenever the economic conditions improve enough to permit sector development. This strategy admittedly does not serve the immediate needs of the unemployed or of the bulk of the present apprentices. No single, focused strategy can alleviate their plight.

The trade associations do not, of course, have the interests of the whole of society at heart, but it is in the nature of political interest groups to advance specific interests. They are exclusive and protectionist but the specific groups they represent have specific need of protection. They cannot be seen as the vectors of democracy on a large social scale, but within their internal structures the essentials of informed, democratic decision-making so lacking in Nigeria as a whole can be found. They are, perhaps, not the Platonic ideal of future society, but they are what they are and we are convinced that what they are is very much worth building upon. It is important to stress that all findings presented here pertain solely to the particular economic and political situation in Nigeria. That is to say that in many other African countries, especially in those where the small enterprise sector is, as yet, much less developed, we might have arrived at completely different conclusions. However, some issues may be generalized in view of future intervention policies.

There is a general need to formulate a coherent, demand-driven and needs-oriented national policy on vocational training, both formal and non-formal. This requires an orientation to the conditions prevailing in the labour market, in order to bring training and education resources more into line with employment opportunities. Basic labour market developments, specific skill demands and labour market opportunities should be identified, in order to determine macro- and micro-levels of intervention.

At the macro-level, programmes and strategies are needed that can enhance people's capacity to become engaged in more productive income-generating activities, meaning both wage-employment and self-employment. A structure will have to be developed that allows effective delivery of skills while recognizing the critical connections between training and other inputs required. None the less, new policies that try to foster micro- and small-scale development need to pay attention to the training needs of small enterprises.

Although micro- and small enterprises are by far the largest mediator of skill transference, they will not alone be able to raise the standard of performance required to meet market demands. Thus, the existent apprenticeship practice should be built upon, and advanced in conjunction with, in-service training and upgrading of master craftspeople. In doing so, it has to be kept in mind that the market in which these micro- and small business people function is not a luxury economy based on individual desires but a standard economy based on universal needs. Any trade master must have a certain level of competence necessary to provide the local, generally accepted standard of quality. A master with a significantly lower level would probably not be able to remain in business, and it is just as probable that a master with somewhat higher than average skills would not gain a corresponding advantage. Thus we must be cautious about assigning technical skills an absolute value, as any assessment of competence must be based on the level and types of skills appropriate to this framework.

Skills training is not easily translated into (self-) employment due to weak linkages with markets, business training, credits and follow-up services. In addition, the lack of capacity as regards administrative as well as technical skills, and poor co-ordination among provider organizations and institutions may easily stand in the way of training success. Again, a strategy is needed to develop and sustain non-formal training activities. This would include intensive dialogue, defined roles and responsibilities, co-ordination of activities, and a government accepting a role as facilitator of this process.

In order to prepare people for productive life, stronger linkages, both structural and curricular, to general education are needed. The first pertains to a multilevel training system that can be entered from various backgrounds. The second requires a more profound technical orientation of the school curricula. This does not mean integrating vocational training into the school setting but making an attempt to adapt topics more to practical needs, e.g. numbers, measures and cuts, time schemes, scales, etc. In this respect it is essential to take into account the student's material environment. Many of them are likely to be unfamiliar with the concepts of industrial culture. They have no experience of the underlying patterns of industrial society on which these concepts are based. Precisely for this reason, it is indispensable for the school curriculum to give students an opportunity to become familiar with various technologies, and provide them with exploratory experiences. A coherent national strategy can provide a framework for micro-level interventions.

The micro-level comprises individual target groups, communities, and regions where the specific skill demands and realistic labour market opportunities will need to be analysed. However, the example of Nigeria, a country in which the informal sector is well developed, shows that solutions must not always be sought through interventions from without. On the contrary, the Nigerian trade associations show that those directly involved are increasingly able and willing to develop their own response to changing economic circumstances. The formation of interest groups indicates self-regulating tendencies in the small enterprise sector, which clearly shows that the 'informal' sector is not a 'non-structured' sector and that external intervention, especially if undertaken with inadequate knowledge of local conditions, may be positively harmful.

Improvements must be made in many areas of society to create the atmosphere of support and human dignity necessary for any specific reform concept to thrive. Competence and training in the informal sector were the subject of our research but, as we have stressed repeatedly, they are part and parcel of much larger social dynamics which they affect and by which they are affected. These problems must be addressed on many fronts in addition to those upon which our work can cast light.

15 Reshaping vocational training: hopeful signs from a Ghanaian experience

LAWRENCE A. HONNY

Introduction

Problems of unemployment among graduates of the Technical and Vocational Education and Training (TVET) system have been exacerbated by the economic and educational reform policies in Ghana, triggering off a policy reform of the TVET system aimed at employment creation, especially through self-employment, income-generation and poverty alleviation.

Vision 2020 (Republic of Ghana 1995: 51) identifies the objectives of employment in terms of increasing productive employment, and sustaining a wages and salaries policy that promotes employment. It outlines the policy objectives of training in terms of strengthening and expanding training facilities through: (1) improving and expanding the infrastructure for training, (2) increasing opportunities for technical and vocational level training, and (3) strengthening linkages between the training sector and industry.

With evidence from a recent study, this chapter examines how the reform of the TVET system might reduce poverty and employment among vocational graduates. It first briefly surveys the consequences of the economic and educational reforms for vocational graduates.

The impact of the economic reform programme

Under the Structural Adjustment Policies, introduced in the early 1980s, Ghana has generally made progress in the major economic indicators, but GDP growth rates dropped to below 5 per cent in 1992, 1993 and 1994 (TCOP 1996). Recent economic growth has been driven very largely by mining and services, but the industrial sector has been relatively weak, and in recent years has declined considerably.

High interest rates and inflation account for high production costs which together with competition from imports, have weakened the productive sector considerably. These effects have also affected the informal productive sector, where most vocational graduates seek employment and incomes.

Unemployment in 1997 was estimated at 25 per cent or about 2.2 million out of a current labour force of about 9 million (Dordunoo 1994: iv).[1] Each

[1] This is considerably in excess of the estimate of about 1 000 000 unemployed contained in the Government's Budget Statement of 1995, but consistent with the 13–24 per cent unemployment estimates of the Statistical Services in their Poverty Study of 1995.

year, at a growth rate of 3.3 per cent per annum, more than 230 000 young people will be added to the labour force. Employment and income-generation through a sharper delivery of the TVET system have thus provoked a major rethinking of policies to encourage the growth of the informal sector and to improve the quality and delivery of education and training at the lower and less formal levels of economic activity.

The impact of the educational reform programme

An Educational Structural Adjustment Programme (ESAP) introduced in 1986 reduced the length of pre-secondary formal schooling from 12 to 9 years. After three years at the junior secondary school (JSS) level, candidates are deemed ready either to enter training for the labour market, or proceed for further schooling at the senior secondary school (SSS) level.

Another major educational reform is the 'Programme for the Provision of Free Compulsory and Universal Basic Education by the Year 2005', the so-called fCUBE, introduced in 1994. This was to make primary education free and compulsory for all children.

The existing system of pre-tertiary education was judged to produce educated but unskilled and unemployed people who were suitable mostly for clerical and other office work. The changes were expected to raise the number and quality of youth with primary or secondary school education before vocational and apprenticeship training. They were also to make them employable after completing either the JSS or SSS level.

The objectives of ESAP were: (1) to reduce excessive emphasis on academic training at the pre-secondary level; (2) to help young people discover their talents, aptitudes, potential, and appreciate the use of the hand and mind; and (3) to make the youth more creative and production-oriented. A significant aspect of the reforms was the integration of general and technical/vocational education to inculcate in the individual an understanding of the world of work.

In practice, the reduction in the years of pre-tertiary education from 17 to 12 years triggered the arrival of thousands of young entrants into the labour market at a much younger age, without preparing them adequately for employment at either the JSS or SSS level. A report on the new system observed that after SSS, candidates were not adequately prepared to enter University (Education Reforms Review Committee 1994).

At present, fewer than 10 per cent of JSS graduates gain admission into the senior secondary schools and of these, only about 2 per cent are absorbed into higher educational institutions. The vast majority of JSS and SSS graduates look forward to some kind of vocational training for either formal or informal employment.

The demand for vocational training

It is important to distinguish vocational training from other forms of skill training. The policy on VOTEC in Ghana (Ministry of Education 1990) characterizes vocational education as that type of education designed to prepare skilled personnel *at lower levels of qualification* for one or a group of occupations, trades or jobs. The emphasis is on practical training at lower levels as part of an overall educational process. By contrast, vocational training aims at developing the particular skills for a specific occupation.

The demand for early skill acquisition to raise the employment prospects of the youth has been expressed in large increases in the numbers of vocational and technical training institutions and in the phenomenal growth of vocational graduates. It has been suggested that real prospects for employment are available to these graduates, but that these may be linked to the identification of markets as a support mechanism (Adam, this volume, 1999)). Mead (this volume, 1999) makes a similar observation from Zambian and Kenyan studies that an approach to education and training that is based on identified market opportunities is likely to be more effective.

Adu-Sarkodie (1995) notes that from 1960 to 1984, the number of VOTEC-trained professionals and semi-professionals increased from 17 900 to 28 700 and the number of skilled persons from these institutions rose from 5836 to 708 800. Vocational enrolment rates are increasing at an average of 7.5 per cent every year, with the private sector accounting for about 95 per cent of total enrolment.

Currently there are about 160 vocational and technical training centres in the public sector (GES technical institutes and Ministry of Education vocational training institutes). Within the private sector there are about 250 registered training centres and more than 700 unregistered private centres operating traditional apprenticeship systems. The informal system is considered to have contributed the vocational skills of about 70 per cent of those who are self-employed.

Between 1987 and the year 2000, VOTEC is expected to turn out over 2 000 000 graduates at the secondary level. A clear picture has therefore emerged that vocational education has now become a major plank in efforts at making the youth fully productive, and reducing levels of unemployment.

Policy objectives of the TVET system

The TVET system that the new policies aim at correcting has shown a number of weaknesses. First, the technical proficiency of graduates is too low and needs to be improved. Under this system, the testing of proficiency takes place only once, that is, at the end of training. It therefore fails to guarantee that a successful candidate at the terminal examination is in possession of all the competencies in which he trained, and is capable of displaying them in a work situation.

Second, the training system as a whole lacks flexibility. Its structure and delivery do not adequately address the challenges of a modernizing economy in a global system in that opportunities for specialization and accumulation of skills in different but related trades do not exist. Trainees are unable to opt out at suitable stages of their training to enter the labour market in the hope of returning for additional training later, because certification and evidence of proficiency at each stage, though essential, cannot be provided. Many instances exist of trainees ending their training prematurely upon finding jobs.

Third, the expectations of self-employment for the majority of graduates are not materializing. The capacity of the trainees to enter into self-employment, even in the most traditional trades, has been constrained by excessive supplies of artisans in those trades (for example, masonry, carpentry), and by the lack of linkages and comments from the market and industry. The training is out of balance in terms of the connectedness of trades with the market.

An Education Reforms Review Committee (1994) concluded that the existing system of VOTEC education lacked flexible strategies that responded to changing demands in the labour market, and proposed competency-based training towards more self-employment and the introduction of an Enterprise Skills Development Programme (ESDP).

Against this background, the focus of future policy for education and skills training is to provide training linked with jobs or self-employment (MESW 1995) and to enable the poor to participate in the economy. Special recognition is given to competency-based training for the acquisition of employable skills.

The *Proposals For The Development of Technical And Vocational Education And Training* (Task Force 1997), made 10 key policy recommendations to improve the management and delivery of the TVET system, four of which are of special relevance to this chapter namely to:

- give training and impart the necessary skills leading to the provision of operatives, craftsmen and women and other middle-level personnel, and improve the technical proficiency, management skills and business efficiency of the workforce
- enable the youth to have an intelligent understanding of the increasing complexity of science and technology, and to keep abreast of changing scientific and technological trends through systematic exposure to modern technology
- equip trainees with entrepreneurial skills for self-employment through the reorientation of existing programmes linked with credit packages
- create flexible linkages and opportunities for continuing education in the system up to the tertiary level.

The competency-based training policy

The competency-based policy recognizes that the informal sector lacks the flexibility to participate effectively in the global economy, and that this is manifested in the low quality of training skills imparted and the type and relevance of training to the market. The major objectives of the competency-based training are therefore to ensure:

- the attainment of high levels of individual proficiency
- that graduates are capable of working under changing market and technological conditions
- the progressive harmonization of training programmes and standards to keep abreast of international developments.

Findings from a study of vocational graduates

In the process of conducting a study to develop a methodology for tracer studies of NVTI graduates (Honny 1997), questions were asked about the incomes, employment experiences and relevance of trades and skills of graduates from 21 NVTI centres trained under the TVET system. Centre managers, instructors and over 180 graduates with work experiences ranging from one year to more than 10 years were interviewed. Through this study it was possible to assess the impact, relevance and usefulness of the training that graduates had been receiving, and determine how far the TVET policy reforms would address the existing defects.

Among the questions investigated were:

- Where do graduates tend to go, and what have been their experiences concerning access to employment and incomes?
- Are the levels of proficiency generally high enough, and in what respects are competencies low and therefore training defective?
- How flexible has the training been in meeting the demands of industry, technology and the market in general?

Relevant among the results of these investigations are an activity profile describing the movements and location of vocational graduates, interest inventories of those still in training, and an identification of factors that affect the employment and income situations of graduates.

Activities of vocational graduates

For employment-seeking graduates, the activity profile shows a spread between securing formal employment, entering into self-employment, undergoing further apprenticeships, abandoning trades acquired to undertake training for a different trade or engage in a new economic venture, and facing prolonged unemployment.

In contrast to the past, recent trends indicate that most graduates do not train in centres located nearest to their places of origin. In some cases, the percentage of candidates from localities around their vocational centres was as low as 2 per cent. Immediately after their training, graduates generally go to their places of origin for about six months to await their examination results. This is usually followed by travel to large towns and cities for a stay of up to three or four months to look for employment.

Most graduates initially go in search of wage employment. The motivations that determine subsequent activities include accumulation of capital to purchase tools (and later set up a workshop), acquisition of work experience, and development of a career in the formal sector.

The most important employers of these graduates are public sector organizations that deal with the construction, provision and maintenance of facilities and utilities, and large private construction firms.[2] Many of them offered 'on-the-job' training to candidates during their training and employed them after their graduation. The investigations suggest that in the past about 40 per cent of graduates found jobs in the formal and semi-formal sectors within a period of one year and that about 10 per cent went into higher institutions for additional training and qualifications. Formal employment is usually concentrated in the regional capitals. The proportion of those who graduated in the last two or three years employed in this way, however, has fallen considerably.

Other studies in Ghana have observed similar levels and trends of employment among vocational graduates. One survey found that 14 per cent of past trainees obtained employment three to six months after graduation, 46 per cent between six and 12 months, 20 per cent between one and two years, with 20 per cent establishing their own businesses (Apraku-Mensah 1995).

Graduates who fail to obtain employment after an initial search may become apprenticed to private workshops. In the large towns and cities some of those not in employment may engage in petty trading. Substantial numbers of the young traders who roam the streets of some regional capitals (the so-called 'street-children') are holders of vocational qualifications.

Other graduates attempt to operate as self-employed artisans in their localities, doing so mostly without tools, workshops or work experience. In the circumstances, they are often unable to sustain their trade, remaining more or less unemployed for about two or three years, and occasionally much longer. Unless early employment possibilities open up for them, those in rural areas enter into food farming, joining the ranks of the rural poor. At this point, they may abandon their trade permanently.

---

2. Employment in these institutions is usually concentrated in the regional capitals. For most graduates, travel to large towns and cities to look for jobs is thus a routine practice that may often follow about six months after training for a stay of up to three or four months. However, new graduates finding jobs in the formal and semi-formal sectors during this search tend to be in the minority.

Such experiences suggest that in many localities a dichotomy exists in the linkages between the training provided and local production possibilities. Where opportunities exist for self-employment in the immediate environment and other conditions prevail, there are more self-employed graduates within the locality, and more trainees appear desirous of setting up their own enterprises. Suitable conditions include post-training support with tools, equipment and finance, group organisation, and assistance in creating access to markets. A few centres manage to attract and retain candidates from immediate localities by creating some of these conditions. A proportion of graduates also enter into technical institutes to upgrade their qualifications.

To determine the likely activities of future graduates, the future plans of trainees were inventoried using samples of simple statements from trainees in a number of centres. Most of the respondents were in their last year of training. The results in Table 4.1 indicate that 35 per cent wished to pursue further training and education, 29 per cent would become self-employed, and 36 per cent would seek wage-employment. In one centre, 80 per cent of final year trainees planned to pursue further studies.

The variability in the percentage distribution of interests at different centres reflects locational experiences such as the availability of centre support for self-employment after graduation, the low-esteem felt by holders of NVTI qualifications seeking formal employment, and low job expectations. However, there is a degree to which interest in further education is growing.

It can be seen, therefore, that vocational graduates may not acquire their training predominantly for self-employment, and that perhaps a larger percentage looks forward to formal employment. Special efforts to develop the spirit of self-employment among vocational graduates will be required.

The work situation and experiences of vocational graduates

Within the rural environment, conditions influencing the employment of graduates include: (a) the level of local development and corresponding demand for different trades, (b) the difficulty of entry into various trades, and (c) post-training support in the form of access to productive resources and human resource development (e.g. entrepreneurship training).[3]

Graduates who settle in centres located where there are development activities involving construction find work early, either as self-employed or wage-employed artisans if they have their own tools. Graduates who establish their own enterprises tend to do so close to their places of origin about five years after graduation, and sometimes in large commercial towns.

Where the pace of local development activities is slow, unemployment may be quite high. Vocational graduates in electronics from one rural centre were

---

[3] 'Local' in this context refers to the political/administrative district and catchment area for which every centre is originally expected to cater. Seventeen of the 21 centres studied were located in areas that could be described as rural settlements.

TABLE 15.1: INTEREST STATEMENTS (FUTURE PLANS) OF VOCATIONAL TRAINEES

	% Distribution Between Likely Future Activities		
Centre	*FURTHER EDUCATION*	*WAGE EMPLOYMENT*	*SELF-EMPLOYMENT*
Comboni	86.67	11.11	2.22
Alavanyo	7.69	3.85	88.46
Yamfo	45.83	45.83	8.33
Tumu	24.59	32.79	42.62
Dormaa	22.22	22.22	55.56
KVTC	24.27	37.86	37.86
TOTAL	35.07	29.10	35.82

Source: Honny 1997: Appendix 12 Abridged

compelled to move out of the area because no demand existed for their skills in that locality, and also because the practice of the technology it entailed was too difficult to sustain and upgrade at the local level. High levels of poverty among local people may also put at risk graduates of certain trades. The weaving of cloths whose quality and price exceed local preferences and 'willingness-to-pay' provides an illustration of this.

Trades that require fewer or cheaper tools and equipment are more readily established by individuals. These include masonry and carpentry, in which self-employed artisans are common. However, the high cost of tools in recent times is putting self-employment in these trades beyond the reach of young graduates.

Graduates in trades that depend on heavy, capital-intensive machinery often find it impossible to establish on a private or individual basis. Such machinery usually has extremely low labour needs. For example, few organizations can afford a lathe, yet it may require not more that one or two operators. Unemployment among graduates in the machining and fabrication trades is thus becoming serious.

The lack of access to capital to procure the tools and equipment necessary for work is another major issue. Generally, graduates are not able to secure the minimum set of tools to engage in work after graduation. Various responses are being attempted to overcome these conditions of joblessness, lack of capital and workshop facilities.

One response in an economically depressed area has been to promote co-operative or group-based interventions and support them with capital equipment and tools. In another response, graduates have formed small production cells of three or four people to access jobs. Centres are also supporting the employment of their graduates through a variety of approaches. Where capital is available, the growth of artisanate enterprises has tended to create more avenues for employment and income.

The evidence suggests there are formidable barriers to the entry of graduates into certain trades after training. This makes it extremely difficult to promote self-employment effectively in certain occupations. Due consideration of processes to alleviate this situation is necessary.

The income situation of vocational trainees

The stability of employment and incomes is another major issue affecting graduates. This is strongly influenced by the form of organization. Large formal organizations tend to offer the highest stability of employment and wages. Successful self-employed graduates frequently earn more than their formally employed mates, but they encounter greater difficulty in maintaining a steady flow of jobs and incomes.

Compared to large public sector organizations, employment with small and medium organizations tends to be considerably less stable, and to last only a few months. This is due primarily to two factors. The first is irregular payment of wages, which causes young employees to quit new jobs even when they have no alternatives. The other factor, as noted below, is a weak-willed acceptance and recognition by employers, of the status of certificates from vocational centres.

Many graduates employed in the formal sector contend that they are not accorded due recognition and placement because of uncertainties among employers and institutions over the status of their qualifications. This may be related to the low proficiency of some of the certificate holders. With the introduction of the competency-based training approach, a new system of certification that is more acceptable to employers will be adopted. The new basis of assessing competency, therefore, will determine the placement and career of the vocational graduate.

Concerning co-operative groups of graduates, a few have achieved exceptionally high incomes, but the members of most groups find their incomes low and the benefits inequitable. Some groups have not managed to secure contracts for a long period but their access to productive assets provides them with obvious advantages.

Besides suffering irregular payments, graduates who are employed with small firms are usually not paid the recommended wages and are among the lowest income earners. They tend to abandon their jobs after a few months to join the unemployed for long periods. Graduates in small production cells usually manage to secure a slightly steadier flow of work and income than those in sole proprietorships, though they remain among the poorest groups. The lowest income group is made up of fully unemployed graduates and those with only occasional jobs.

The picture of graduate incomes, therefore, is one in which different types of work engagement dictate the capacity of the graduates to be occupied most of the time and earn suitable wages. To understand the income situation of graduates, therefore, not only the size and level of income, but also the occupational forms (that is, status and size of organization) in which the graduate operates must be studied.

Training, technology and the market.

Issues also exist regarding how training affects employment and income. Training in some trades is also not responding well to important changes in the market. The trades concerned include building construction, weaving, dressmaking and electronics. For example, most modern houses require floors with tiles, yet graduates are not taught this technique. The market for builders in the rural areas generally demands that masons are able to execute all plumbing works as well, but masons are not given this training. Carpenters acquire proficiency in using machines to which they may have little access in many situations, especially when self-employed. Thus, they may be incapable of high quality work using only hand tools [4].

In the weaving trade, in certain markets inferior products are preferred to the higher quality the graduates are trained to produce, leading to difficulties in the marketing of their products. Dressmakers are trained to use patterns and designs when cutting but in practice have to resort to freehand methods to which they have had no exposure.

The issue of technology and training is more acute with the 'modern trades' of electronics auto mechanics, electricals and printing. The designs of modern engines, appliances, equipment and parts met in the market vary markedly from those on which graduates train. In printing, for example, graduates who went on to work with new technologies found that they were almost completely unable to operate them.

The evidence pointed to a lack of adaptability of training to market trends and technology, affecting the delivery and access of graduates to jobs. Graduates nursed the hope that their centres would organize courses to familiarize them with modern practices and industry skill needs.

Conclusions: hopeful signs and challenges for the future

Under the training reforms, candidates will be required to provide evidence of competence by building up portfolios, based on standards supplied by industry, institutions, or the markets at which the training is targeted. Competency-based and phased tests would play a major role in the evaluation and assessment procedures. Standards of proficiency will therefore be developed for each trade at different levels. In place of the present instructor-centered and pedagogic system, the reform will introduce a trainee-centered system, in which the candidate acquires proficiency at his own pace. This method of training and skill attainment will improve proficiency considerably.

---

[4] The study identified several types of machinery, equipment, and hand tools which young graduates were not able to use properly, as well as several tasks for which they had been trained but were not able to perform.

The new training policies and reforms can therefore be seen as addressing the right issues and, with effective implementation, should result in improvements to the employment prospects of vocational graduates. However, more needs to be done to enhance the relevance of training provided to secure employment that offers satisfactory earnings for graduates. Adaptations to the trades, structure and content of training are required. From this analysis at least three major challenges emerge.

First, greater proficiency is necessary in the trades in which candidates specialize. This implies familiarity with modern technologies, ability to adapt to different work situations, and capacity to perform a range of tasks competently. In this context, the value of tracer studies of graduates in identifying concerns relating to the adequacy of training is evident from the results presented. Such a response process has been set in motion in Ghana as part of efforts to consolidate the competency-based training system.

The requirements here will include modern training facilities and equipment, exposure to new work techniques and a breed of well-trained instructors who understand the shift in training emphasis. In Ghana, these concerns are also being addressed through the competency-based training system which is being introduced into the NVTI Centres. On a wider scale, the establishment of VOTEC resource centres, which will increase access of trainees to modern and well-equipped workshops, is planned.

Second, greater consideration should be given to replacing the supply-oriented output of graduates with a fully demand-driven strategy that is based on a careful combination of trades and a flexible adaptation of modules and skills to fit the needs of the market. Connectedness of the training institutes with major clients and institutions will ensure that candidates acquire a relevant variety of skills to enable them to work independently when necessary. Employer linkages and studies of the job market can provide the inputs for training institutions to realize this.

Finally, post-training support mechanisms will be required to promote self-employment and enhance the survival of the informal sector. The introduction of ESDP to satisfy the need for basic skills in business planning, entrepreneurship and marketing as part of the TVET system should be supported by other strategies. Apart from providing and, if necessary, subsidizing access to physical and financial resources for investment, these should incorporate schemes that groom and assist businesses for a period. There is little evidence that efforts to enhance the employment prospects for vocational trainees in all these areas have gone far enough. Training in the wider context suggested above would be more effective.

16 The role and potential of technical and vocational education in formal education systems in Africa

BONAVENTURE WANJALA KERRE

Introduction

The concern for national development has, over the decades, underscored the need to improve the quality of life of the citizenry of a given nation. This was Adam Smith's concern when he observed that indeed a society cannot be flourishing and happy if the majority of her citizens are poor and miserable (Smith [1776] 1937). Today, this concern remains so true as the level of poverty seems to be on the increase, particularly in Africa, despite continued development aid. Education has been recognized as playing a pivotal role in the alleviation of poverty. African leaders at an education conference in Addis Ababa in May 1961 recognized that education was a basic factor in economic and social development and in particular observed that:

> the African countries, in a century characterized by technological progress, should embark on a very broad expansion of technical and vocational education and specialized training in the interests of their own development and especially for their industrialization. (ECA / UNESCO 1961: 9.37)

In subsequent meetings of Education Ministers organized by UNESCO (UNESCO 1976; 1991), technical and vocational education and training (TVET) have continued to receive greater emphasis in an effort to prepare Africa's youth for the world of work. Despite these worthwhile efforts, both from within and without Africa, education has reached a crisis level, where participation has dwindled and illiteracy once more threatens a continent that must, *inter alia*, enter and face the challenges of the twenty first century (UNESCO BREDA 1995). In February 1995, an international meeting entitled 'Audience Africa' was convened in Paris, France and attended by several African heads of state and other interested parties to re-examine the whole question of development and development priorities in their continent in the light of the new challenges facing the world (Audience Africa 1995: 6).

The meeting recommended that basic education should be given priority, and a law on compulsory schooling should be introduced wherever this had not been done. The meeting further recommended that secondary education should also give a prominent place to technical and vocational education. While sufficient evidence exists for us to accept the important contribution that TVET makes toward national and individual development, it is not clear which approaches are most appropriate given the challenges facing us in the twenty-first century.

In this chapter we shall examine and discuss some of the most common approaches used in selected African countries, with the aim of identifying any concrete evidence linking vocational and technological education to national development and the nurturing and growth of an entrepreneurial culture. We shall also make an attempt to address the challenges faced in the workplace and communities as we face the dawn of the twenty-first century.

TVET in national development policy frameworks

The true test of the importance ascribed to technical and vocational education in any nation lies in its accommodation in the legal policy frameworks and the place it is accorded in the national school curriculum. In the majority of African states, the legislation stipulating the establishment of technical and vocational education came much later, after the promulgation of the education Acts (UNESCO BREDA 1996). This happened naturally after realizing that the graduates of mainly liberal arts-oriented curricula could not easily find employment, because the few clerical and other administrative jobs had already been filled and they lacked basic skills required in the employment sector. It is also important to recognize that most of Africa's post-colonial education systems were heavily criticized as mere adaptations of the élitist colonial education systems where vocational education and training were meant for African manual labourers. This resulted in the total rejection of TVET by élitist Africans, resulting in what Ki Zerbo (1990: 63) described as educational systems producing 'large numbers of people who are just underproductive precisely because they have been to school'. To avoid the debilitating effects of such educational systems, it was deemed necessary, first and foremost, to provide vocational training to produce the much needed skilled manpower in various trades. This led to the establishment of Vocational Training Acts in an attempt to regularize such training. This, for example, happened with Ghana in 1970, Kenya (1971), Uganda (1979), Zimbabwe (1978) and Swaziland (1982).

Later on in the 1980s it was felt that technical and vocational education should become an integral aspect of general education if the continued supply of technical manpower was to be guaranteed in the future. This led to major educational reviews leading to the vocationalization of the school curriculum in Africa. This trend, however, was felt all over the world as states grappled with youth unemployment in a technologically competitive era. In Nigeria, the national education policy, effected in 1982, laid emphasis on a restructured (6–3–3–4) school system. In Kenya, a new vocationalized (8–4–4) curriculum was launched in 1985. Ghana's new constitution in 1992, through articles 25 and 38, reviewed the education system and revitalized technical and vocational education.

By the mid-1990s, Swaziland, Uganda and Zimbabwe had already established mechanisms for incorporating technical and vocational education into their general education systems (UNESCO BREDA 1996). The Francophone countries of Africa had similar developments, with Senegal's orientation law of national education leading the way as early as 1971, and culminating in a reviewed and more comprehensive law in 1991. In Burkina Faso the 1991–95 development plan put emphasis on diversified professional and vocational training to address prevailing socio-economic needs. A closer examination of educational structures of some of the cases discussed in this chapter reflects a major trend toward the inclusion of technical and vocational education and training in modern education systems.

The TVET curricula

An effective policy framework for technical and vocational education with appropriate legislative backing must ultimately be implementable at the curricular level. Subsequently, the nature and type of TVET curricula depend on the level and type of learning required. In Africa, a wide range of technical and vocational subjects are offered across the school curriculum. Most countries do not emphasize the inclusion of the subjects at the primary level. Kenya is one of the very few countries that have several subjects (six) offered at this level; Cameroon has three.

It is at the secondary school level that most TVET subjects are commonly offered, and to a limited extent at the upper primary or junior secondary levels. The role of higher education, and particularly that of the African University, has recently been subjected to closer scrutiny. Much criticism has been levelled against it as being too academic and largely oblivious to national development needs. The university has been called upon to broaden its vocational field and address more effectively the concrete problems facing the African people (Thiam 1992: 109). The minimal attention accorded to technical and vocational education programmes by the university has contributed to the negative attitudes that TVET has earned due to the lack of opportunities for further education (Kerre 1990). Educational reforms at the university have been most minimal in addressing the TVE component.

Currently, there is talk about an education master plan in Kenya. This is as far as it has gone. The stakeholders and professionals in education have not been involved, and are least informed about it. More recently a national commission has been established to review the entire education system in Kenya, thus shelving any ideas about a master plan.

Despite the fact that TVET has found a place in the school curriculum, several issues–some outstanding over the years and others emerging–still challenge both the educationists and development experts. These challenges can be viewed in two major domains. First, is the philosophical conceptualization, the understanding of which is critical to our decisions on the plans for content and the levels and modes of intervention in formal education and training systems. Second, is the determination and validation of the TVET effects, both short term and long term, on the development of economies and human resources.

The philosophical underpinnings of TVET

In order to understand the total concept of Technical and Vocational Education and Training (TVET), it is important to separate and delineate the concepts of education and training, as their understanding influences the type of curricula that we may order for a given group of learners or trainees. Technical and vocational education (TVE) is a comprehensive term referring to an integral aspect of general education which introduces technical/technological and vocational subjects to learners at primary, secondary and post-secondary levels. Such subjects may include: drawing and design, construction technology, communications technology, electrical and electronics technology, etc., on the one hand, and business studies, home science, agricultural education, music, art, etc., on the other.

TVE as part of general education lays emphasis on the general educational aspects of learning where awareness and orientation are imparted at the primary level and exploration and basic preparation are given at secondary level. At post-secondary level, higher education and more preparation are preferred. At both levels vocational training should be phased in at an incremental rate emphasizing occupational awareness through basic practical skills. During the education cycle, vocational training is phased in at an incremental rate.

Technical and Vocational Training (TVT), on the other hand, is the imparting of technical and vocational skills aimed at occupational preparation. Training aims at the acquisition of skills and relevant knowledge required either for direct or self-employment in the world of work. TVT is thus ideal for post-school preparation as practised in Kenyan Technical and Vocational Training Institutions (Republic of Kenya 1988). However, continuing adult education is necessary to enable TVET personnel to benefit from the changing work environment. The greatest problem on the part of policy makers and the public at large has been the misconception that the school system should provide technical and vocational training (TVT) to alleviate the unemployment problem. Schools are best placed to provide education but least equipped to provide vocational training. Furthermore, unemployment is a problem to which many causes can be attributed. The provision of TVET may not necessarily guarantee employment if, for example, the economy is on the decline or there is some political instability. It seems quite obvious from the list of subject offerings in the school curriculum that the focus is more on vocational training than on the provision of vocational education as a general requirement for all learners. However, it makes sense when we learn that a meagre 20–30 per cent of school leavers at primary level in most of these African nations will proceed to secondary school. What preparation can one then give to the majority (70–80 per cent) that will not continue with any form of education or training? (UNESCO BREDA 1995). Frequently, confusion reigns when major government policy statements on education and employment mix up the roles of education and training as implied in the following recommendation:

> It is important to recognize that education is the process and means of acquiring practical skills, whether through traditional or modern systems of education. (Ibanda 1993: 63)

It is important, therefore, that the role of TVET in the formal education curriculum is clearly understood and that the expected performance of the products of such a system be understood by all stakeholders so as to be in agreement with that role.

The questions to pose ought to be: (a) whether schools have succeeded in imparting positive work habits and attitudes; (b) whether technical and vocational institutions have adequately responded to the preparation of trainees for the changing world of work; and (c) whether TVET has the capacity to prepare one for a productive and fulfilling life. With regard to positive work attitudes, it has been found in Kenya that the majority of entrepreneurs in the informal sector have had some orientation to TVET either through technical and vocational institutions or apprenticeship in the *jua kali* sector. New entrants into the sector who are graduates of TVET institutions have often lacked the necessary experience due to the lack of resources and qualified instructors in the institutions. However, after a short apprenticeship, they often adjust much faster than those without the exposure (MRTTT 1994). The introduction of entrepreneurship education in Kenya's TVET system of education has yielded positive results. An evaluation report (Kerre 1994) found that graduates of these institutions look forward to self-employment in the informal sector and that interest in pursuing entrepreneurship education at higher levels has increased. At present all TVET institutions in Kenya offer courses in entrepreneurship education besides the technical courses. The university has also established enterpreneurship education courses in the programmes. Some other universities have also introduced similar courses.

TVET programmes, however, have been found lacking in keeping pace with technological changes in the workplace due to the lack of appropriate facilities and resources. Nations have found the rising costs of TVET difficult to contain at a time when they have to service heavy foreign debts and operate within stringently imposed structural adjustment programmes. A major problem affecting about 50 per cent of Africa's population has been the lack of access and participation by girls and women in scientific and technological programmes and careers. In Kenya, for example, women's enrolment and participation in wage employment in TVET programmes and related occupations fall below 40 per cent and 25 per cent respectively (Kerre 1996). A similar trend is depicted in most of the other African countries, with some states having little or no involvement at all (Logan and Beoku-Betts 1996). Major factors contributing to this problem include low participation rates in mathematics and science at lower levels of education and some inhibitive traditional or cultural practices (Kerre 1996; Otunga 1997).

TVET prospects for industrialization and human resource development

The phenomenal growth of the informal sector (popularly known as *jua kali* in Kenya) in Africa is closely linked to the acquisition and eventual utilization of TVET knowledge and skills. These may have been acquired either through formal training or informally through apprenticeships in the *jua kali* sector. Most activities in this sector are based on the production of a wide range of goods and services requiring the possession and proper application of technical knowledge and skills. The impacts of the informal sector were felt shortly after independence as youth unemployment emerged. It was as a result of the pressures from this sector that the Brigades movement in Botswana and the Village Polytechnics in Kenya, for example, were started at the community level. Today these grassroots movements still exist but whether or not they have earned respect from both governments and the communities in which they still operate is very much debatable due to the many constraints emanating from the political, environmental, economic and social structures prevalent today. Zambia, like many other African states that have achieved independence over the last three decades, has experienced some of the most acute problems in its economic and social welfare. It has experienced a rapid economic decline since the mid-1970s and with a high annual population growth of 3.3 per cent. A large number of youth, around 200 000 every year, leave the school system and enter the labour market without any opportunities for acquiring skills for a productive life. In addition, existing TVET institutions have inadequate resources and personnel to respond effectively to the needs of the employment sector (Mukuni and Kalunga 1997). In response to this deficiency, the Zambian government has, since 1996, formulated and is currently implementing a broader national policy aimed at improving TVET and linking it to the requirements of the employment sector. The new policy incorporates entrepreneurship development, encompassing all types of TVET programmes including nursing, agriculture, community development and engineering. It covers training being conducted at all levels in both the formal and the informal sectors (Republic of Zambia 1996).

Kenya is one of the frontier African nations in terms of supporting the development and growth of small-scale enterprises in both the urban and rural areas. In 1986, a sessional paper on 'Economic Management for

Renewed Growth' (Republic of Kenya 1986) was published, setting a national development strategy up to the year 2000. In this document, the small enterprise sector was identified as a primary means of strengthening Kenya's economy.

In 1988, another sessional paper was published, in which TVET was recognized as pivotal in the preparation and supply of technical manpower for various economic sectors in the country. It also recommended the establishment of entrepreneurship education at all levels of training programmes to promote self-employment in small-scale enterprises and provide managerial skills in the *jua kali* sector.

In 1992, a comprehensive policy framework was established by the government to target the development of the *jua kali* sector, which at the time accounted for approximately 70 per cent of all new jobs for the new entrants in the job market (Republic of Kenya 1992). The government, in collaboration with the private sector, had already helped the *jua kali* sector to stage annual provincial exhibitions at which various products and services were marketed to the public. This also accorded the entrepreneurs an opportunity to share ideas, knowledge and skills in a competitive manner. Towards the end of 1996, the Government of Kenya established another major national strategy to help the country become industrialized by the year 2020 (Republic of Kenya 1996). In this strategy, the role of TVET was once more emphasized and the commitment to sessional paper no. 8 of 1988 on 'Manpower Training for the Next Decade and Beyond' was reaffirmed. Today Kenya stands at a crossroads; clear in her vision as to where she wants to be by the year 2020 but confounded by a myriad of obstacles from within her own political, social and economic milieu.

Achievements

Despite the fact that most African states have had to cope with various problems emanating from political instability, economic malaise and social unrest, *inter alia,* major strides have been made in the promotion of TVET for national development.

TVET legislation

It is evident from discussions in this chapter that most states have recently established legislative backing to guide policy on TVET. This brings together all stakeholders to collaborate in ensuring that TVET is relevant to their needs.

Policy orientation

Most policies support the orientation of TVET toward self-employment and the improvement of the skills of those who seek or have employment in existing organizations. As a result, the emphasis has been placed on teaching entrepreneurship skills and on the support of the informal sector with technical and managerial skills.

TVET curricula review

Education reviews have often included TVET. It is now common knowledge that TVET must respond to the needs of the changing work place and that in most African situations the need for fulfilling basic needs is still high. This means that vocational training associated with basic needs is still relevant. There is also a growing need for continuing adult TVET to enable future workers to cope with changing skill demands in the workplace.

Financing TVET

Financing TVET programmes is one of the most difficult aspects when it comes to implementing the policies so well articulated. However, some innovative ways of cost sharing on a more sustainable level are emerging. These include sharing costs through training levies, and charging nominal fees to the beneficiaries. There have also emerged alternative means through which TVET institutions themselves generate funds based on their expertise. These include the introduction of production units through which products and services are offered to the local communities. These units also function as workstations for industrial attachment of trainees in the TVET programmes. Examples of successful production units include those of the automotive service shop at the Malawi Polytechnic in Malawi and the furniture and bakery units at Kiambu Institute of Technology in Kenya. These, however, have adversely impacted upon business for local producers. Some collaboration through sub-contracting can improve the relationship.

TVET links with small and medium-scale enterprises

Increased attempts at partnerships between TVET institutions and enterprises have emerged as a result of direct policy initiatives and interest at the institutional level. Collaborations through industrial attachments for both students and teaching staff have been reported. These are bringing together institutions and industry, thus enhancing the learning and training processes (UNESCO-UNEVOC 1996). Small Business Centres have been established in TVET institutions in Kenya, for example, to offer consultancy services in both technical and managerial skills to entrepreneurs in the *jua kali* sector. The experiences shared by TVET staff and students with business and industry personnel are valuable in promoting the relationships between the institutions and enterprises. However, the full impact of these SBCs is yet to be realized due to the declining economy.

TVET for personal development

Today, it is not difficult to see the distinctive advantages that TVET has over general education. As an integral aspect of general education, it has the potential of lending intelligibility to education, where theory and practice are enhanced. This inevitably leads to more options in the selection of career opportunities for the learners TVET has, further, a greater potential in imparting technological literacy and enhancing the productive capacities of the modern labour force, a desirable characteristic in the modern technologically oriented workplaces in business and industry.

Conclusion

It can be observed from the discussions in this chapter that while criticisms are often levelled against African states and their leaders for not responding quickly to the changing demands of the workplace and the needs of their populations, serious attempts, despite prevailing adverse circumstances, have been made to revamp the education systems in order to produce the right manpower for national development. The high cost of TVET programmes notwithstanding, most states now have legal provisions to ensure that TVET is given due emphasis in the formal education system, and that it is poised to play a leading role in the transformation of the respective states from agrarian to industrial status. It is thus further worth noting that most educational reviews in Africa are still relatively new compared to those in Europe or America. Most have taken place only in the 1980s and 1990s after struggling to shed a long, debilitating colonial influence. The results of these changes and renovations have yet to be determined. This should be possible within the next decade as most systems mature through the various education cycles.

17 Learning to grow? The importance of education and training for small and micro-enterprise development

SIMON MCGRATH AND KENNETH KING

Revisiting the African small and micro-enterprise

Recent reports on international development from the UK and Sweden underline the potential interrelatedness of small and micro-enterprises (SMEs) in Africa with the broader macroeconomic context of development trajectories and growth strategies (DFID 1997; Sweden, Ministry for Foreign Affairs 1997). Small and micro-enterprises are intimately connected to larger enterprises, whether positively through linkages or negatively through exclusion and isolation from the larger industrial economy. The productivity of the small-scale economy is fundamentally bound up with the fortunes of the economy as a whole. Development co-operation policies also directly and indirectly impact upon SMEs, and new trends in the donor community in the 1990s make it likely that for those countries with appropriate national small enterprise policies, there will be increasing evidence of sector programme support from external sources. In particular, both national and donor strategies for the promotion of SMEs are more than ever coupled with concerns about the appropriate role of education and training (Working Group for International Cooperation in Vocational and Technical Skills Development 1997).

It is timely to revisit the growth potential of Africa's small-scale economy at the end of the 1990s. The second half of the decade has heard increasing talk of an African economic renaissance. A substantial number of countries began to show real GDP growth, and foreign direct investment has been improving in several cases (Holman 1997; Sweden, Ministry for Foreign Affairs 1997; Killick 1999, this volume). Moreover, nearly two decades of structural adjustment has profoundly affected the small and micro-enterprise sector and education and training institutions, both formal and informal. Furthermore, as donors increasingly talk of poverty eradication and pro-poor growth, it is necessary to attempt a revisiting of existing policies and programmes for small-scale pro-capitalist development and for developing the skills necessary for its sustainability.

Small and micro-enterprises: between poverty and growth

The current focus on poverty eradication/alleviation raises serious questions about sectoral development strategies for small and micro-enterprises.

Because the beneficiaries of small enterprise policy could arguably be identified both as the poor and as the emergent entrepreneurs, it has been possible to suggest that donor support to small enterprise development (SED) could have multiple goals. Thus the previous UK administration's SED policy had the following rationale:

> Small and microenterprises are an important source of off-farm employment and self employment for the poor. Growth and productivity increase in this sector thus make a significant contribution to poverty reduction. Moreover, some small and microenterprises expand into medium and even large scale enterprises through investment and skill acquisition, and thus contribute to the vigour of private sector development. (ODA 1995: 2)

SMEs have been seen by some constituencies, and particularly by many Northern NGOs, as a haven of the poor. NGOs have been more frequently involved with income generation schemes for community groups, and especially poor women, than they have been identified with the support of economic growth via individual entrepreneurs, although the world of the technology NGO is a partial exception here (Jeans 1999, this volume).

Beyond NGO support to survivalist or subsistence micro-enterprises, there has been a growing concern about emergent enterprises. In several African contexts, the policy dilemmas in encouraging this segment relate not only to the long-standing debates about the characteristics and determinants of success or 'graduation' among micro-enterprises, but they also acknowledge that successful enterprises emerge into a situation where they often face very severe competitive challenges from established white, Asian or other formal small and medium sized industry (King 1996; Rogerson 1998). In other words, the emergent entrepreneur debate is linked in some countries in sub-Saharan Africa to discussions of 'level playing fields', positive discrimination and securing niches in modern industrial areas where there are sometimes very few indigenous entrepreneurs.

Another aspect of the emergent entrepreneur argument is contained in the flexible specialization literature (Piore and Sabel 1984; McGrath and King 1996; Barr 1999, this volume; McCormick 1999, this volume). There a claim is made that small enterprises are typically better able to respond positively to the challenge of the alleged new global, post-Fordist production than are bureaucratically constrained large corporations.

The third major strand of the pro-small and micro-enterprise literature is that which sees it as the uncertain beneficiary of wider international trends, including structural adjustment. In these accounts, a series of decisions taken by, or imposed upon, formal sector firms has led to outsourcing, informalization of the workforce or the complete collapse of formal firms. Equally, a range of constraints present in protected and state-driven economies have been removed by liberalization and privatization. In this light, the SME sector appears very much as the knock-on sector, dependent to quite a significant extent for its health and vitality on trends that are beyond its direct control.

It is essential that a clearer picture be developed of whether the different strands of small and micro-enterprise support policy are compatible with each other and under which circumstances. Equally, it is necessary to address whether each of the major policy strands can be adopted for SMEs in general, or whether different policies must be adopted for different segments. Moreover, it is vital that strategies for support to, and intervention in, the small and micro-enterprise sector should be consistent and coherent with programmes focused on large and formal enterprises. Finally, it is our concern in this chapter to examine the implications of such explorations for policy and practice in the fields of education and training.

Describing the small and micro-enterprise sector

Since the 'discovery' of the informal sector, much effort has gone into the definition of it and other variants (see Mead and Morrison 1996). While there is a plethora of distinctions and definitions, the degree of informality and the size of employment have been the two principal criteria on which classification has rested. Using a broad brush, it is possible to paint three categories of enterprise that emerge from this debate:

- Formal and small: the classic small enterprises of the literature on Northern economies are also a feature of the economies of the South. Such enterprises conform to regulations to a significant extent, exhibit relatively (and often absolutely) high levels of human capital and are integrated into the structures of the formal economy. Although largely excluded from discussions of the informal sector and poverty alleviation, they are potentially significant players, particularly as sources of skills or as part of the 'glass ceiling' for our next category.
- Informal and small: elements of the informal sector, which are given descriptions such as 'successful' or 'sustainable'; 'emergent' or 'entrepreneurial'. It is in these enterprises that informal sector incomes can outstrip those in the lower reaches of the formal sector (Mead 1999, this volume; Oketch and Otieno 1998). Although outside formal sector structures, often the owner-operators of such enterprises have had significant exposure to both formal education and training and to formal employment. Such enterprises are seen as central to the poverty-growth debate as important producers of goods, services and employment. This does not mean, of course, that they are necessarily part of any industrial growth project of their respective states. Indeed, they are at least as likely to have been discriminated against as promoted by the state (Mkandawire 1999, this volume).

- Survivalist: enterprises in which the commonly perceived relationship between poverty and informal sector is most apparent. Engaged primarily in commerce, but also in basic and low-quality forms of production, those running these enterprises are typically at the level of subsistence, with enterprise income being only one part of income (Mead 1999, this volume).

The extent to which these types represent discrete segments with significant barriers between each of them (and with the medium and large formal sector too) or are simply modal points along a continuum, is one that continues to be debated. King (1996) and Mead (1999, this volume) point to the frequency of enterprise between categories: a movement that can take place in both directions. Rogerson (1999, this volume), however, emphasizes the massive disparities between the segments and the particular racial nature that the division between the first two categories has taken historically in South Africa. This is an important debate in that it highlights the need to look carefully at the intended targets and beneficiaries of specific policies. Crucially here it is necessary to consider whether targeting a policy on current realities is to reinforce inequalities (Rogerson 1999, this volume) or whether it is possible actively to target those with potential–basing interventions both on where they are now and on where they might be in the future (Mead 1999, this volume).

In the light of the current uncertainty about the relationship between poverty and growth, the decision on which types of enterprise to target with which kind of intervention is a major challenge for policy makers and practitioners. Should the principal focus, for instance, be on those who have the greatest potential to employ others (Jeans 1999, this volume; Manu 1999, this volume), or should it be on the poorest of the poor? A decision on this will have serious implications for the kind of interventions to be contemplated. However, it must be remembered that the resources available for any such interventions are very limited and that many in the policy community have serious reservations about the desirability of interventions.

What is clear is that it is untenable to consider small and micro-enterprises in isolation from either macroeconomic trends or the health of larger enterprises. Mead (1999, this volume) points to a growing realization that such a picture is complex. He notes thats in an economic upswing the informal sector jobs being created are more 'growth'-focused, while in a downswing survivalist self-employment is dominant. How can such a dynamic best be taken account of in programmes of support to, and intervention in, the small and micro-enterprise sector, but also in programmes that aim at influencing the vitality of the economy as a whole?

While the extension of flexible specialization debates to Africa has not resulted in any firm evidence of world-class clusters, the literature of networks and linkages can, nevertheless, throw up some important issues for discussion in the light of a debate about poverty and growth. It is important to remain mindful that vertical relationships based on outsourcing are designed primarily to allow larger firms to evade labour regulations. Equally, disagreement exists about the extent to which such vertical relations promote skill transfer (Adam 1999, this volume; Jeans 1999, this volume) and thus constitute an important source of learning for growth within SMEs. None the less, high quality vertical relations based on mutuality, as is alleged to take place in Japan, does seem an attractive vision. While this seems likely to be a very limited possibility in Africa, it is still worth considering which mechanisms would foster and support such relationships.

Barr's chapter suggests that vertical networks of African small and micro-enterprises tend to be risk-minimizing. Such enterprises have small, cohesive networks designed to minimize risk, for instance through failure to honour contracts. These networks, however, do not encourage enterprises to innovate and, when innovation does take place, do not allow them to take advantage of this in anything more than the very short run. The risk minimization strategy of African SMEs arises out of the chronic failures of infrastructure, market institutions and support services from which African economies suffer (Rogerson 1998; Barr 1999, this volume; Pedersen 1999, this volume). Such supports to production and trade are inadequate and discriminate in favour of larger enterprises which, therefore, have less need of risk-reduction strategies.

The role of education and training in enterprise development

The Donor Committee for Small Enterprise Development has recently popularized the notion of Business Development Services (Gibson 1997). This concept places non-financial services alongside credit as part of a menu of inputs, which can then be tailored to individuals' needs. Among these, education and training are increasingly factors that are being given attention in the whole promotion of small and micro-enterprises, particularly as donors to education are increasingly seeing the SME sector as an appropriate location for their own interventions (Working Group for International Cooperation in Vocational and Technical Skills Development 1997).

The challenge for educational researchers from this new conjuncture is to integrate their own lessons about the relationship between education and work in Africa with new insights about the new dynamics of the small-scale economy across the continent. This challenge can be met adequately only with rigorous research. However, in the next few pages, we shall seek to identify some of the key themes that may require attention.

The poverty-growth debate sheds a particular light on this exploration. It highlights a concern with policy coherence and consistency: between learning and SED policies within African countries, and between the new trends in aid policies, including those for learning and SED, and those of African governments. It also promotes an awareness of the linkages and the desire for intersectoral connections between learning systems and SED within and across the agencies (Working Group for International Cooperation in Vocational and Technical Skills Development 1997; McGrath 1998b).

One possible starting point for a re-evaluation of the relationship between education and training, and SMEs and development, would be the policy of Education for All, the global educational orthodoxy of the 1990s. EFA fails to reflect critically on the future livelihoods of those passing through education systems. Thus, it seems to undermine the awareness highlighted in the previous paragraph. The final declaration of the Jomtien conference (WCEFA 1990) appears to assume implicitly that there is a core set of educational attainments which will prepare graduates for their lives ahead. Yet, in reality, those future lives will be extremely varied. It is necessary, therefore, to examine whether there is indeed a set of universal, or even national, competences, skills and attainments that is capable of delineation. If there is not, then it must be considered whether there are different needs for different communities.

If the likely livelihoods of the majority of African children are to be informal sector-related, then does the kind of basic education on offer post-Jomtien address their needs for sustainable livelihoods? In spite of the evidence against vocational education, and questions about the efficacy of preparation of school students for self-employment, are there answers in these areas? Such questions have not been addressed seriously enough in the past decade.

Honny's contribution to this book highlights the problems that Ghana has found in addressing both 'relevance' and quality in its school curriculum. Kerre (1999, this volume) notes the aspirations towards relevance, particularly to self-employment, embodied in the Kenyan 8–4–4 reforms. Skills development for self-employment remains a clear and acknowledged need in Kenya, but the 8–4–4 system is the subject of a Presidential Education Commission which seems likely to reduce the number of subjects on the grounds of efficiency (McGrath 1998d). In South Africa, however, it appears that a very different path is being taken. There, the new Curriculum 2005 reforms have a very strong emphasis on enterprise education (King 1997). Whether South Africa is simply following a post-independence tradition of stressing relevance, only to abandon it as unfeasible in the future, remains to be seen.

For those outside the formal education system, too, there is a need to consider the appropriate form of basic education, if this is to become more widespread. Here also there is a major challenge in making learning relevant to socio-cultural experience and economic activities, while still allowing for socio-economic movement. But the central challenge may be to construct an Adult Basic Education and Training (ABET) curriculum that allows for appropriate combinations of vocational and academic teaching that will facilitate learners to participate more critically and effectively across their range of activities. In this regard, the South African attempt to integrate ABET into a National Qualifications Framework and to incorporate informal sector activities and actors into the national system of learnerships (see below) is an exciting, though highly ambitious, emerging example of what may be possible.

The Copenhagen Summit has already rescheduled (and arguably narrowed) the Jomtien targets. It may also be time to reassert the importance of preserving their connections to a broader vision of an integrated education and training sector. There is a considerable danger that the current growth in a pro-poor focus will be allowed to further emphasize the primary sub-sector at the expense of other subsectors which should be seen as complementary to it. The findings of the GEMINI surveys suggest that small amounts of education do little to enhance productivity in the informal sector (Mead 1999, this volume). Rather, this work seems to suggest, albeit tentatively, that the returns on education to those in the SME economy may be greater for the post-basic level. None the less, while causal relationships between education, employment and productivity remain unproven, it is dangerous to suggest that higher education levels in the SME sector will lead to better productivity. Rather, the growing levels of education in the SME sector may best be viewed from the standpoint of their potential implications for the livelihoods of those who have only a basic education, or none at all.

If a pro-poor strategy is to be followed then it is inconceivable that it should fail to address those out of school as well as those in it. A balanced view of poverty and growth priorities may also help to highlight the crucial developmental roles of other aspects of education and training and cause a re-evaluation of the importance of broader notions of what learning is about, in both vocational and cultural terms. Far more thought is required about the goals of learning and about the contexts in which it takes place and is utilized.

In the OECD countries the current fascination with the notion of a new work organization has led to a multitude of calls for a radically restructured form of education (Reich 1991; Cummings and McGinn 1997; Ilon 1997; McGrath and King 1997). This education would be convergent with training, the new work organization having undermined the archaic distinctions between the two domains (de Moura Castro and de Oliveira 1994). It would also focus on the new skills required for the new workplace: problem-solving, creativity, team working (Reich 1991). For those interested in education in Africa, and for its links to the working realities of the majority of Africans, it is important to consider whether there is any relevance in such a model for African needs.

Whether poverty- or growth-focused, interventions for those in, or likely to enter, the SME sector need to consider the enhancement of livelihoods. Newer or better skills and knowledge have been associated with better livelihoods in a number of ways. Improved education has been linked to a greater ability to adapt to new market conditions; to access wider social networks; to utilize more productive technologies, although the precise mechanisms operating are poorly understood and evidence is insufficient.

Education and training are also seen as potentially assisting in the maximization of future life choices. While the importance of socializing youth for future employment niches is often given considerable prominence in educational strategies, it is important that a balance be struck between socialization for the most likely labour market destination and empowerment to have more than one viable option for future (self) employment.[1]

It is crucial for educationalists to re-evaluate the ability of schooling to deliver on these twin imperatives of enhanced livelihoods and maximized choices. A critical and detailed reading of the nature of the SMEs, of the sector as a whole, and the place of both in national and global economies, allows and necessitates a review of the intentions of education and training systems. What are the appropriate knowledges that education systems in Africa should be developing among students? These remain largely under-debated and researched. What types of skills do these students need when they enter the labour market full time?

Just as it has been difficult to sift out the impact of several rounds of 'successful' micro-credit programmes on individual entrepreneurial development, so it has been difficult to escape from what may be termed minimalist descriptions of the education–enterprise interaction. The tradition in many studies of entrepreneurs' experience over the years has been to rely on measures such as 'years of education', or of bald educational stages: 'complete primary' or 'secondary' or 'technical training', without attempting to take account, in any way, of the modality, content or quality of that education or training experience. This minimalist use of education or training as an explanatory variable in discussing enterprise success neglects the political attention historically given in many African countries to deliberately altering the content of basic, secondary and vocational education. In addition to what Mead calls 'the standard problems of associating more education with more productivity' (1999, this volume), there must also be a problem in treating education-designed-for-enterprise as if it were identical to ordinary academic schooling.

Thus it would be valuable to assess, for instance, the enterprise consequences of 14 years of Kenya's educational reform (1985–1998). This may still be worth attempting even if this enterprise and self-employment-oriented reform will be abandoned without a shred of evidence from post-school experience, just as it was launched without any. This Kenyan example points up a more general challenge to policy coherence in education–enterprise initiatives: that for any particular set of current small enterprise clients, their education is no longer a policy manipulable variable; it is a 'given'. Knowledge of the particular deposit of skills and attitudes from different reform phases in the education and training systems is something that could be built

[1] This point is reinforced in Northern economies by arguments about the erosion of jobs-for-life, whether in the narrow Japanese sense of employment with one company or in a broader sense of a single linear career path.

upon in principle, but the variety and diversity of prior learning are such that it is probably very unusual for small enterprise schemes to consider them.

The impact of education and training on employability and productivity is further complicated by what appears to be a powerful synergistic relationship between formal learning and on-the-job experience. Mead (1999; this volume) suggests that more education and training may allow workers to take better advantage of what they learn through doing. Equally, as a worker becomes more experienced, so it is possible that he or she is better able to put their theoretical and practical understandings together. Other evidence points to the importance of time in facilitating access to sustainable informal sector livelihoods (Grierson 1993; McGrath and King 1995). While the quality and quantity of the initial distillation of education and training may be important, it can improve with age through being fermented with experience, networks and capital accumulation. Thus, to attempt to research the linkage between initial education and training and subsequent (self) employment performance must grasp this important dimension to understand the relationship in its complexity.

An additional layer of complexity is added to this national education–enterprise equation by the influence of the donor community. This influences the national equation in two inter-related ways. Internationally, during the 1990s, the dominance within donor thinking of basic education has had a very marked knock-on effect on agencies' intellectual and financial support to other education and training sub-sectors, such as vocational and higher (and even on the composition of their own personnel). Second, within countries, the donor community has been rather influential in the national adoption of new education reforms, and in the case of Kenya, again, it is interesting that this reform is intended to reduce the subjects in the basic cycle from 10 to four, and at a stroke remove the orientation towards practical skills at this level.

It is not clear that what was originally introduced as part of a national project to develop technical capacity is being abandoned because of the adoption of a new project. Nor is it evident in what way it is related to Kenya's desire to achieve technological capacity at higher levels of education, or indeed industrial transformation more generally (Government of Kenya 1996). As we suggested earlier, there is some danger that the poverty focus (which may be one element in the simplification of the basic cycle) of donor agencies can result in a policy fragmentation whereby particular sub-sectors are given attention both externally and nationally because they are in the international development targets. This may then make more difficult the achievement of a comprehensive national project of industrial development.

In some ways this illustration of quite sudden change from Kenya could be repeated in other countries, and in many other aspects of the supply side of skills for the economy and in particular for the small-scale world of self-employment. There have been one-off initiatives, sometimes from governments, sometimes from donors. They have focused attention on schools, on post-school training, on vocational training, on local apprenticeship systems, and even on universities, and they have sought through some additionality to make the institutions serve two worlds: employment and self-employment. Thanks to a number of researchers who have tried to tease out the achievements of these ventures, we are now better informed about a series of these different initiatives (e.g. Grierson and McKenzie 1996; McGrath and King 1995; Grierson 1997; Adam; Honny; Kerre – all 1999, this volume). But too often one has had the sense that the research or evaluation is examining a phenomenon which is short-lived, and which will end with the exhaustion of the external (or less commonly the national) funds that made it possible. Not surprisingly, therefore, the record of these initiatives is very mixed.

The lack of linkage to the labour market in so many of these initiatives and the inevitable time lapse before tracer studies could be helpful (but see Honny 1999, this volume) have meant that in one sense the evidence about the capacity of these programmes to change attitudes, provide skills or secure work is no better than when Philip Foster did his well-known research on the vocational school fallacy in development planning in the early 1960s in Ghana (Foster 1965). Indeed, in some sense the record is less robust, because the research capacity of many universities has haemorrhaged very severely over the past 20 years. There is not therefore available any major national research study of the education reform (8–4–4) which would give a sense of the skills and attitudes acquired by young people in Kenya.

In the light of the lack of data it is possible that the arguments on both sides of the vocationalization debate are context-specific. The Ghana undergoing independence of Foster's writings is very different in certain key respects from the Ghana attempting to respond rapidly to globalization in the late 1990s. It is important to consider how globalization and rapid technological change alter the argument at the general level, and at the level of their specific manifestations in locations such as Suame Magazine or Gikomba.[2] If education is to contribute to enhanced livelihoods, to maximized choices and to African competitiveness, as policy makers intend, this debate is urgently in need of updating.

Formalizing the informal sector: a skills-driven development project

South Africa does not have the same level of coverage or internal formalization[3] in its non-formal training as other African countries. For this, and other

[2] Areas of major SME concentration in Kumasi and Nairobi, respectively.

[3] By internal formalization we refer to the presence of structures within the non-formal system, such as contracts, certificates and graduation ceremonies that are internally policed. This contrasts with the external formalization of the South African attempt to develop common qualifications across the formal and non-formal training systems.

reasons, it is the country in which attempts to bring all training under a single system are most radical (Department of Labour 1997).

One of the core elements in South Africa's ambitious Green Paper (on skills development) is a new system of learnerships (King 1997; McGrath 1998a and c). A key challenge will be to ensure that the new training instruments will no longer operate primarily in the traditional industrial sector, e.g. in seeking to halt the declining number of apprenticeships, but should apply across a variety of employment and self-employment sites, including the small and micro-enterprise sector as defined in South Africa.[4] This has meant thinking how to deliver to small and micro-enterprises the crucially important work experience and other requirements of these new learnerships.

This commitment will be difficult to put into practice; but what is clear about the South African proposals, is that in contrast to many other countries in Africa where there are effectively two training systems, 'traditional' and 'modern', the intention is clearly to have a single national system, if at all possible.

Enough has been said to suggest that this formalizing and inclusive aspiration, though hugely ambitious, should attract research attention from its earliest stages. Whether a common national qualification currency will be sufficiently persuasive to draw all skills into a single system is still unclear. But what is important with this South African initiative is that it will send out signals about the small-scale economy becoming part of a nationally accredited system.[5]

Putting the small-scale economy at the heart of the national economy

Although they may numerically contain the bulk of the economically active population, both male and female, in many countries, the employers and workers in these informal small-scale economies most certainly do not feel themselves to be an integral part of the national economy. Equally, those in the informal sector probably do not feel themselves to be part of

[4] South African policy literature more generally uses the term small, medium and micro-enterprise. However, the Department of Labour excludes the formal medium sized firm from its discussions about target groups.

[5] This position, developed in response to the particular historical trajectory of South Africa, is also reflected in some agency statements. One of the most recent and unequivocal comes from Sweden:

> For the small-scale economy to be genuinely capable of contributing to lasting growth in Africa, it must be formalised. Links must be incorporated that are capable of transmitting macroeconomic signals and generating incentives for expansion. Such links may consist of more comprehensive credit systems, reliable regulatory systems and functioning institutions. Accordingly, the small-scale economy and the informal sector become more amenable to economic measures – no longer 'just' a means of livelihood for poor groups in the population, but also an important pillar of the country's economic future. (Sweden, Ministry for Foreign Affairs 1997: 119)

any developmental project of the sort described by Mkandawire, in this book. Whether, by contrast, they would prefer to feel themselves to be part of a new poverty focus of their state is doubtful. Across Africa, the very idea of a poverty focus or framework for their government may seem rather surprising. But if that focus were to involve any sense of their options for upward mobility being somehow foreclosed, they would likely have none of it.

The previous (1975) White Paper of the UK government captured very nicely the danger of a policy that was carefully shaped for the poor of the rural areas (or for that matter of the informal sectors of Africa):

> We must beware of adopting policies which while intended to meet the needs of the poorest people, and especially those in rural communities, imply that poorer people and people living in the country can expect only a standard of education lower than those who happen to live in towns. There is a need for education about education. (Ministry of Overseas Development 1975: 22)

This points to the dilemma at the heart of much of what we are discussing here: the danger of slipping into ghettoization or, conversely, that 'neutral' policies will leave existing power imbalances in place. It is to be hoped that the renewed attention being given to both poverty and growth in the African context, whether in the education sector or beyond, can be the catalyst for careful re-examination of principles and practices that affect, both directly and indirectly, the majority of African workers; those located in small and micro-enterprises.

Bibliography

Introduction

Adam, S. 1999, 'Competences and other factors affecting the small enterprise sector in Ibadan, Nigeria'. This volume.

Barr, A. 1999. 'Do SMEs network for growth?' This volume.

Charmes, J. 1999. 'Micro-enterprises in West Africa. The need for a follow-up survey of their dynamics and role in job creation within the continuous expansion of the informal sector'. This volume.

Chossudovsky, M. 1997, *The Globalization of Poverty*. Zed, London

CPAG (Consultative Group to Assist the Poorest) 1995, 'A policy framework for the Consultative Group to Assist the Poorest – a micro-finance program'. CGAP, World Bank, Washington DC.

de Soto, H. 1989, *The Other Path.* I.B. Tauris, London.

Fine, B. 1998, 'Neither Washington nor Post-Washington Consensus: an introduction'. Unpublished paper, SOAS, University of London.

Fluitman, F. 1994, 'Traditional apprenticeship in Africa'. In Husen, T. and Postlethwaite, N. (eds.) *The International Encyclopaedia of Education.* Pergamon , Oxford.

Frimpong-Ansah, J. 1992, *The Vampire State in Africa.* James Currey, London.

Gibbons, M. et al. 1994, *The New Production of Knowledge.* Sage, London.

Gibson, A. 1997, 'Business development services for SMES: preliminary guideline for donor-funded interventions'. Donor Committee on Small Enterprise Development, Washington DC.

Holman, M. 1997, 'Cultivating the seeds of recovery in Africa'. Japan's Overseas Development Assistance Seminar, *Financial Times*, London, November.

Honny, L. 1999, 'Reshaping vocational training: hopeful signs from a Ghanaian experience'. This volume.

Jeans, A. 1999, 'Technology, NGOs and small enterprise: securing livelihoods through technical change'. This volume.

Joekes, S. 1999, 'Gender, property rights and trade: constraints to African growth'. This volume.

Kerre, B.W. 1999, 'The role and potential of technical and vocational education in formal education systems in Africa'. This volume.

Killick, A. 1999, 'Have Africa's economies turned the corner?' This volume.

King, K. 1977, *The African Artisan.* Heinemann, London.

King, K. 1996, *Jua Kali Kenya.* James Currey, London.

King, K. 1997, 'Policy coherence in education, training and enterprise development in South Africa: the implementation challenge of new policies'. Papers in Education, Training and Enterprise No. 4, Centre of African Studies, University of Edinburgh.

King, K. and Buchert, L. (eds.) 1999, *International Aid to Education: Global Patterns and National Contexts.* UNESCO/NORRAG, Paris.

McCormick, D. 1999, 'Enterprise clusters in Africa: linkages for growth and development'. This volume.

McGinn, N. 1996, 'The impact of globalization on national education systems'. *Prospects* 27/1, pp. 41–54.

McGrath, S. 1997, 'From national project to sectoral policies: examining Ghana's 2020 vision'. Papers on Education, Training and Enterprise 9, Centre of African Studies, University of Edinburgh.
McGrath, S. 1998a, 'Further education and training in South Africa: the acid test for the integrated approach'. Papers in Education, Training and Enterprise No. 14, Centre of African Studies, University of Edinburgh.
McGrath, S. 1998b, 'No easy walk to industrialization: reflections of the reform of Kenyan education and training'. Papers in Education, Training and Enterprise No. 18, Centre of African Studies, University of Edinburgh.
McGrath, S. 1999, 'Education, development and assistance: the challenge of the new millennium'. In King, K. and Buchert, L. (eds.) *International Aid to Education: Global Patterns and National Contexts.* UNESCO/NORRAG, Paris.
McGrath, S. and King, K. 1999, 'Learning to grow? The importance of education and training for small and micro-enterprise development'. This volume.
Manu, G. 1999, 'Enterprise development in Africa: strategies for growth and impact'. This volume
Marais, H. 1998, *Limits to Change.* Zed, London.
von Massow, F. 1999, 'Inherent gender inequities in small and micro-enterprise development in rural Africa?' This volume.
Mead, D. 1999, 'MSEs tackle both poverty and growth (but in differing proportions)'. This volume.
Mkandawire, T. 1999, 'Developmental states and small enterprises'. This volume.
North, D. 1990, *Institutions, Institutional Change and Economic Performance.* Cambridge University Press, Cambridge.
Pedersen, P. O. 1999, 'Trading agents and other producer services in African industrialization and globalization)'. This volume.
Powell, J. 1995, *Survival of the Fitter.* Intermediate Technology Publications, London.
Riddell, R. 1997, 'The changing concepts of aid and development'. In Cummings, W. and McGinn, N. (eds.) *International handbook on education and development.* Pergamon, Oxford.
Rogerson, C.M. 1999, 'Small enterprise development in post-apartheid South Africa'. This volume.
UNESCO 1999, 'Lifelong learning and training: a bridge to the future. Draft main working document'. UNESCO, Paris.
World Bank 1997, *World Development Report 1997.* World Bank, Washington DC.
WCEFA (World Conference on Education for All) 1990, 'Declaration of the World Conference on Education for All'. WCEFA. New York.

Chapter 1

Adam, C. 1998, 'Investing in Africa: a question of risk'. Centre for the Study of African Economies, University of Oxford.
Aryeetey, E., Harrigan, J. and Nissanke, M. (eds.) 1999 (forthcoming), *The Economy of Ghana*. James Currey, Oxford.
Burnside, C. and Dollar, D. 1997, 'Aid, policies and growth'. Policy Research Working Paper 1777, World Bank, Washington DC.
Collier, P. and Gunning, J.W. 1997, 'Explaining economic performance'. Centre for the Study of African Economies, Working Paper WPS/972, University of Oxford.

Devarajan, S. 1997, 'Real exchange rate misalignment in the Franc Zone'. *Journal of African Economies* 6/1.

Dhonte, P. 1995, 'Three propositions on African economic growth'. International Monetary Fund Paper on Policy Analysis and Assessment PPAA/95/9, Washington DC.

Easterly, W., Kremer, M., Pritchett, L. and Summers, L. 1993, 'Good policy or good luck? Country growth performance and temporary shocks'. *Journal of Monetary Economics.* 32/3.

Easterly, W. and Levine, R. 1997, 'Africa's growth tragedy: a retrospective, 1960–89'. World Bank Policy Research Working Paper 1503, Washington DC.

Easterly, W. and Levine, R. 1998, 'Troubles with the neighbours: Africa's problem, Africa's opportunity'. *Journal of African Economies* 7/1.

Elbadawi, I., Ndulu, B.J. and Ndung'u, N. 1997a, 'Debt overhang and economic growth in Sub-Saharan Africa'. In Iqbal, Z. and Kanbur, R. (eds.) *External Finance for Low-Income Countries.* International Monetary Fund, Washington DC.

Elbadawi, I., Ndulu, B.J. and Ndung'u, N. 1997b, 'Macroeconomic performance in sub-Saharan Africa in a comparative setting'. African Economic Research Consortium conference paper, Nairobi.

Fischer, S., Hernandez-Cat, E. and Khan, M. 1998, 'Africa: is this the turning point?' International Monetary Fund Paper on Policy Analysis and Assessment PPAA/98/6, Washington DC.

Fosu, A.K. 1996, 'Primary exports and economic growth in developing economies'. *The World Economy* 19/4.

Ghura, D. 1995, 'Macro policies, external forces, and economic growth in Sub-Saharan Africa'. *Economic Development and Cultural Change* 43/4.

Hadjimichael, M.T. et al. 1995, 'Sub-Saharan Africa: growth, savings and investment, 1986–93'. International Monetary Fund Occasional Paper 118, Washington DC.

Hadjimichael, M.T. and Ghura, D. 1995, 'Public policies and private savings and investment in Sub-Saharan Africa: an empirical investigation'. International Monetary Fund IMF Working Paper WP/95/19, Washington DC.

Hayami, Y. and Platteau, J.-P. 1997, 'Resource endowments and agricultural development: Africa vs. Asia'. Centre de Recherche en Economie et Développement (CRED), Belgium.

International Monetary Fund 1992, *World Economic Outlook.* IMF, Washington DC.

International Monetary Fund 1998, *World Economic Outlook.* IMF, Washington DC.

Iqbal, Z. and Kanbur, R. (eds.) 1997, *External Finance for Low-Income Countries.* International Monetary Fund, Washington DC.

Joekes, S. 1999, 'Gender, property rights and trade: constraints to African growth'. This volume.

Khan, M.S. and Kumar, M.S. 1997, 'Public and private investment and the growth process in developing countries'. *Oxford Bulletin of Economics and Statistics* 59/1.

Killick, T. 1994, 'Africa's post-independence development experiences'. In Grilli, E. and Salvatore, D. (eds.), *Economic Development.* Greenwood Press, Westport, CT.

Killick, T. 1999 (forthcoming), *Aid and the Political Economy of Policy Change.* Routledge, London.

Ng, F. and Yeats, A. 1997, 'Open economies work better! Did Africa's protectionist policies cause its marginalisation in world trade?' *World Development* 25/6.

Oshikoya, T.W. 1994, 'Macroeconomic determinants of domestic private investment in Africa'. *Economic Development and Cultural Change* 42/3.

Ram, R. 1997, 'Tropics and economic development: an empirical investigation'. *World Development* 25/9.

Sachs, J.D. and Warner, A.M. 1997, 'Sources of slow growth in African economies'. *Journal of African Economies* 6/3.

Stasavage, D. 1997, 'The CFA Franc Zone and fiscal discipline'. *Journal of African Economies* 6/1.

United Nations 1997, *The World Economy at the Beginning of 1998*. UN–Dept. of Economic and Social Affairs, New York.

United Nations 1998, *Africa Recovery* 11/3.

World Bank 1981, *Accelerated Development in Sub-Saharan Africa*. World Bank, Washington DC.

World Bank 1997a, *World Development Report: The State in a Changing World*. Oxford University Press for World Bank, Oxford.

World Bank 1997b, *World Development Indicators, 1997*. World Bank, Washington DC.

World Bank 1998, *World Development Indicators, 1998*. World Bank, Washington DC.

Chapter 2

Amsden, A. 1995, 'Like the rest: South-east Asia's 'late' industrialization'. *Journal of International Development* 7/5.

Aron, J. 1996, 'The institutional foundations of growth'. In Ellis, S. (ed.) *Africa Now*. James Currey, London.

Biggs, T. and Srivastava, P. 1997, 'Structural aspects of manufacturing in sub-Saharan Africa: findings from a seven country enterprise survey'. ATD Discussion Paper 356, World Bank, Washington DC.

Boahen, A. 1985, 'Colonialism in Africa: its impact and significance'. In Boahen, A. (ed.) *Africa under Colonial Domination*. UNESCO, Paris.

Chang, H-J. 1996, *The Political Economy of Industrial Policy*. Macmillan, London.

Chazan, N. 1987, 'Disengagement from the state in Africa: reflections on the experience in Ghana and Guinea'. *Comparative Studies in Society and History* 19/1.

de Soto, H. 1989, *The Other Path*. Harper and Row, New York.

Dondo, C.A. 1998, 'The dynamics of the informal sector in Kenya'. Paper presented to the 'Enterprise in Africa' conference, Edinburgh, May.

Evans, P. 1992, 'The state as problem and solution: embedded autonomy and structural change'. In Haggard, S. and Kaufman, R. (eds.) *The Politics of Structural Adjustment*. Princeton University Press, Princeton.

Evans, P. 1997a, 'Introduction: development strategies across the public–private divide'. In Evans, P. (ed.) *State–Society Synergy*. University of California Press, Berkeley.

Evans, P. 1997b, 'Transferable lessons? Re-examining the institutional prerequisites of East Asian economic policies'. UNCTAD, Geneva.

Haggard, S. 1998, 'Business, politics and policy in East and Southeast Asia'. In Rowen, H. (ed.) *Behind East Asian Growth*. Routledge, London.

Hsaio, H.-H. 1995, 'The state and business relations in Taiwan'. In Fitzgerald, R. (ed.) *The State and Economic Development.* Frank Cass, London.
Jomo, K.S. 1994, 'Privatisation and public sector reform: the political economy of state intervention'. *Pakistan Development Review* 33/4.
Kim, L. and Nugent, J. 1994, 'The Republic of Korea's small and medium-size enterprises and their support systems'. World Bank, Washington DC.
Koo, H. and Kim, E. 1992, 'The developmental state and capital accumulation in South Korea'. In Henderson, R. and Applebaum, J. (eds.) *State and Development in the Asian Pacific Rim.* Sage, London.
Lewis, P. 1994, 'Economic statism, private capital and the dilemmas of accumulation in Nigeria'. *World Development* 22/3.
Marx, K. 1962, *Capital.* Foreign Languages Publishing House, Moscow.
Mkandawire, T. 1994, 'The political economy of privatisation in Africa'. In Cornia, A. and Helleiner, G. (eds.) *From Adjustment to Development in Africa.* Macmillan, London.
Mkandawire, T. 1998, 'Thinking about developmental states in Africa'. UNCTAD, Geneva.
Moore, M. and Hamatal, L. 1993, 'Economic liberalisation, political pluralism and business associations in developing countries'. *World Development* 21/12.
Root, H. 1998, 'The distinctive institutions in the rise of industrial Asia'. In Rowen, H. (ed.) *Behind East Asian Growth.* Routledge, London.
Steel, W. 1993, 'Analysing the policy framework for small enterprise development'. In Helmsing, A. and Kolsteee, T. (eds.) *Small Enterprises and Changing Policies.* IT Publications, London.
Steel, W., Aryeetey, E., Hettice, H. and Nissanke, M. 1997, 'Informal finance markets under liberalisation in four countries'. *World Development* 25/5.
World Bank 1993. *East Asian Miracle.* World Bank, Washington DC.
World Bank 1994. *Adjustment in Africa.* World Bank, Washington DC.
World Bank 1995. *Bureaucrats in Business.* World Bank, Washington DC.
World Bank 1997. *World Development Report 1997.* World Bank, Washington DC.
Yanagihara, T. 1997, 'Economic system approach and its applicability'. In Yanagihara, T. and Sambommatsu, S. (eds.) *Economic System Approach and its Applicability.* Institute of Developing Economies, Tokyo.

Chapter 3

Berge, K, Daniel, P., Evans, D., Kennan, J., Owens, T., Stevens, C. and Wood, A. 1994, 'Trade and development options for the poorest countries: a preliminary investigation'. Working Paper 12, IDS, University of Sussex.
Bredie, J.W.B. and Beeharry, G.K. 1998, 'School enrollment decline in Sub-Saharan Africa'. World Bank Discussion Paper No 395, World Bank, Washington DC.
Dolan, C. 1997, *Tesco is King: Gender and Labor Dynamics in Horticultural Exporting, Meru District, Kenya.* PhD thesis, State University of New York, Binghampton.
Fontana, M., Joekes, S. and Masika, R. 1998, 'Global trade expansion and liberalisation: gender issues and impacts'. BRIDGE Report No 42 for DFID, IDS, University of Sussex.
Goetz, A-M. 1997, *Getting Institutions Right for Women.* Zed, London.
Hamner, L., Pyatt, G., and White, H. nd. 'Poverty in Sub-Saharan Africa. What

can we learn from the World Bank's poverty assessments?' Institute of Social Studies, The Hague.

Jamison, D.T. and Lau, L.L. 1982, *Farmer Education and Farm Efficiency*. Johns Hopkins University Press, Baltimore.

Joekes, S., Green, C. and Leach, M. 1996, 'Integrating gender into environmental research and policy'. Working Paper 27, IDS, University of Sussex.

Kennedy, E. 1989, 'The effects of sugarcane production on food security, health and nutrition in Kenya: a longitudinal analysis'. IFPRI Research Report no 78, Washington DC.

Koopman. J. 1992, 'Neo-classical household models and modes of household production: problems in the analysis of African agricultural households'. African Studies Center, Boston University, Working Paper No. 166.

Lastarria-Cornhiel, S. 1997, 'Impact of privatization on gender and property rights in Africa'. *World Development* 25/8.

Leach, M. and Fairhead, J. 1995, 'Ruined settlements and new gardens: gender and soil-ripening among Kuranko farmers in the forest–savanna transition zone'. *IDS Bulletin* 26/1.

MacKenzie, F., 1994, 'Land rights and labour rights in Kenya: issues for research'. In Yngström. I., et al. (eds.) *Gender and Environment in Africa: Perspectives on the Politics of Environmental Sustainability*. Centre of African Studies, University of Edinburgh.

Meinzen-Dick, R., Brown, L., Feldstein, H.S. and Quisumbung, A.R. 1997a, 'Gender and property rights: resources'. *World Development* 25/8.

Meinzen-Dick, R., Brown, L., Feldstein, H.S. and Quisumbung, A.R. 1997b, 'Gender, property rights, and natural resources'. *World Development* 25/8.

Palmer, I. 1991, 'Gender and population in the adjustment of African economies: planning for change'. ILO/UNFPA, Geneva.

Quisumbing, A. 1994, 'Improving women's productivity as farmers and workers'. Education and Social Policy Department, ESP Discussion Paper Series No 37, World Bank, Washington DC.

Quisumbing, A. 1996, 'Male-female differences in agricultural productivity: methodological issues and empirical evidence'. *World Development* 24/10.

Roberts, P. , 1988, 'Rural women's access to labour in West Africa'. In Sticher, S. and Parpart, J. (eds.) *Patriarchy and Class: African Women in the Home and the Workforce*. Westview, Boulder.

Thrupp, L-A. et al. 1993, *Bittersweet Harvest*. World Resources Institute, Washington DC.

UNCTAD 1994, *Statistical Pocket Book*. UNCTAD, Geneva.

UNCTAD 1998, *Trade and Development Report 1998*. UNCTAD, Geneva.

Wood, A. 1994, 'Land, skill and trade: a simple analytical framework'. Working Paper 1, IDS, University of Sussex.

Wood, A. and Berge, K. 1994, 'Exporting manufactures or human resources?' Working Paper 4, IDS, University of Sussex.

World Bank 1995, *Towards Gender Equality: the Role of Public Policy*. World Bank, Washington DC.

Chapter 4

Daniels, L. 1995, *Entry, Exit, and Growth Among Small-Scale Enterprises in Zimbabwe*. PhD Dissertation, Department of Agricultural Economics, Michigan State University.

Daniels, L. (1999 forthcoming), 'The role of small enterprises in the household and national economy of Kenya: a significant contribution or a last resort?' *World Development*.

Daniels, L and Mead, D.C. 1998, 'The contribution of small enterprises to household and national income in Kenya'. *Economic Development and Cultural Change*, October.

McPherson. M.A. 1992, *Growth and Survival of Small Southern African Firms*. PhD Dissertation, Dept. Of Economics, Michigan State University.

McPherson, M.A. 1996, 'Growth of micro and small enterprises in Southern Africa'. *Journal of Development Economics* 48.

McPherson, M.A. 1998, 'Changes in Zimbabwe's micro and small enterprise sector, 1991–1998: evidence from a third country-wide survey'. Unpublished paper.

Mead, D.C. 1994, 'The contribution of small enterprises to employment growth in Southern and Eastern Africa'. *World Development* 22.

Mead, D.C. and Morrisson, C. 1996, 'The informal sector elephant'. *World Development* 24.

Parker, J. 1995, *Patterns of Business Growth: Micro and Small Enterprises in Kenya*. PhD Dissertation, Department of Agricultural Economics, Michigan State University.

Parker, J. 1996, 'Micro and small-scale enterprises in Zambia: results of the 1996 nationwide survey'. Unpublished paper.

Chapter 5

Charmes, J. 1984, 'Place and role of the informal sector in development planning and employment policies in Tunisia' (in French). Appendix to the World Bank report *Tunisia Industrial Employment*. No 5564–TUN, June 1985.

Charmes, J. 1996a, 'The informal sector in Burkina Faso. Trends in long term and follow-up in the short term' (in French). Ministry of Economy, Finance and Planning / GTZ, Ouagadougou.

Charmes, J. 1996b, 'Situation and perspectives of labour force and employment in Benin (1979–2002)' (in French). Ministry of Planning, Economic Restructuring and Employment Promotion / UNDP, Cotonou.

Charmes, J. 1996c, 'Progress in measurement of informal sector employment'. *Regional Development Dialogue* 17/1.

Charmes, J. 1997, 'Informal sector and micro-enterprises in Tunisia: towards a renewed approach (in French)'. National Institute of Statistics, Tunis and Paris.

Charmes, J. 1998, 'Contribution of women working in the informal sector in Africa: a case study'. Paper prepared for WIEGO and the United Nations Statistics Division 'Umbrella Gender Statistics Programme' and presented at the second meeting of the Delhi Group on Informal Sector Statistics. Ankara, April.

ILO, 1993a, *Statistics of Employment in the Informal Sector: XVth International Conference of Labour Statisticians. Report III*. ILO, Geneva.

ILO, 1993b, *XVth International Conference of Labour Statisticians. Report of the Conference*. ILO, Geneva.

Marniesse, S. 1998, *Dynamics of Micro-enterprises in Developing Countries* (in French). PhD thesis, University of Paris I-Pantheon-Sorbonne.

Chapter 6

Budlender, D. and Theron, J. 1995a, 'Report on home-based work'. Community Agency for Social Enquiry, Cape Town.

Budlender, D. and Theron, J. 1995b, 'Working from home: the plight of home-based workers'. *South African Labour Bulletin* 19/3.

Bukula, S., Memani, M. and Fakudze, N. 1998, '"My region, my province– it's my business": institutional and legal framework for SMME promotion in the Gauteng Province'. Unpublished Report for the Directorate of Economic Empowerment, Gauteng Provincial Government, Johannesburg.

Clark, I., Hofmeyr, A. and Hawken, L. 1996, 'Horizontal linkages intervention'. Unpublished report.

Harrison, P. , Todes, A. and Watson, V. 1997, 'Transforming South Africa's cities: prospects for the economic development of urban townships'. *Development Southern Africa* 14.

Horn, P. 1995. 'Self-Employed Women's Union: tackling the class-gender intersection'. *South African Labour Bulletin* 19/6.

Karungu, P. , Rwigema, H. and Ngeleza, B. 1997, 'A study on development, management and needs analysis of small, medium and micro enterprises in the Southern Metropolitan Local Council'. Unpublished report prepared for the Southern Metropolitan Local Council, Johannesburg.

Liedholm, C. and Mead, D. 1993, 'The structure and growth of microenterprises in Southern and Eastern Africa: evidence from recent surveys'. GEMINI Working Paper No. 36, Bethesda, MD.

Manning, C. 1993a, 'Informal manufacturing in the South African economy'. Working Paper No 11, Centre for Social and Development Studies, University of Natal, Durban.

Manning, C. 1993b, 'Subcontracting in the South African economy: a review of evidence, and an analysis of future prospects'. Unpublished paper prepared for the Taskgroup Workshop 21–23 May.

Manning, C. 1996, *Market Access for Small and Medium Sized Producers in South Africa: the Case of the Furniture Industry.* PhD dissertation, University of Sussex.

Manning, C. and Mashego, P. 1993, 'Manufacturing in microenterprises in South Africa'. Industrial Strategy Project, University of Cape Town.

Manning, C. and Mashego, P. 1994, 'Manufacturing in South African microenterprises'. *IDS Bulletin* 25/1.

May, J. (ed.) 1998, *Poverty and Inequality in South Africa.* Praxis, Durban

May, J. and Rogerson, C.M. 1995, 'Poverty and sustainable cities in South Africa; the role of urban cultivation'. *Habitat International* 19.

Mead, D.C. and Liedholm, C. 1998, 'The dynamics of micro and small enterprises in developing countries'. *World Development* 26/1.

Ntsika Enterprise Promotion Agency 1997a, 'The state of small business in South Africa: annual review 97'. Centre for Small Business Promotion, -Pretoria

Ntsika Enterprise Promotion Agency 1997b, 'Markets in the state sector: procurement guidelines for small, medium and micro enterprises (SMMEs) and service providers'. Ntsika and Department of Trade and Industry, Pretoria

Pityana, S.M. 1997, 'Determinants of the low employment absorptive capacity of the economy: is the labour market the culprit?' Paper presented at the Conference on Labour Markets and Enterprise Performance in South Africa, 30 January.

Republic of South Africa 1995, *National Strategy for the Development and Promotion of Small Business in South Africa.* Department of Trade and Industry, Cape Town

Republic of South Africa 1996, *Growth, Employment and Redistribution: A Macroeconomic Strategy.* Department of Finance, Pretoria.

Republic of South Africa 1997, *Green Paper on Public Procurement Reform.* Department of Public Works, Pretoria.

Rogerson, C.M. 1991, 'Deregulation, subcontracting, and the (in)formalisation of small scale manufacturing'. In Preston-Whyte, E. and Rogerson, C. (eds.) *South Africa's Informal Economy* Oxford University Press, Cape Town.

Rogerson, C.M. 1994, 'Flexible production in the developing world: the case of South Africa'. *Geoforum* 25.

Rogerson, C.M. 1995, 'Looking to the Pacific Rim: production subcontracting and small scale industry in South Africa'. *International Small Business Journal* 13/3.

Rogerson, C.M. 1996a, 'Rethinking the informal economy of South Africa'. Development Paper No. 84, Development Bank of Southern Africa, Halfway House.

Rogerson, C.M. 1996b, 'Urban poverty and the informal economy in South Africa's economic heartland'. *Environment and Urbanization* 8.

Rogerson, C.M. 1997a, 'SMMEs and poverty in South Africa'. Unpublished input report for the National Project on Poverty and Inequality.

Rogerson, C.M. 1997b, 'Globalisation or informalisation?: African urban economies in the 1990s'. In Rakodi C. (ed) *The Urban Challenge in Africa: Growth and Management of Its Large Cities.* United Nations University, Tokyo.

Rogerson, C.M. 1997c, 'Local government and the SMME economy in South Africa'. *Africa Insight* 27.

Rogerson, C.M. 1998a, 'The Gauteng manufacturing SMME economy: present status and future prospects'. Papers in Education, Training and Enterprise No. 12, Centre for African Studies, University of Edinburgh.

Rogerson, C.M. 1998b, 'The Gauteng SMME economy: profile, needs and constraints'. Unpublished report for the Directorate of Economic Empowerment, Gauteng Provincial Government, Johannesburg.

Rogerson, C.M. and Reid, K. 1997, 'Towards a framework for rural small business support'. Discussion Paper, Ntsika Enterprise Promotion Agency, Pretoria.

Rogerson, C.M. and Rogerson, J.M. 1997, 'The changing post-apartheid city: emergent black-owned small enterprises in Johannesburg'. *Urban Studies* 34.

SEWU (Self-Employed Women's Union) 1995, 'SEWU submission to the Portfolio Committee on Trade and Industry for the 1996 Budget Bill'. SEWU, Durban.

SEWU (Self-Employed Women's Union) 1996, 'Submission to Finance Portfolio Committee on ways in which the budget could address poverty'. SEWU, Durban.

Steven, J. 1998, 'Manufacturing advice from govt paying off'. *Engineering News* 7 August, 8.

Tendler, J. 1994, 'Strengthening the capabilities of (largely informal) manufacturing micro/small enterprises'. Paper prepared for the Workshop on Small, Medium and Micro Enterprise Development and Financing, Verwoerdburg, 2 November.

Tendler, J. and Amorim, M. 1996, 'Small firms and their helpers: lessons on demand'. *World Development* 24/4.
World Bank 1993, 'Characteristics of and constraints facing black businesses in South Africa: survey results'. World Bank, Washington DC.

Chapter 7

Barr, A. 1999, 'Do SMEs network for growth?' This volume.
Berger, M. 1989, 'An introduction to the importance of a focus on women'. In Berger, M. and Buvinic, M. (eds.) *Women's Ventures*. Kumarian Press, W. Hertford, CT.
Buvinic, M. 1986, 'Projects for women in the Third World: explaining their misbehaviour'. *World Development* 14/5
Chambers, R. 1998, 'Forward'. In Guijt, I and Shah, M. (eds.) *The Myth of Community: Gender Issues in Participatory Development*. Intermediate Technology Publications, London.
Commonwealth Secretariat 1989, *Engendering Adjustment for the 1990s*. Commonwealth Secretariat, London.
Dawson, J. 1992, 'The relevance of the flexible specialisation paradigm for small-scale industrial restructuring in Ghana'. *IDS Bulletin* 23/3.
Downing, J. 1991, 'Gender and the growth of microenterprises'. *Small Enterprises Development* 2/1.
DPU, 1997, 'DPU gender policy and planning training materials'. Development Planning Unit, University College London.
Elson, D. 1992, 'Male bias in structural adjustment'. In Afshar, H. (ed.) *Women and Adjustment Policies in the Third World*. Macmillan, London.
FAO 1988, 'The impact of development strategies on the rural poor' World Conference on Agrarian Reform and Rural Development 1979–1989, FAO, Rome.
Gaidzanwa, R.B. 1993, 'Women entrepreneurs, donor promotion and domestic policies'. In Helmsing A. and Kolstee T. (eds.) *Small Enterprises and Changing Policies: Structural Adjustment, Financial Policy and Assistance Programmes in Africa*. Intermediate Technology Publications, London.
Grown, C. and Sebstadt, J. 1989, 'Introduction: toward a wider perspective on women's employment' *World Development* 17/7.
Hulme, D. and Turner, M. 1990, *Sociology and Development: Theories, Policies and Practices*. Harvester Wheatsheaf, London.
Jazairy, I. 1996, *ACORD Annual Report*. ACORD, London.
Jolly, R. 1997, 'Eradicating poverty early in the 21st Century' Report for the UN Secretary General.
Kabeer, N. 1991, 'Gender, production and well-being: rethinking the household economy' IDS Discussion Paper No 288
Kabeer, N. 1994, *Reversed Realities: Gender Hierarchies in Development Thought*. Verso, London.
Levy, C. 1996. 'The process of institutionalizing gender in policy and planning: the "web" of institutionalisation'. DPU Working Paper No. 74, University College London.
Levy, C. 1999 (forthcoming), 'The operational components of gender policy and planning'. Development Planning Unit Working Paper, University College London.
Liedholm, C. and Mead, D. 1987, 'Small Scale industries in developing countries:

empirical evidence and policy implications'. MSU International Development Paper No 9, Michigan State University.
von Massow, F. 1992, 'The palm wine drinkers: an analysis of male underemployment within the framework of the gender and development approach to planning' MSc Dissertation, London School of Economics
von Massow, F. 1995, 'WID/gender implementation under Lome IV, Malawi'. Report for the Commission of the European Communities, DGVIII.
von Massow, F., Turner, K., Beall, J. and Acton, H. 1993, 'Gender aware enterprise development in FLEC, Sierra Leone'. Report to CARITAS, Switzerland.
McCormick, D. 1999, 'Enterprise clusters in Africa: linkages for growth and development' This volume.
Mayoux, L. 1995, 'From vicious to virtuous circles? gender and microenterprise development'. UNRISD, Geneva.
Molyneux, M. 1985, 'Mobilization without emancipation? Women's interests, states and revolution in Nicaragua'. *Feminist Studies* 11/1.
Moser, C. 1989, 'Gender planning in the third world: meeting practical and strategic gender needs'. *World Development* 17/11
Moser, C. 1993, *Gender Planning and Development: Theory, Practice and Training*. Routledge, London.
Munachonga, M. 1988, 'Income allocations and marriage options in urban Zambia'. In Dwyer, D. and Bruce, J. (eds.) *A Home Divided: Women and Income in the Third World*. Stanford University Press, Palo Alto, CA.
NCWID 1993, 'Women and the law in Malawi'. National Council for Women in Development, Ministry of Women, Children, Community Services and Social Welfare, Lilongwe.
Nieuwenhuys, O. 1994, 'The children of the rural poor'. In Nieuwenhuys, O. (eds.) *Childrens' Lifeworlds: Gender, Welfare and Labour in the Developing World*. Routledge, London.
Schmink, M. 1984, 'Household economic strategies: a review and research agenda'. *Latin American Research Review* 19/3.
TGNP 1993, 'Gender profile of Tanzania'. Tanzania Gender Networking Programme, P. O. Box 8921, Dar es Salaam.
Tinker, I. 1987, 'The human economy of microentrepreneurs'. Paper presented at the International Seminar on Women in Micro- and Small-Scale Enterprise Development, Ottawa, Canada
United Nations 1996, 'UN Platform for Action and the Beijing Declaration'. UN Department of Public Information, New York.
UNDP 1995, *Human Development Report, 1995*. UNDP, New York.
UNDP 1997, *Human Development Report, 1997*. UNDP, New York.

Chapter 8

Birdsall, N. and Jaspersen, F. (eds.). 1998, *Pathways to Growth: Comparing East Asia and Latin America*. Inter-American Development Bank, Washington D.C.
Cagliano, R., Voss, C. and Blackmon, K. nd, 'Manufacturing practice and performance in small companies: preliminary findings from the Microscope database'. Unpublished Paper, Milan Polytechnic.
Cullen, J. and Sommerlad, E. 1997, 'Making sense of "organisational learning" in small to medium enterprises'. Discussion Paper, Tavistock Institute, London.
ILO (International Labour Office). 1998, *World Employment Report 1998–99*. ILO, Geneva.

Liedholm, C. and Mead, D.C. 1987, 'Small scale industries in developing countries: empirical evidence and policy implications'. MSU International Development Paper No. 9, Michigan State University Department of Agricultural Economics, East Lansing, Michigan.
Little, I.M.D., Mazumdar, D. and Page, J.M. 1987, *Small Manufacturing Enterprises.* World Bank Research Publication, Oxford University Press, New York.
Manu, G. 1995, 'Which clients to serve with training, extension and other support services for small and medium-sized enterprise development?' *IYB Bulletin*, Harare.
Manu, G., Nelson, R. and Thiongo, J. 1996, *Know About Business: Entrepreneurship Education in Vocational and Technical Training.* International Training Centre of the ILO, Turin.
McGrath, S. and King, K. 1996, 'Learning to compete: African education, training and small enterprise development in the era of globalisation'. Papers on Education, Training and Enterprise No. 1, Centre of African Studies, University of Edinburgh, October.
Mead, D. and Liedholm, C. 1998, 'The dynamics of micro and small enterprises in developing countries'. *World Development* 26/1.
Papoutsis, C. 1996, 'Promoting the development of fast-growing companies'. *Monthly Newsletter*, European Commission, Brussels, June.
Piore, M.J. and Sabel, C.H. 1984, *The Second Industrial Divide.* Basic Books, New York.
Pyke, F. 1988, 'Co-operation among small and medium-sized establishments'. In *Work, Employment and Society* 2/3.
Reich, R. 1991, *The Work of Nations.* Simon and Schuster, London.
Senge, P. 1990, *The Fifth Discipline.* Doubleday, New York.
Sengenberger, W. and Pyke, F. 1991, 'Small firm industrial districts and local economic regeneration: research and policy issues'. *Labour and Society* 16/1.
Storey, D.J., Keasey, K., Watson, R. and Wynarczyk. 1987, *The Performance of Small Firms* Croom Helm, London.
Storey, D.J., Watson, R. and Wynarczyk. nd, 'Fast growth small businesses: case studies of 40 small firms in North East England'. Department of Employment Research Paper No. 67.

Chapter 9

Aeroe, A. 1992, 'New pathways to industrialisation in Tanzania: theoretical and strategic considerations'. *IDS Bulletin* 23/3.
Alderman, H. and Paxson, C. H. 1994, 'Do the poor insure? A synthesis of the literature on risk and consumption in developing countries'. In Bacha, E. L. (ed.) *Economics in a Changing World: Proceedings of the Tenth World Congress of the International Economic Association.* International Economic Association, London.
Barr, A. M. 1997, 'Social capital and technical information flows in the Ghanaian manufacturing sector'. Centre for the Study of African Economies, University of Oxford.
Barr, A. M. 1998, 'Enterprise performance and the functional diversity of social capital'. Centre for the Study of African Economies, University of Oxford.
Bräutigam, D. 1997, 'Substituting for the state: institutions and industrial development in Eastern Nigeria'. *World Development* 25/7.

Dawson, J. 1992, 'The relevance of the flexible specialisation paradigm for small scale industrial restructuring in Ghana'. *IDS Bulletin* 23/3.

Fafchamps, M. 1992, 'Solidarity networks in preindustrial societies: rational peasants with a moral economy'. *Economic Development and Cultural Change* 41/1.

Fafchamps, M. 1996a, 'The enforcement of commercial contracts in Ghana'. *World Development* 24/3.

Fafchamps, M. 1996b, 'Ethnicity and markets: suppliers credit in African manufacturing'. Stanford University Working Paper wopstanec 96016.

Hansohm, D. 1992, 'Small enterprise flexibility in Sudan'. *IDS Bulletin* 23/3.

Holmström, M. 1993, 'Flexible specialisation in India?' *Economic and Political Weekly*, 28 August.

Livingstone, I. 1991, 'A reassessment of Kenya's rural and urban informal sector'. *World Development* 19/6.

Nadvi, K. and H. Schmitz 1994, 'Industrial clusters in less developed countries: review of experiences and research agenda'. IDS Discussion Paper, No. 339, University of Sussex.

Pattillo, C. 1997, 'The impact of uncertainty on the investment behaviour of Ghanaian manufacturing sector firms'. In Collier, P. and Pattillo, C. (eds.) *Risk and Agencies of Restraint: Reducing the Risks of African Investment.* Macmillan, London.

Posner, R. A. 1980 'A theory of primitive society, with special reference to law'. *Journal of Law and Economics* 23.

Rasmussen, J. 1992, 'The small enterprise environment in Zimbabwe: growing in the shadow of large enterprise'. *IDS Bulletin* 23/3.

Schmitz, H. 1982, 'Growth constraints on small scale manufacturing in developing countries: a critical review'. *World Development* 10/6.

Schmitz, H. 1995, 'Collective efficiency: growth path for small scale industry'. *Journal of Development Studies* 31/4.

Schmitz, H. 1997, 'Collective efficiency and increasing returns'. IDS Working Paper 50, University of Sussex.

Sverrisson, A. 1992, 'Flexible specialisation and woodworking enterprises in Kenya and Zimbabwe'. *IDS Bulletin* 23/3.

van Dijk, M.P. 1992, 'How relevant is flexible specialisation in Burkina Faso's informal sector and formal manufacturing sector?' *IDS Bulletin* 23/3.

Chapter 10

Abuodha, C. and King, K. 1991, 'The building of an industrial society: change and development in Kenya's informal (*jua kali*) sector 1972–1991'. IDS Discussion Paper No. 292, Institute for Development Studies, University of Nairobi.

Alila, P. O. and McCormick, D. 1997, 'Firm linkages in Kenya's tourism sector'. Paper presented as part of the *Multi-Country Study of Private Enterprise Development, Kenya Case Study.* Institute for Development Studies, University of Nairobi.

Barr, A. 1995, 'The missing factor: entrepreneurial networks, enterprises and economic growth in Ghana'. Working Paper WPS/95–11, Centre for the Study of African Economies, University of Oxford.

Becattini, G. 1989, 'Sectors and/or districts: some remarks on the conceptual foundations of industrial economics'. In Goodman, E.G. and Bamford, J. (eds.) *Small Firms and Industrial Districts in Italy*. Routledge, London.

British Aid to Small Enterprise. 1998. 'A five-year strategy for the British Aid to Small Enterprise (BASE) Programme in Kenya'. Department for International Development, Nairobi.

Dawson, J. 1988 'Small-scale industry development in Ghana: a case study of Kumasi'. (For presentation to ESCOR, Overseas Development Administration, London).

Hart, M. 1994 'Study to profile Jua Kali Associations relevant to the FIT programme'. Farm Implements and Tools (FIT), Nairobi.

Humphrey, J. 1995 'Industrial reorganisation in developing countries: from models to trajectories'. *World Development* 23/1.

Jones, P. and Barr, A. 1996 'Learning by doing in Sub-Saharan Africa: evidence from Ghana'. *Journal of International Development* 8/3.

Kinyanjui, M.N. 1997, 'Tapping opportunities in enterprise clusters in Kenya: the case of enterprises in Ziwani and Kigandaini'. Paper prepared for research project on *Collective Efficiency and Small Enterprise in Kenya* and presented at Institute of Development Studies, University of Sussex, UK. Institute for Development Studies, University of Nairobi.

Kinyanjui, M.N. 1998, 'Vehicle repair clusters in Kenya: alternative strategies for slowly industrialising countries'. Report prepared for research project on *Collective Efficiency and Small Enterprise in Kenya.* Institute for Development Studies, University of Nairobi.

Marshall, A. 1890, *Principles of Economics*. Macmillan & Co., London.

McCormick, D. 1997, 'Industrial district or garment ghetto? Nairobi's mini-manufacturers'. In van Dijk, M.P. and Rabellotti, R. (eds.) *Enterprise Clusters and Networks in Developing Countries.* Frank Cass, London.

McCormick, D. 1998, 'Enterprise clusters in Africa: on the way to industrialisation?' IDS Discussion Paper No. 366, Institute of Development Studies, University of Sussex.

McCormick, D. and Atieno, R. 1997, 'Firm linkages: importance for industrial structure and performance'. Paper presented as part of the *Multi-Country Study of Private Enterprise Development, Kenya Case Study.* Institute for Development Studies, University of Nairobi.

Mitullah, W.V. 1998, 'Lake Victoria's nile perch fish industry: the politics of joint action'. IDS Working Paper No. 519, Institute for Development Studies, University of Nairobi.

Nadvi, K. 1997, 'The cutting edge: collective efficiency and international competitiveness in Pakistan'. IDS Discussion Paper No. 360, Institute of Development Studies, University of Sussex.

October, L. 1996, 'Sectors, clusters and regions: a study of the Cape clothing industry'. Working Paper No. 2, Development Policy Research Unit, University of Cape Town.

Piore, M.J. and Sabel, C.F. 1984, *The Second Industrial Divide: Possibilities for Prosperity.* Basic Books, New York.

Porter, M. 1990, *The Competitive Advantage of Nations.* The Free Press, New York.

Schmitz, H. 1992, 'On the clustering of small firms'. *IDS Bulletin* 23/3.

Schmitz, H. 1997, 'Collective efficiency and increasing returns'. IDS Working Paper 50, Institute of Development Studies, University of Sussex.

Sengenberger, W. and Pyke, F. 1992, 'Industrial districts and local economic regeneration: research and policy issues'. In Pyke, F. and Sengenberger, W.

(eds.) *Industrial Districts and Local Economic Regeneration.* International Institute for Labour Studies, Geneva.
Storper, M. and Walker, R. 1989, *The Capitalist Imperative: Territory, Technology, and Industrial Growth.* Basil Blackwell, New York and Oxford.
Zeitlin, J. (ed.) 1989, 'Local industrial strategies'. Special Issue of *Economy and Society* 18/4

Chapter 11

Biggs, T., Shah, M and Srivastava, P. 1995, 'Technological capabilities and learning in African enterprises'. World Bank Technical Paper, No. 288, Washington DC.
von Bülow, D., Damball, E. and Maro, R. 1995, 'Supporting women's groups in Tanzania through credit: is this a strategy for empowerment?'. CDR Working Paper 95.10, Centre for Development Research, Copenhagen.
Daniels, L. 1994, 'Changes in the small scale enterprise sector from 1991 to 1993: results of a second nationwide survey in Zimbabwe'. GEMINI Working Paper No. 71, Bethesda, MD.
Daniels, L., Mead, D.C. and Musinga, M. 1995, 'Employment and income in micro and small scale enterprises in Kenya: results of a 1995 survey'. Gemini Working Paper No.92, Bethesda, MD.
Dicken, P. 1994, 'The Roepke Lecture in Economic Geography: global-local tensions: firms and states in the global space economy'. *Economic Geography* 70/2.
Fafchamps, M. 1992, 'Solidarity networks in preindustrial societies: rational peasants in a moral economy'. *Economic Development and Cultural Change* 41/1.
Ferrand, D. 1997, 'Discontinuity in development: the case of Kenya's "missing middle"'. Paper presented to a IDS/CDR Conference on African Business Systems: Institutionalising Industrialisation in the Era of Economic Reform, Mombasa, June.
Gereffi, G. 1994, 'Contending paradigms for cross-regional comparison: development strategies and commodity chains in East Asia and Latin America'. In Smith, P. H. (ed.) *Latin America in Comparative Perspective: New Approaches to Method and Analysis.* Westview, Boulder.
Granovetter, M. 1985, 'Economic action and social structure: the problem of embeddedness'. *American Journal of Sociology* 91.
Humphrey, J. 1995, 'Industrial reorganisation in developing countries: from models to trajectories'. *World Development* 23/1.
Humphrey, J. and Schmitz, H. 1996, 'Trust and economic development'. IDS Discussion Paper 355, University of Sussex.
Kaplinsky, R. 1995, 'Technique and system: the spread of Japanese management techniques to developing countries'. *World Development* 23/1.
Kinyanjui, M. 1997, 'Employment in small scale enterprises in Nairobi: job search procedures and labour force characteristics'. Institute of Development Studies, University of Nairobi.
Knorringa, P. 1997, 'Transferability of industrial district models and policies'. Paper presented at the final EMOT Conference, ISTUD, Stresa, Italy, September.
McCormick, D. 1997, 'Enterprise clusters in Africa. on the way to industrialisation?' Working Paper No. 518. Institute of Development Studies, University of Nairobi.

McCormick, D. and Pedersen, P. O. 1997, 'African business systems in a globalising world'. Occasional Paper No. 11. Department of Intercultural Communication and Management, Copenhagen Business School.
Mwamadzingo, M. 1997, 'Technological capabilities and performance of small and medium sized enterprises in Kenya'. Institute of Development Studies, University of Nairobi.
Nadvi, K. and Schmitz, H. 1994, 'Industrial clusters in less developed countries: review of experiences and research agenda'. IDS Discussion Paper 339, University of Sussex.
North, D. 1990, *Institutions, Institutional Change and Economic Performance.* Cambridge University Press, Cambridge.
Paldam, M. 1997, 'Dansk u-landshjœlp: altruismens politiske økonomi' (Danish development aid: the political economy of altruism). Aarhus Universitetsforlag, Copenhagen.
Pedersen, P. O. 1997a, *Small African Towns: between Rural Networks and Urban Hierarchies*. Avebury, Aldershot.
Pedersen, P. O. 1997b, 'Foreign direct investment and aid: capacity building or capacity exploitation?' Paper presented at the conference of the Nordic Association of Development Geographers in Sandö, Sweden, June.
Sassen, S. 1994, *Cities in a World Economy*. Pine Forge Press, Thousand Oaks, CA.
Schmitz, H. 1995, 'Small shoemakers and Fordist giants: tales of a supercluster'. *World Development* 23/1.
Shafaeddin, S.M. 1996, 'Risks of further marginalisation of Sub-Saharan Africa in international trade'. *Journal of Developing Societies* 6/2.
Sørensen, P. 1997, '*Money is the true Friend*'*–Trust, Morality and Economic Practice among the Iganga Maize Traders in Uganda.* PhD dissertation, Department of Anthropology, University of Copenhagen and Centre for Development Research.
Sverrisson, A. 1997, 'Enterprise networks and technological change: aspects of light engineering and metal working in Accra'. In van Dijk, M.P. and Rabellotti, R. (eds.) *Enterprise Clusters and Networks in Developing Countries.* EADI/Frank Cass, London.
Trulsson, P. 1997, 'Strategies of entrepreneurship: understanding industrial entrepreneurship and structural change in northwest Tanzania'. Department of Technology and Social Change, Linköping University.

Chapter 12

Afenyadu, D. 1996a, 'Participatory evaluation of exchange visits between food processing women's groups in Togo and Ghana'. Consultancy Report, FIT Programme, ILO/TOOL, Geneva/Amsterdam, restricted.
Afenyadu, D. 1996b, 'Exchange visits between food processing women's groups in Kassem-speaking areas in Ghana and Burkina Faso'. Consultancy Report, FIT Programme, ILO/TOOL, Geneva/Amsterdam, restricted.
Amenuvor, B. 1998, 'Impact monitoring of FIT activities in Ghana 1994–98'. Consultancy Report, FIT Programme, ILO/TOOL, Geneva/Amsterdam, restricted.
Aryetee, E. and Appiah, E. 1995, 'Associations of informal producers in Ghana:

report of a study of 6 informal associations in the agro-metal and food processing subsectors'. FIT Working Document No. 13, FIT Programme, ILO/TOOL, Geneva/Amsterdam.

Burger, K. and Haan, H.C. 1996, 'Rapid market appraisal for micro and small enterprises'. FIT Manual No. 2, FIT Programme, ILO/TOOL, Geneva/Amsterdam.

Craig, K. and Oneko, M. 1994, 'Strengthening the Kenyan informal sector through exchange forums'. Draft FIT Consultancy Report, ILO/TOOL, Geneva/Amsterdam.

Esbin, H.B. 1994, 'Marketing of the jua kali sector in Kenya: analysis and strategic plan'. FIT Working Document No. 5, FIT Programme, ILO/TOOL, Geneva/Amsterdam.

Gibson, A. and Havers, M. 1994 'The role of small business membership organisations (SBMOs) in small enterprise development'. Overseas Development Group, Small Business Centre, Durham University Business School, Durham.

Haan, H.C. 1989, 'Issues in informal sector development with special reference to the technology factor'. In Fluitman, F. (ed.) *Training for Work in the Informal Sector*. ILO, Geneva.

Haan, H. 1995 'Informal Sector associations in Africa'. TOOLConsult Working Paper No. 1, Amsterdam.

Hileman, M. 1995, 'An evaluation of the PRIDE/FIT exchange visit programme'. Consultancy Report, FIT Programme, ILO/TOOL, Geneva/Amsterdam, restricted.

Hossenmamode, H. 1993, 'Les petites entreprises, les associations professionelles en Afrique: perspectives de consolidation du secteur privé'. AFREDI, UNDP/ILO, Douala.

ILO 1972, *Employment, Incomes and Equality in Kenya*. ILO, Geneva

ILO/TOOL 1994, 'Information demand, supply and transfer in relation to the development of the micro and small enterprise sector'. Draft Final Report, ILO/TOOL, Geneva/Amsterdam.

Kordylas, J.M. 1997, 'The glass jar project: development of the Glass Jar Users Association with the FIT Programme in Ghana'. Consultancy Report FIT Programme, ILO/TOOL, Geneva/Amsterdam, restricted.

Kyerematen, A. 1993, 'Improving the access of SMEs to new technologies'. Paper prepared for the Small and Micro Enterprise Conference 'Agents of Change in Policy Development and Implementation for Small Enterprises', Abidjan, November–December

Levitsky, J. 1992, 'Private-sector organisations and support for small and microenterprises'. In Helmsing, P. and Kolstee (eds.) *Small Enterprises and Changing Policies: Structural adjustment, financial policy and assistance programmes in Africa.* IT Publications, London.

Levitsky, J. 1994, 'Business associations in countries in transition to market economies'. *Small Enterprise Development* 5/3.

Livingstone, A.-M. 1996, 'A study on associations of small scale producers in Ghana'. FIT Working Document No. 17, FIT Programme, ILO/TOOL, Geneva/Amsterdam.

Maldonado, C. and Sethuraman, S.V. (eds.) 1992, *Technological Capability in the Informal Sector*. ILO, Geneva.

Mathuva, J.M. 1996, 'Identification and profiling of groups of metalworkers and foodprocessors in Kenya: a case study of Machakos, Thika and Bugoma

Districts'. Consultancy Report, FIT Programme, ILO/TOOL, Geneva/Amsterdam, restricted.

Njagi, J.K. 1994, 'Study of the potential for sectoral associations in Kenya'. Draft Consultancy Report, FIT Programme, ILO/TOOL, Geneva/Amsterdam, restricted.

Nzioka, T.M. 1994, 'Manual on the organisation of jua kali exhibitions'. FIT Manual No. 1, ILO/TOOL, Geneva/Amsterdam.

Pedersen, P. O., Sverrisson, A. and van Dijk, M.P. 1994, *Flexible Specialization: the dynamics of small-scale industries in the South.* IT Publications, London,

Schmitz, H. 1998, 'Fostering collective efficiency'. *Small Enterprise Development.* 9/1.

World Bank 1993, 'Micro and small enterprise training and technology project: staff appraisal report'. World Bank, Washington DC.

Zoomers, E.B. (ed.) 1995, *Supporting Small Scale Enterprise: Case Studies in SME Interventions.* Bulletin 338, Royal Tropical Institute, Amsterdam.

Chapter 13

Barnett, A. 1995, 'Technology and small scale production'. *Small Enterprise Development Journal* 6/4.

Barton, C. 1997, 'Microenterprise business development services: defining institutional options and indicators of performance'. Microenterprise Best Practice Project, Development Alternatives Inc., Bethesda MD.

Biggs, T., Shah, M. and Srivastava 1995, 'Technological capabilities in African enterprises'. World Bank Technical Paper No. 288, Washington DC.

Bush, A. 1997, (unpublished) submission by ITDG to DFID for a review of its support for Appropriate Technology.

Dawson, J. and Jeans, A. 1997, 'Looking beyond credit: business development services and the promotion of innovation among small producers'. IT Working Papers, IT Publications, London.

Gibson, A. 1997, 'Business development services for SMEs: preliminary guidelines'. Summary Report to the Donor Committee on Small Enterprise Development, World Bank Washington DC.

Jeans, A. 1997, 'Small workshops: supporting a production pyramid'. *Appropriate Technology Journal* 24/1.

Jeans, A., Hyman, E. and O'Donnell, M. 1990, 'Technology: the key to increasing the productivity of microenterprises'. GEMINI, Bethesda MD.

Schmitz, H. 1995, 'Collective efficiency: growth path for small scale industry'. *Journal of Development Studies* 31/4.

Tanburn, J. and Osumba, M. 1997, 'User-led innovation'. *Appropriate Technology Journal.* 24/1.

Chapter 14

Birks, J. S. and Sinclair C. A. 1991, 'Education and training for skills and income in the urban informal sector in Sub-Saharan Africa, the case of Ibadan, Nigeria'. ILO, Geneva.

Centre for African Settlement Studies and Development/Friedrich Ebert Stiftung 1992, 'Improving the fortunes of small scale industries in Nigeria: policy guidelines'. CASSAD, Ibadan.

Fapohunda, O. J. 1978, 'Characteristics of the informal sector of Lagos'. Research Bulletin, No.78/01, University of Lagos.
Fapohunda, O. and Lubell H. 1978, 'Lagos: urban development and employment'. ILO, Geneva.
Fashoyin, T. (ed.) 1994, *Economic Reform Policies and the Labour Market in Nigeria*. Nigerian Industrial Relations Association/Friedrich Ebert Foundation, Lagos.
Fluitman, F. 1989, 'Training for work in the informal sector: an agenda item for the 1990s'. Vocational Training Branch, ILO, Geneva.
Fluitman, F. 1992, 'Rediscovering traditional apprenticeship: lost world or promised land'. ILO, Geneva.
Ihonvbere, J. O. 1993, 'Economic crisis, structural adjustment and social crisis in Nigeria'. *World Development* 21/1.
Meagher, K. and Yunusa M-B. 1991, 'Limits to labour absorption: conceptual and historical background to adjustment in Nigeria's urban informal sector'. United Nations Research Institute for Social Development Discussion Paper 28, Geneva
Obi, A. W. 1991, 'Prospects for small scale industries, development under a structural adjustment programme: the case of Nigeria'. *Africa Development* 16/2.
Oni, B. 1989, 'Patterns and processes of vocational/technical skill acquisition in formal and informal institutions in Nigeria and in Ibadan in particular'. Submitted as part of the Report of World Bank/NISER Project on Education and Training for Skills and Income in the Urban Informal Sector in Sub-Saharan Africa: the Case of Ibadan, Nigeria.
Osoba, A. M. (ed.) 1987, *Towards the Development of Small Scale Industries in Nigeria*. NISER, Ibadan.
Oyejide, T. A. 1991, 'Adjustment with growth: Nigerian experience with structural adjustment policy reform'. *Journal of International Development* 3/5.

Chapter 15

Adam, S. 1999, 'Competences and other factors affecting the small enterprise sector in Ibadan, Nigeria.' This volume.
Adu-Sarkodie, K.A. 1995 'The role of VOTEC in development'. Paper prepared for the workshop on the preparation of business plans for NVTI Centre managers under the auspices of the ODA. Ministry of Employment and Social Welfare, Accra.
Apraku-Mensah 1995, 'Analysis of responses to performance of NVTI graduates working in various establishments'. National Vocational Training Institute, Accra.
Dordunoo, C. K. 1994, 'A macroeconomic analysis of output and employment in Ghana'. Ministry of Employment and Social Welfare / UNDP / ILO Umbrella Programme: Sustained Employment Generation (GHA/89/007), Accra.
Education Reforms Review Committee 1994, *Report of the Education Reforms Review Committee on Pre-tertiary Education*. Ministry of Education, Accra.
Government of Ghana 1994, *Programme for the Provision of Free Compulsory and Universal Basic Education by the Year 2005*. Ministry of Education, Accra.
Honny, L. A. 1997, 'A methodology for tracer studies of NVTI graduates'. Ministry of Employment and Social Welfare / Department For International Development, U.K., Accra.

Mead, D. 1999, 'MSEs tackle both poverty and growth (but in varying proportions)'. This volume.
Ministry of Education 1990, 'Policy on technical and vocational education and training in Ghana'. Ministry of Education, Accra.
Republic of Ghana 1995, *Ghana-Vision 2020. Coordinated Programme of Economic and Social Development Policies* Assembly Press, Accra.
Republic of Ghana. Technical Committee On Poverty (TCOP) 1996, *Policy Focus for Poverty Reduction.* Technical Secretariat, National Development Planning Commission, Accra.
Task Force 1997, 'Proposals for the development of technical vocational education and training (VOTEC) system in Ghana'. Ministry of Employment and Social Welfare, Accra.

Chapter 16

Audience Africa 1995, *Social Development: Africa's priorities. Final Report.* UNESCO, Paris.
ECA/UNESCO 1961, *Final Report of the Conference of African States on the Development of Education in Africa.* ECA, Addis Ababa.
Ibanda, S. 1993, *A Study of Human Resource Development in Uganda*. Ministry of Finance and Economic Planning/United Nations Development Programme, Kampala
Kerre, B.W. 1990, 'The university's future role in vocational education in Kenya'. In Achola, P. , Gray, K. and Kerre, B.W. (eds.) *Trends and the Future of University Education in Kenya*. Masaki Publishers, Nairobi.
Kerre, B.W. 1994, 'Promoting entrepreneurship education in technical training institutions: an evaluation report'. UNDP, Nairobi.
Kerre, B.W. 1996, 'Promotion of the equal access of girls and women to technical and vocational education in Kenya'. In UNESCO (ed.) *Promotion of the Equal Access of Girls and Women to Technical and Vocational Education.* Unesco, Paris.
Ki Zerbo, J. 1990, *Educate or Perish*. UNESCO/UNICEF, Paris.
Logan, B.I and Beoku-Betts, J.A 1996, 'Women and education in Africa: an analysis of economic and socio-cultural factors, influencing observed trends', *Journal of Africa American Studies* 31/3–4.
MRTTT (Ministry of Research, Technical Training and Technology) 1994, 'Jua kali symposium reports, 1992–94'. MRTTT, Nairobi.
Mukuni, J.S. and Kalunga, J. 1997, 'Training for the informal sector in Zambia'. In UNESCO/UNEVOC (eds.) *National Policy Definition in Technical and Vocational Education: Beyond the Formal Sector*. UNESCO, Nairobi.
Otunga, R.N. 1997, 'School participation of gender: implication for occupational activities in Kenya'. *African Development* 22/1.
Republic of Kenya 1986, *Economic Management for Renewed Growth*. Government Printer, Nairobi.
Republic of Kenya 1988, *Sessional Paper No. 8 of 1988 on Education and Manpower Training for the Next Decade and Beyond.* Government Printer, Nairobi.
Republic of Kenya 1992, *Sessional Paper No. 2 of 1992 on Small Enterprise and Jua Kali Development in Kenya.* Government Printer, Nairobi.
Republic of Kenya 1996, *Sessional Paper No. 2 of 1996 on Industrial Transformation to the Year 2020*. Government Printer, Nairobi.
Republic of Zambia 1996, 'Technical Education, Vocational and Entrepreneur-

ship Training (TEVET) Policy'. Ministry of Science, Technology and Vocational Training, Lusaka.
Smith, A. [1776] 1937, *Wealth of Nations*. Modern Library, New York.
Thiam, I.D. 1992, 'Innovations and reforms in higher education: paths to renovation'. In UNESCO/BREDA (ed.) *Higher Education in Africa: Challenges for the 21st Century*. UNESCO-BREDA, Dakar.
UNESCO 1991, *Final Report of the Sixth Conference of Ministers of Education and those Responsible for Economic Planning (MINEDAF VI) in Africa*. UNESCO, Dakar.
UNESCO/BREDA 1995, *Report on the State of Education in Africa: Education Strategies for the 1990s: Orientations and achievements*. UNESCO, Dakar.
UNESCO/BREDA 1996, *The Development of Technical and Vocational Education in Africa: A synthesis of case studies*. UNESCO, Dakar.
UNESCO/OAU/ECA 1976, *Final Report of the Conference of Ministers of Education of African Member States*. UNESCO, Lagos.
UNESCO-UNEVOC 1996. *Establishing Partnerships in Technical and Vocational Education: Cooperation between educational institutions and enterprises in technical and vocational education*. UNESCO, Berlin.

Chapter 17

Adam, S. 1999, 'Competences and other factors affecting the small enterprise sector in Ibadan, Nigeria'. This volume.
Barr, A. 1999, 'Do SMEs network for growth?'. This volume.
Cummings, W. and McGinn, N. (eds.) 1997, *The International Handbook of Education and Development*. Pergamon, Oxford.
de Moura Castro, C. and de Oliveira, J. 1994, 'Convergence between training and education'. In Husen, T. and Postlethwaite, N. (eds.) *The International Encyclopaedia of Education*. Pergamon , Oxford.
DFID (Department For International Development) 1997, *Eliminating World Poverty: a Challenge for the 21st Century*. HMSO, London.
Department of Labour 1997, *Green Paper: Skills Development Strategy for Economic and Employment Growth in South Africa*. Department of Labour, Pretoria.
Foster, P. J. 1965, 'The vocational school fallacy in development planning'. In Anderson, C. and Bowman, M. (eds.) *Education and Economic Development*. Aldine, Chicago.
Gibson, A. 1997, 'Business development services for SMES: preliminary guideline for donor-funded interventions'. Donor Committee on Small Enterprise Development, Washington DC.
Government of Kenya 1996, *Sessional Paper no 2 of 1996 on Industrial Transformation to the Year 2020*. Government Printer, Nairobi.
Grierson, J. 1993, 'Self-employment in developing countries: analysing the effectiveness of enterprise-based training approaches'. Paper presented at the 'Development and the Strategies of SMEs in the 1990s' Conference, Mikkeli, Finland, July.
Grierson, J. 1997, *Where there is no Job*. SKAT, St. Gallen.
Grierson, J. and McKenzie, I. (eds.) 1996, *Training for Self-employment through Vocational Training Institutions*. International Training Centre of the International Labour Office, Turin.
Holman, M. 1997, 'Cultivating the seeds of recovery in Africa', Japan's Overseas Development Assistance Seminar, Financial Times, London, November.

Honny, L. 1999, 'Reshaping vocational training: hopeful signs from a Ghanaian experience'. This volume.
Ilon, L. 1997, 'Educational repercussions of a global system of production'. In Cummings, W. and McGinn, N. (eds.) *The International Handbook of Education and Development.* Pergamon, Oxford.
Jeans, A. 1999, 'Technology, NGOs and small enterprise: securing livelihoods through technical change'. This volume.
Kerre, B.W. 1999, 'The role and potential of technical and vocational education in formal education systems in Africa'. This volume.
Killick, A. 1999, 'Have Africa's economies turned the corner?' This volume.
King, K. 1996, *Jua Kali Kenya.* James Currey, London.
King, K. 1997, 'Policy coherence in education, training and enterprise development in South Africa: the implementation challenge of new policies'. Papers in Education, Training and Enterprise No. 4, Centre of African Studies, University of Edinburgh.
Manu, G. 1999. 'Enterprise development in Africa: strategies for impact and growth'. This volume.
McCormick, D. 1999, 'Enterprise clusters in Africa: linkages for growth and development'. This volume.
McGrath, S. 1998a, 'Further education and training in South Africa: the acid test for the integrated approach'. Papers in Education, Training and Enterprise No. 14, Centre of African Studies, University of Edinburgh.
McGrath, S. 1998b, 'Towards a new paradigm: donor discourses of skills development'. Paper presented to the Education Faculty Seminar, University of the Western Cape, April.
McGrath, S. 1998c, 'Reforming South African technical and vocational education and training'. *Journal of Vocational Education and Training* 50/4.
McGrath, S. 1998d, 'No easy walk to industrialisation: reflections of the reform of Kenyan education and training'. Papers in Education, Training and Enterprise No. 18, Centre of African Studies, University of Edinburgh.
McGrath, S. and King, K. 1995, *Education and Training for the Informal Sector.* Education Papers 11, Education Division, ODA, London.
McGrath, S. and King, K. 1996, 'Learning to compete: African education, training and small enterprise development in the era of globalisation'. Papers in Education, Training and Enterprise No. 1, Centre of African Studies, University of Edinburgh.
McGrath, S. and King, K. 1997, 'The future of technical and vocational education and training' In Cummings, W. and McGinn, N. (eds.) *The International Handbook of Education and Development.* Pergamon, Oxford.
Mead, D. 1999, 'MSEs tackle both poverty and growth (but in differing proportions)'. This volume.
Mead, D. and Morrison, C. 1996, 'The informal sector elephant'. *World Development* 24/10.
Ministry of Overseas Development 1975 *Overseas Development: the Changing Emphasis in British Aid Policies: More help for the poorest.* cmd. 6270 HMSO, London.
Mkandawire, T. 1999, 'Developmental states and small enterprises'. This volume.
Oketch, H. and Otieno, A.A. 1998, 'Education, technical training and enterprise: case studies of micro and small enterprise growth, productivity and competitiveness in Kenya'. Draft report, K-Rep/Centre of African Studies, Nairobi/Edinburgh.

Overseas Development Administration (ODA) 1995, 'Strategy for ODA support for small enterprise development'. ODA, London.
Pedersen, P. O. 1999, 'Trading agents and other producer services in African industrialization and globalization)'. This volume.
Piore, M. and Sabel, C. 1984, *The Second Industrial Divide.* Basic Books, New York.
Reich, R. 1991, *The Work of Nations.* Simon and Schuster, London.
Rogerson, C. M. 1998, 'The Gauteng manufacturing SME economy: Present status and future prospects'. Papers in Education, Training and Enterprise No. 12, Centre of African Studies, University of Edinburgh.
Rogerson, C.M. 1999, 'Small enterprise development in post-apartheid South Africa: gearing up for growth and poverty alleviation'. This volume.
Sweden, Ministry for Foreign Affairs 1997, *Partnership with Africa: proposals for a new Swedish policy towards Sub-Saharan Africa*. Stockholm.
Working Group for International Cooperation in Vocational and Technical Skills Development, 1997, *Donor Policies Skills Development. Discussion Paper No. 2.*, Berne.
WCEFA (World Conference on Education for All) 1990, 'Declaration of the World Conference on Education for All'. WCEFA: New York.